PRAISES F

"**A FUN, ENTERTAINING STORY** about life on the road—the life of a true-hearted hobo—when America felt itself toppling into decline. This book gives you a sense of the soul-searching quests many went on during the tail end of the so-called 'Me Decade.'"

- **Kevin Mattson**, author of eight books including *What the Heck Are You Up To, Mr. President?* TV and radio commentator. Featured historian in *The Seventies*, the Tom Hanks-produced miniseries on CNN.

"**PERSONAL...WELL-WRITTEN...DEEP...** reveals what it was like to be a restless and adventurous youth in a bygone time."

- **Tom Grimm**, author of *The Hitchhiker's Handbook*.

"**LIKE KEROUAC AND STEINBECK**, it takes us on a thrilling journey through the heart of America. Although it takes place in 1979, the book offers a snapshot of who we are right now in the twenty-first century.

"As readers enjoy its breezy spirit and its sharp, often bemused observation, they will be challenged to consider with fresh eyes the current wrestling match for America's soul.

"Those on all sides of the political divide—even those with the 'sex, drugs, and rock 'n' roll' mentality—are not judged but treated with compassion. Most significant of all, the author presents everyone as yearning for the same thing: something deeper and richer beyond the shenanigans."

- **Louis Markos**, author of seven books, including *On the Shoulders of Hobbits: The Road to Virtue with Tolkien and Lewis*.

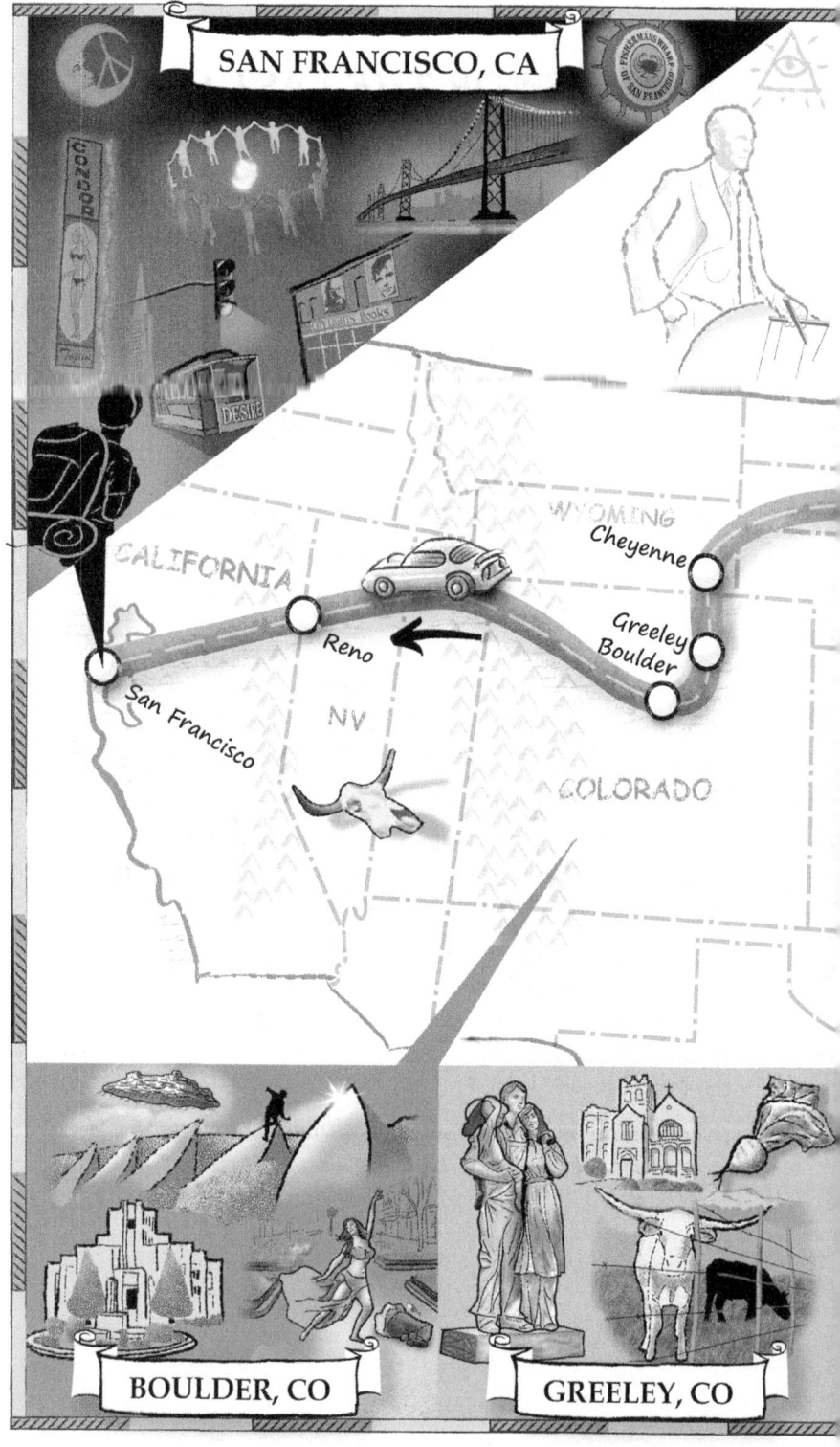

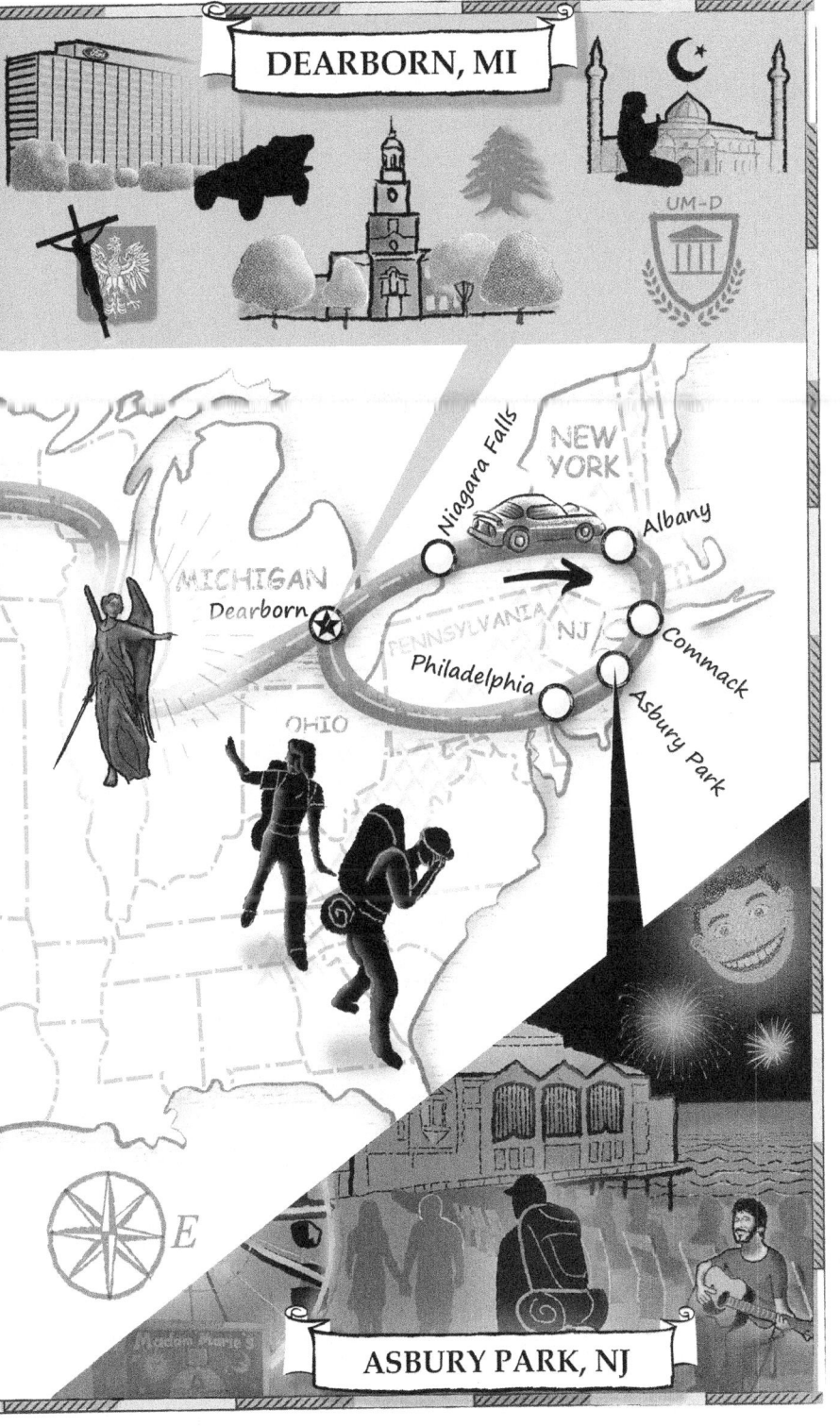

Dan Grajek

MOON People

A smug Dearborn college kid gets schooled by the road and the cult

Maureen — I hope you enjoy this book! Dan

Dearborn, Michigan 2024

MOON PEOPLE: *A smug Dearborn college kid gets schooled by the road and the cult*

Copyright © 2024 by Dan Grajek

All rights reserved. No part of this document may be reproduced or transmitted in any form or by any means, electronic, mechanical, photocopying, recording, or otherwise, without prior written permission of the publisher, except by a reviewer who may quote brief passages.

Published by Round Barn Media LLC
P.O. Box 23048
Dearborn, Michigan 48123
Contact: dpgrajek@icloud.com
Website: dan-grajek.com

All illustrations by Dan Grajek, except front cover by Dale Trujillo and Dan Grajek; and map by Dan Grajek with Tim Grajek

Chief Editor: Joe Cheff
Printed in the United States of America

ISBN: 978-0-9973247-1-6
ASIN: 0997324716

TABLE OF CONTENTS

AUTHOR'S NOTE	ix
PROLOGUE: ESCAPE FROM PARADISE	1
PART I: THE ROAD	7
"OHHH, MOTHER!"	9
A Lucky Break	11
Fall From Grace	15
Greeley, CO	19
How Randal and I Got the Idea to Hop a Train	24
The Miracle	29
The Batcave	34
Conversation With Rosie	38
The Apron Strings Speech	41
Dorna	47
THE HOLY CITY	51
The New York Trip	53
John Hancock	55
Commack, NY	59
Moon Gulch	61
Asbury Park, NJ	65
The End of the Line	68
Return With Elixir	70
Breakfast at Sambo's	72
Karma™	76
Randal's Republic	80
A TALE OF TWO COLLEGE TOWNS	83
Welcome to Boulder	85
Dearborn, MI	88
Vanity Fair	91
Go Blue!	95
The People's Republic of Boulder	102
Brave New World	105
The Gypsy	108
Sister Mary Fisher	111
The Shadow of Death	116
A Sign From Heaven	119
The Red Dragon	121
Christmas of '78	124
Ma Prem Nando	127

New Years 131
Who Is the Antichrist? 133

GOLDEN GATE CITY 135
Caliph-ornia 137
North Beach Crossroads 142
The Dinner Meeting 145

PART II: THE CULT 151

THE GREENHOUSE EFFECT 153
The Ride to Boonville 155
(Dis)Orientation 157
Sin Revisited 162
Durst Returns 165
Sunday Night Testimonies 167
The Last Man 171
"I'm a Prisoner..." 173
"I'm Your Spiritual Father" 177
Heavenly Deception 181

SPIRITUAL BOOTCAMP 185
Mrs. Durst 187
Kristina's Big Announcement 191
Letter to Randal 193
Politics, Politics 195
Charlie 198
The Two Me's 200
Letter from Randal 201
The Rescue Team 203
The Roaring Silence 206
The Infant of Prague 211
My Final Day at Camp K 213
Piper 216
Pete Meets Jim 217
The Last Temptation 219
Harry and Marge 222
Home at Last 224

EPILOGUE 227

AFTERWORD A: THE VANISHED IMAM 234
AFTERWORD B: THE POLISH POPE 239

ENDNOTES 243

ACKNOWLEDGEMENTS 255

BONUS SECTION: *THE LAST HOBO* EXCERPT 257

AUTHOR'S NOTE

THIS TALE FOLLOWS THE TRADITION of Homer's *Odyssey*, except you won't find a swashbuckling Odysseus, a man-eating cyclops, or seductive sirens. It's based on a true story, so its heroes, monsters, and seducers are of a different order. It draws on my travel journal and the eyewitness accounts of my traveling buddies. The Endnotes section shows the extensive research done to verify background information. The reader is invited to use it as a springboard for further study.

Artistic license was used to make autobiographical material (which this book is mostly) more user-friendly. Fictional elements and characters are used sparingly to accentuate the factual. Their main function is to clarify, simplify, and explain things, not to spice up the story.

Regarding genre, file this book under "Novelized Memoir." "Coming of Age" and "Adventure" fit as well as "Travel Writing." This may be a stretch but *Moon People* can also be placed in the "Local History" category since it mostly takes place in 1978 and 1979, a pivotal time for Dearborn regarding religion.

Truth is stranger than fiction, so expect the most outlandish, fantastic, and unbelievable elements of this story to be true and the more mundane and low-key elements to be fudged.

— Dan Grajek

Other books by Dan Grajek

THE LAST HOBO: A clueless Detroit kid hitchhikes across America the summer the seventies ran out of gas

MOON PEOPLE

A smug Dearborn college kid gets
schooled by the road and the cult

*Dedicated to Lori, Andy,
Justin, and Ron Crajak*

PROLOGUE

ESCAPE FROM PARADISE

Ten miles east of Healdsburg, California; August 20, 1979, two hours past midnight.

S*TAY AWAKE, TED!* I EXHORT MYSELF as I lay staring at the ceiling. My eyelids grow heavier. The soothing rhythm of the crickets worries me as much as the guards outside. A beam of light streaming through the window reveals the face of my wristwatch.

1:45 a.m. Fifteen more minutes. Why did I choose the top of the hour to break out of here? I guess I just figured it's when most people are asleep.

1:59 a.m. . . . *10, 9, 8, 7, 6, 5, 4, 3, 2, 1. TWO A.M. GO!*
Ever. So. Slowly. I peel off my sleeping bag. *Pause. . . Sit up. Pause. . . Stand up. Pause. . . Grab sleeping bag. Pause. . .* Each action is as stealthy as a cat. Each extended pause between moves is like a chess player carefully weighing his options. Toward the door, I cautiously step over several young men.

Warily, I rotate the doorknob. . . *Crrrrrreeeeeek.* . . *Whew!* Out. Then. . . *Brrrrrrr!* Moist, fifty-degree air!

I look up and see silhouettes of the guards on top of the hill.

Around midnight, I had seen them up-close sitting in metal folding chairs just beyond the compound's back porch. I met them as I started to head back to my cabin after finishing kitchen duty. They are two attractive women in their early twenties. One's probably Korean; the other, German, judging by her accent. While saying goodnight, I took a quick glance at the valley below from their vantage point. Particularly noted were the guards' blind spots: swatches of darkness around the lighted private road. I mentally sketch out my route from the cabin to the bridge.

The place is called Camp K, a former Camp Fire Girls camp found amid rolling hills and dense forest. You could probably determine a number of ways out. But all of them appear torturous except one—the path across the Maacama Creek bridge and onto California Highway 128. The two-lane road is right there on the other side.

Looking at a map, the seven-mile-long stream forms an almost impregnable natural barrier between Camp K and 128. It's 250-350 feet wide and curves along the west and north sides of the property creating a peninsula.

Next, I retrieve my backpack from the crawlspace under the cabin. The cobweb-covered pack had been freshly restocked the day before with provisions for a long journey ahead. I then roll up the sleeping bag and fasten it to the pack's aluminum frame. Once that's done, I position the pack along my posterior, secure the shoulder straps, and take a deep breath.

Show time!

I imagine myself as the lead character in a Hollywood movie. After the opening credits, the camera pans across the rustic setting and then I eventually appear. The movie soundtrack is like the one heard in countless war flicks like *The Great Escape*. It has drum parts that create tension during nail-biting scenes where the protagonist executes clandestine operations under the very nose of his captors. I'm teary-eyed from laughing about how my friends back home are going to react to the story of my breakout. However, despite my giddiness, I'm extremely nervous. My heart is pounding in my chest at the realization that getting caught might not be so hilarious.

"Rat-tat-tat-tat-tat-tat!" pound the drums of the movie soundtrack in my head.

Hightail it to the creek! There, the cottonwood trees along its bank supply cover.

Rat-tat-tat-tat-tat-tat!

Follow the riverbank toward the bridge! The sloped ground and thickets along the creek are hard to tread. In some spots, you must cling perilously close to the water's edge to avoid being seen. I need to grab a shrub or two to keep myself from falling in. This would be a tricky maneuver even without a heavy mass on your back.

Rat-tat-tat-tat-tat-tat!

Cross the bridge! As I take stock of the situation. I feel like daredevil Evel Knievel revving up his motorcycle to jump over the Snake River Canyon. *This is it, Ted. Your big move. Make-it-or-break-it time.* The structure spans at least 300 feet. It's reddish-brown and barely wide enough to accommodate a pickup truck. To my relief, I see no one at the entrance, but I still know crossing it would be chancy. The guards could probably spot me a mile away on the light-drenched section of the bridge, the side adjacent to the camp. And besides, I'm imagining more guards on the other side.

Pretty risky but nothing in life is one-hundred percent safe. At that thought, I decide to make a break for it. I step up the embankment into the light and flee across the Maacama Creek Bridge into the darkness.

Done.

Whew! No Family members out here. No alarm bells or sirens. I did it! I did it! I'M FREE. The only thing waiting for me is the State Highway, my only connection to the outside world.

I HEAD EAST DOWN CA-128. The lonely country road takes many twists and turns as it clings to the snakelike creek for about four miles. I'm serenaded by rushing water and crickets. The waxing crescent moon and the stars emit just enough light for me to track the yellow line. The next town going this direction is Calistoga, twelve miles away.

Darkness of course cloaks the majestic Mayacamas and Palisades straight ahead. They form the western wall of the celebrated Napa Valley, one of the best wine-producing regions in the United States.

The highest peak is Mt. St. Helena. The mountains are in a state park which is named after Robert Louis Stevenson. In 1880, he spent his honeymoon at nearby Silverado, an abandoned mining camp. Some of his descriptions of the rugged terrain ended up in *Treasure Island*. This makes me think of Dr. Mose Durst, my favorite lecturer at the camp. In his speech back in San Francisco, the former English professor associated the romantic quest for buried treasure with mankind's search for meaning. "There's gold in them thar hills!" he proclaimed as he impersonated an old prospector. The hill country he was referring to is the area where Camp K is located. It's the place where you can "strike it rich spiritually." The idea one could discover all of life's answers there intrigued me. I've long aspired to possess the ultimate Tao that transcends and permeates everything. I wanted to have complete and thorough knowledge of it. However, when "Truth" told me to stay there, I started to panic.

My surroundings suddenly brighten. *Headlights!* I lunge rightward into the brushes to let the car pass. The way the road curls around makes it especially treacherous for pedestrians, even in the daytime. Fortunately, traffic is light. After the first vehicle goes by, it occurs to me that someone *local* might be behind the wheel—someone from Camp K!

What would happen if they caught me? Family members would certainly not ambush me, at least not *physically*. However, they know how to persuade. The words of my member-buddy Jim Corner could make me feel as uplifted as a robin in springtime, or as guilty as a scolded puppy with its tail between its legs. And Family members could do to me what they call "love bomb." That means they would encircle me, barrage me with complements, and sing "We love you Ted-dy. Oh yes, we do. . ."

Despite their questionable tactics, the Family seemed to have ancient wisdom on their side. And they based everything on scientific principles. They championed self-evident truths such as humans are meant to be happy all the time, love is the cure to all of society's ills, values should guide your life, and so on. They seemed to have solutions to everything.

"Ask yourself one question," Jim had once said to me cogently. "Why would *anyone* want to leave *Paradise*?" It's the same question asked in last night's movie *Lost Horizon*. It's the one always asked regarding Adam and Eve's colossal screw-up.

No easy answer. If any Family member asked me that point blank, I'd stammer like a schoolboy caught cheating on a test. I may have even surrendered! I'd fall to my knees and, in tears, beg them for forgiveness.

Why?

You could call the Family anything you like—naive, corny, manipulative, phony, robotic, creepy, evil, etc.—and each adjective could be spot-on correct. But I have to say, they had a leg up over all outsiders regarding one thing:

They'd built Heaven on Earth, the perfect world!

Mankind had long tinkered with the idea of creating a place or state called *Utopia*. This concept recalls Plato's *Republic*, the works of Karl Marx, B. F. Skinner, and of course St. Thomas More who coined the term. Like many in my generation, one song captured the notion more than anything else—John Lennon's "Imagine." Philosophers have long debated about whether Utopia is even possible, given humanity's wretched state. (The word *utopia* literally means "no place.") Now, I know the answer. During my month-long stay in Boonville and Camp K, I found out that the perfect world is not only attainable, but it's an observable reality! Yes, my unworthy feet had touched holy ground! I had tasted its delectable fruit!

After basking in a state of spiritual bliss for so long, I left Camp K utterly conflicted. Part of me felt glad to get away; the other part felt extreme regret and sorrow. Nonetheless, at 2:17 a.m. Pacific Time, I walked down Highway 128 with a new bounce in my step, confident I'd made the right decision. I'm feeling exhilarated, jittery. But, for the first time, I'm besieged by another emotion: dread. I wonder what's going to happen to me in the outside world. I hear Jim's voice warning me that Satan and his minions will surely ambush me if I ever decide to exit Camp K on my own.

The dread also stems from a different source: my parents back in Detroit. The Family had assigned me "spiritual parents." Jim, my "spiritual dad," once reminded me of Jesus' shocking words: "If anyone comes to me and does not *hate* his own father and mother... he cannot be my disciple (Luke 14:26)." But now, I have a strange desire to reunite with the pair who brought me into this world. I can't wait to see them! What's more, I'm thinking, *Man, they're going to kill me when I get home!*

Then there's Randal Stark, my close buddy since seventh grade. My folks blamed him for everything. One incident dramatizes this. Sometime in the near future, my mom tells party guests about my Camp K experience. (Jaws drop, the typical reaction of most people.) As she's talking, she spots Randal sitting at another table.

"THERE HE IS!" she exclaims pointing to him with her accusing finger. Those within ear's shot hold their breath as if they're about to witness the unmasking of the Phantom of the Opera.

"It's all HIS fault," Mom mutters with nervous laughter. Mortified, my buddy squirms. Poor Randal looks like he wants to crawl under the table. She then continues to mercilessly lay into him. "YOU'RE the one who instigated the hitchhiking. You and your philosophy crap! YOU'RE the reason Ted got mixed up with those MOON PEOPLE."

Randal Stark the puppet master!

By the way, the "Moon people" she's talking about—those I was running away from on that fateful night in August of 1979—are commonly called "Moonies." The term refers to their leader, Reverend Sun Myung Moon, the Korean preacher/businessman who founded The Holy Spirit Association for the Unification of World Christianity, in short, the Unification Church or Unificationists.

Nowadays, most people have heard of the Kool-Aid-drinking Jim Jones cult, but few remember (or even heard of) the Unification Church, the first religion to be called a "doomsday cult." Its recruitment techniques were once considered to be the most sophisticated among the many other cults that sprang up in the 1970s.

☾ ☾ ☾

2:33 A.M. PLODDING ALONG California Highway 128, I'm exhausted. On top of that, I'm hyper-anxious about getting home fast to straighten everything out.

Here comes another car! An orange '74 AMC Gremlin.

Ah, what the heck. I'll raise my thumb in the air.

The Gremlin stops. As I approach to see who's inside, my stomach begins to turn.

PART I: THE ROAD

"OHHH, MOTHER!"

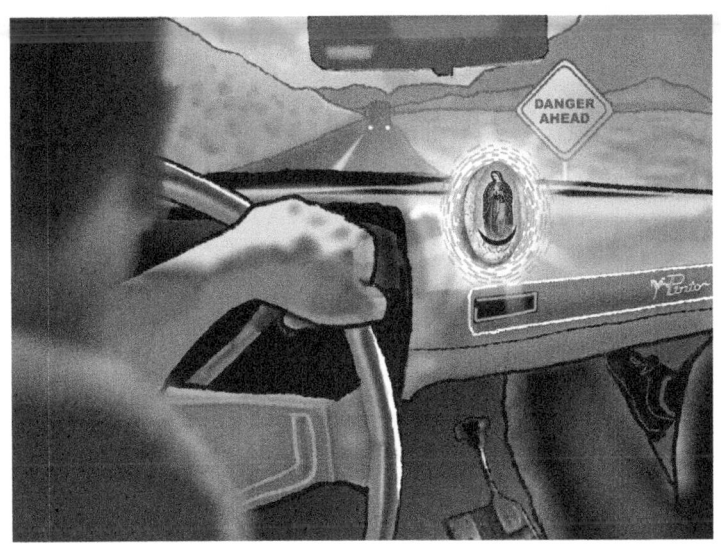

CHAPTER 1

A LUCKY BREAK

Cheyenne, Wyoming; the morning of July 9, 1979.

THREE WEEKS BEFORE MY INVOLVEMENT in the Moonies, I was on the southern outskirts of Cheyenne. Cowboy country! As I awake to a blustery morning, it dawns on me: *We are going to see Rosie again at last!* Rosalynn Smith—"Rosie" for short—is the fellow hitchhiker we'd befriended back in Wisconsin. She is now staying with her friend Dorna in Greeley, Colorado just an hour south of us.

Beyond the hotels, gas stations, and restaurants near the Interstate 80 and Highway 85 intersection, miles and miles of rolling grassland surround us. We had opted to camp close to civilization to avoid rattlesnakes, scorpions, and antelope poop. My jeans are still sooty from the freight train we had jumped the day before.

I, along with my blond, blue-eyed traveling companion, Peter Jean-Baptiste LeBlanc aka Pete, hold up my thumb along 85 in front of a livestock supplies store. It will take over three hours to get picked up. As typical during long waits, the mind ruminates. One insight floors me:

Maybe I'm never going back home.

Up to that point, I had assumed I'd return to the Motor City to resume my studies at the University of Michigan, Dearborn (aka U of M Dearborn and UM-D), but now I'm not so sure. If I'm having so much fun, why stop?

Joy and pride well up inside. What I'm doing is such a thrill. I could do this for months and even years. Heck, I could remain a wandering nomad for the rest of my life! Exotic, faraway places could be thoroughly explored for dirt cheap. I'd always have the option to settle down somewhere if I wanted. After a while, I could pull up the stakes and move on again if I got the itch.

College? Who needs it? Rosie is right. The road is the best school. I had learned so much from it already.

What will my parents think? I doubt they'll approve of my being a professional hobo.

☽ ☽ ☽

THE FIRST CAR THAT PULLS OVER gives me pause. It's a '71 Pinto, Ford Motor's problem child. It had been considered one of the worst cars ever made.

The motorist who stopped is the nervous type. After we pile our backpacks into his trunk, the middle-aged Hispanic man looks Pete and me over up-and-down before we enter his vehicle. "Man, I'm glad I picked you guys up!" he exclaims. "It's not safe around here. The rednecks and cowboys are crazy. They'd beat the snot out of guys like you and leave you to die in the desert just for fun. You're lucky to be alive!"

"*You're lucky to be alive!*" Words coming from a man named Lucky and one who rides a notoriously unsafe car! Even a minor rear-end collision could turn his Pinto into a flaming deathtrap. Since the model went on sale on September 11, 1970, Ford Motor, at one point, had to drop the slogan from its radio ads: "Pinto leaves you with that warm feeling."

"What's *wrong* with you guys? Don't you know hitchhiking is dangerous."

"Yeah, we know," Pete replies lackadaisically.

"Oh you *do* huh?"

As usual, Pete and I wax philosophical. Not yet twenty, we think we're smarter than anyone who ever existed. "We don't worry about that," Pete replies. "If we did, we'd spend our lives locked away in our houses."

"Yeah, practically everything you do in life is a risk," I add dismissively. "Heck, you could get struck by lightning by just walking down the street."

"Oh, come on," responds Lucky. "You can't compare . . ."

"Look," says I, "The only time you're perfectly safe is when you're dead. Maybe life is meant to be lived dangerously. Danger is how you find God."

"Danger is how you *find God?*" Lucky winces like he just got clobbered in the head with a brick. Of course, he has no idea what I said paraphrased Bhagwan Shree Rajneesh, an Indian guru I was seriously looking into at the time.

"You guys are crazy!" our concerned driver chokes. Then he shakes his head and puts in rather ominously, "All I can say is I'll *pray* for you."

I notice Our Lady of Guadalupe glued to his dashboard.

In tough times, people turn to religion. Back in '79, anxiety swept the nation. Gas prices and overall inflation were through the roof. Crime was up. Conflicts were breaking out across the globe and President Carter seemed too inept to do anything. A *Time* magazine article spoke of a fad called "disastermania." People suddenly got religion to deal with a sense of impending doom. One example was the huge success of the book *The Late Great Planet Earth* by Hal Lindsey which discussed Bible prophecies coming true before our very eyes.

ᏞᏞᏞ

I'M SITTING IN FRONT. PETE HAD JUST DOZED OFF in the back seat, the most vulnerable spot in Lucky's Pinto. If we get rear-ended, he is toast. But, then again, the same thing could happen to the rest of us. However, we have Our Lady protecting us! The Guadalupe car magnet on the dash is oval-shaped, 7" high and 4" wide. I'd seen that image plastered all over along Bagley Street in Detroit's Mexican Village. If you look at it closely, you'll see it's the picture of a praying woman wearing a rose-colored tunic covered by a turquoise mantle. Sun rays stream out from her and she's standing on a crescent moon.

"Do you know the *story* of Guadalupe?" Lucky inquires. He should ask. I was raised Polish and Catholic. The two adjectives are practically synonymous. Mother Mary was not only queen of our household but also of our country of origin. Just as Guadalupe symbolizes Mexico, Częstochowa signifies Poland.

"Vaguely," I answer. "My mom told it to me when I was a kid... Hmmm, let's see, that's when the Virgin appears to some Mexican dude named..."

"Juan Diego."

"Yeah, that's it! Juan Diego. How did that go again?"

"Well, it happened in what's now Mexico, just after the Spaniards came and conquered the Aztecs. Juan Diego is walking to Mass on a rustic trail when he's approached by Our Blessed Mother. She sends Juan on a mission: 'Tell the bishop to build me a church here.'"

"Yeah, yeah, now I remember. He does exactly what the Virgin tells him, but the bishop doesn't buy Juan's story, so Mary later appears to Juan again. She tells him, 'This time pick a bunch of roses and take them back to the bishop.' When Juan returns to the bishop's house, he unties the corners of his poncho in which he's carrying the roses and *voilà*! Red flower petals tumble down to the floor and everyone standing there is blown away. Mary's picture is on the poncho!"

I blankly stare out at the desolate prairie whizzing by. "Look, sir, Mary's picture couldn't just appear on some guy's cloak. It's obviously fake." Predictably, I sound off some of the atheist arguments I'd learned recently at UM-D.

But to be honest, I am "complaining too loudly." Over the past few months, I have been moving from skepticism and toward a faith of some kind. A "miracle" occurred the day before. But that's a whole other story that we'll come back to later.

CHAPTER 2

FALL FROM GRACE

Reminiscing about Detroit on the way to Greeley.

LUCKY HAD JUST CROSSED INTO COLORADO when it hit me. It's Randal Stark's birthday! He played a major role in the hobo origin story, though he did so unwittingly I must say.

He was probably waiting on some customer or stocking shelves at Schneider's, a sporting goods store back home. It's in Dearborn's brand-new shopping mall—Fairlane Town Center aka Fairlane Mall or simply Fairlane. I pitied him being all cooped up in that shop sucking up to some boss. Me? I'm my own boss.

Randal and I grew up two miles apart on Detroit's west side, just north of Dearborn. We attended the same Catholic schools and graduated in the same class. His family, like mine, came from durable Eastern European stock. Randal's grandparents were from Hungary. We were each blessed with two devoted parents who were actively involved in our lives. Of the working class, they were quite conservative. Brown-haired, brown-eyed Randal had what it takes to fit in with the cool kids at school—good looks, self-confidence, and above-average intelligence—but, for some odd reason, he preferred to hang out with misfits like me. We had known each other since fourth grade but didn't become friends until seventh grade when we served as altar boys and did a science project together.

Randal Stark was complex like Raskolnikov in Dostoevsky's *Crime and Punishment*. Raskolnikov's name literally means split (as in split personality) which fits Randal. On the one hand, Randal had the traits of a driven, competitive, type-A personality. (For example, he ran for Class President.) On the other hand, he was the exact opposite extreme: a type B—laid-back, apathetic, and even lazy. The lackadaisical way he sauntered into the classroom and slouched in his chair prompted Sister Mary Matilda to declare him the "idlest person" she'd ever met. He was serious yet unserious. If you didn't know him very well, he'd appear as reserved and somber as a cancer surgeon with heartburn. However, you'd eventually discover he's as funny, playful, and mischievous as the class clown.

It's ironic that my mother would later blame Randal for leading me down the wrong path. When I befriended him, Mom was pleased I finally had the good sense to fraternize with the right people. An honor roll student, former boy scout, and even vice-president of the altar boys, Randal seemed poised for success. He was a born leader, and what's more, a righteous man. Like a younger version of Atticus Finch in *To Kill a Mockingbird*, he gallantly spoke his mind whenever he met injustice, real or imagined, regarding, say, a questionable call of an umpire or the cruel actions of a bully. Whether you liked it or not, he told you the truth and did so in its most brutal fashion. I suppose my mother was at least partly right about him getting me to do things I otherwise wouldn't do. Randal knew how to persuade people using sound reason and logic. He approached things scientifically. However, to suggest that he was controlling every move I made like some puppet master is a bit of a stretch.

An argument can be made that I had corrupted Randal, not the other way around. I familiarized him with the shadowy dominion near my house called the Tracks. The place consisted of railroad tracks going east and west. But it also included the region surrounding the railroad tracks known as the "right-of-way." This narrow tract of land—owned by the Chesapeake and Ohio Railway Company (C&O)—was thick with wild vegetation. For safety and liability reasons, C&O fenced it off from the public, except for a few spots such as road crossings. Our parents would never approve of us going there.

The Tracks was much more than a physical place. It was Hades from ancient Greek legend, a "world of darkness" if you will. To understand its essence, it's helpful to compare it to the "world of light" just outside of it, namely the community I grew up in. The district is called Cody Rouge because it features Cody High School to the east and River Rouge Park to the west.

During my formative years, Cody Rouge was a relatively safe place to live. Practically everyone kept their bushes trimmed and lawns cut. Neighbor looked after neighbor. Many attended our local parish, St. Suzanne. Like Emil Sinclair in Hermann Hesse's novel *Demian*, Randal and I were products of the "realm of brilliance, clarity, cleanliness, gentle conversations, washed hands, clean clothes, and good manners."

To the degree sensible people avoided the Tracks, young teenage boys like us were drawn to it as we were attracted to rock music and girls. In Sinclair's world of light, you were supposedly *forced* to be good all the time. In the world of darkness, you were free to do whatever you wanted. The Tracks were a symbol for the world of darkness. It was a hideout where you could smoke, drink, and swear to your heart's content. Unlike its goody-two-shoes counterpart, this realm was unpredictable. At the Tracks you'd chance upon odd and morbidly fascinating things like dead cats hanging from nooses; underground forts stocked with porn; and foreign objects purported to be related to notorious robberies, murders, and suicides. The very fact the Tracks was off-limits and potentially dangerous made it even more enticing like forbidden fruit. Naturally, it inspired risky behavior like climbing on top of buildings, playing chicken with moving freights, and perpetrating crime.

Randal and I, in a relatively short time, went from being dedicated altar servers to conniving crooks who planned and executed misdemeanors and out-and-out felonies, namely vandalism, breaking-and-entering, and theft. We were fallen angels. At one point, Randal became the chief instigator of our delinquent acts. When I began to express reservations, he coaxed me to stay focused on bold capers he had concocted. Like Frank Sinatra's character in *Ocean's Eleven*, he was talking about heists, not run-of-the-mill robberies.

What made us sink to this level? My first response is the adrenaline high induced by the act of getting away with something, a sense of power. Our future Psychology professors would claim our adolescent selves were merely acting out a normal stage of development. According to Erik Erickson's theory, teens searching for identity enjoy testing society's rules. While this and other explanations make sense, I'm still confused by the fact that Randal and I found evil so irresistible.

Whatever the case, what occurred on the day of reckoning would effectively thwart our wayward behavior. I recoil when I mentally relive getting arrested for taking part in a robbery of a warehouse adjacent to the Tracks. (What were we intending to steal? I have no idea.) Being subjected to good cop/bad cop was bad enough, but Mom and Dad arriving to pick me up at the police station was one of the most humiliating experiences in my life. The worst part was beholding my parents' beleaguered faces, my mother in tears repeatedly crossing herself and saying "Matko Jedyna!" (Polish for "Oh Mother!") as she hysterically tried to reassure the law that I was really a good kid. "But officers, he's an altar boy!" she shrieked several times. In her mind, that fact alone proved I was innocent.

Not long afterwards, Randal got caught doing something equally stupid, but it's not worth getting into the details. Thankfully, we weren't involved with each other's infractions. Otherwise, our folks would've permanently forbidden us from hanging out together.

Our life of crime would come to a screeching halt—or would it?

CHAPTER 3

GREELEY, CO

Greeley; the afternoon of July 9, 1979.

P ETE LEBLANC AND I MADE IT safely to our destination by noon. The most impressive spot in downtown Greeley is Lincoln Park, two city blocks of well-maintained grass, trees, and playgrounds. On the paved ground encircling the fountain and the gazebo-style bandstand are the names of seven ideals or virtues cast in bronze: Temperance, Cooperation, Agriculture, Irrigation, Education, Faith, Home, and Family.

Not far from the gazebo is a life-sized bronze statue of a farm family: a husband, wife, and child in 1870s-style work clothes. It's called "The Promise of the Prairie." It reminds me of the Holy Family, except they appear distinctively American. The pioneer man and woman look resolutely into the distance as if facing an approaching dust storm or locust plague. The overalls-wearing "St. Joseph" supports his little boy with his strong right arm and holds his wife close to his side with his left. The woman clings close to her husband, resting her head on his shoulder. The plaque below reads:

"*Where there is no vision, the people perish.*" (Proverbs: 29:18)

Residents of Greeley are very proud of their city. One named James A. Michener based his best-selling novel *Centennial* on it. The sweeping multi-generational epic saga (1,068-pages long!) was eventually made into a popular miniseries on NBC.

Greeley citizens' pride parallels that of the people of Dearborn who are pleased by the fact that they live in Henry Ford's hometown. Instead of celebrating a local-boy-made-good, Greeley-ites relish the fact their town originated as an idealistic community striving to be a utopia.

The much talked about political philosopher Sayyid Qutb (1906-1966) lived in Greeley in the year 1949. The 43-year-old Egyptian had a utopian vision of his own. Across the street from "The Promise of the Prairie" is St. Patrick Presbyterian Church

(formerly First Congregational Church). Qutb's scathing account of a chaperoned dance held in the church basement is known all over the Muslim world! People laugh at his depiction of us Americans as perpetually horny primitives living "in jungles and caves." He's called a prude. But nowadays his vehement rant about our cavalier, disrespectful attitude toward sex doesn't seem far off the mark!

☾ ☾ ☾

ONCE WE ARRIVED THERE, OUR FIRST IMPULSE was to find a payphone to contact Rosie. Looking around, we spot a "Bell System" sign at the nearby Sunoco gas station and sprint toward it. Another sign, a handwritten one, captures the desperate situation in 1979. It read "$5 LIMIT ON GAS." As I said, times were bad.

Pete eagerly feeds the slot with coins, punches the numbers, and anxiously clasps his ear to the earpiece. After telling Rosie our whereabouts, he scribbles down her directions. Thankfully, she is within walking distance. Her "turn lefts" and "turn rights" refers to streets labeled with letters and numbers—O Street, 35th Street, and so on—much like the grid pattern of the game Battleship.

We spent most of the hike along O Street which runs east-west on the northern outskirts of town. The north side features sugar beet farms and cattle feedlots. On a clear day with temperatures in the 80s, the pungent smell of hay, manure, and nitrogen fertilizer fills the air. I find that most of the people driving by—many in pickups and wearing cowboy hats—work in either livestock or agriculture.

After traversing a stretch of O, we turn left on 35th, then right on C, and there we are: the Sunnybrook Mobile Home Park. We make our way to Unit 11D, the home of one Dorna Platte, the close friend Rosie had said she's staying with. Compared to the other mobile homes, I'd give Dorna's dwelling place a B-minus. It's made from white aluminum and has a redwood-stained porch with some patio furniture. An air conditioner droops out of a window like a sagging breast.

Pete pounds on the door with his fist.

"HHHEEEYYY! WHAT'S GOIN' ON?" Rosie explodes with delight as she sees us standing there. She lets us in and smothers us each with a monstrous hug.

GREELEY, CO   21

Since we last saw Rosie, I had fantasized about what the big reunion would be like. Now she is standing right there wearing an apron and flip-flops (a term that aptly describes what my heart is doing at the time). I feel anxious not knowing what to expect next. I had seen her as more than a friend, rather than as a potential girlfriend. She is my muse, my *donna ideale!*

☾ ☾ ☾

AGAIN, ROSIE SMITH WAS THE HITCHHIKER Pete and I had befriended back in Wisconsin. We met her a few miles outside of Mad City, the nickname for Madison, the state's premier college town. In my imagination, she is the "child of God" in the Joni Mitchell (and CSNY) song "Woodstock." Like the mystery person in the lyrics, Rosie invited us to a big bash that was about to begin in the hinterland, a place called "Poverty Gulch." My joy over this development was eclipsed by my insane jealousy over Pete and Rosie hitting it off romantically from the start, leaving me out in the cold, so to speak. Even now—a little over a week later—the intense feeling still lingers like a bad toothache.

Rosie was what one might call a "hippie chick" (I can hear her now quoting Kierkegaard: "Once you label me, you negate me."). Those in my generation (the so-called Baby Boomers) would tag her as such because of the way she dressed, talked, and acted. Hippies like her wore their radical individualism on their sleeves. Rosie sported a white embroidered smock top and mid-thigh length cut-off jeans. Her straight auburn hair was trimmed short and sculpted like rocker Joan Jett. She was as tanned as a saddle, indicative of all the hitchhiking she had done. Sure, she was good looking, but her attractiveness had much to do with her spellbinding effervescence. She was light, cheerful, and bubbly. Her face beamed. She was as energetic as a puppy and chatty as a cockatoo. You could expect her to break out in song or dance at any moment.

"Make yourself at home!" she entreats. Pete and I, taking her cue, take off our backpacks and plop our weary frames on a brown sofa. The mobile home, a double-wide type, looks surprisingly spacious inside. The décor is pure '70s. Screaming orange shag carpeting clashes with the gold- and avocado-colored fabrics. By today's standards, it is hideous. Several elements hint at the local culture's overarching theme: The Old West. These include a lamp base shaped like a cowboy boot, wagon-wheel wall hangings, and rodeo-rider knickknacks.

There is a little girl and a little boy present—about age five and seven respectively—each crouched on the living room floor. Once wrapped up in a game of Cootie, they stare profusely at us as if we're two space aliens who'd just fallen from the sky. "Wendy" and "Kenny," as they'd be introduced, resume playing after their curiosity ebbs.

"I'm babysitting for Dorna," Rosie explains.

As the three of us adults engage in conversation, Rosie occasionally interrupts the flow to see if the cookies in the oven are ready. I have to say, seeing her in the role of Suzy Homemaker is a stunning revelation. It is so incongruous with my image of her as the ultimate free-spirit, one who'd never settle down in a million years.

Incredibly, she had been "on the road" for a whopping year-and-a-half (at least that's what she claimed). From the most populous cities along the West Coast to the most remote village in Alaska, she'd seen America inside out! But now, to my dismay, she seems downright *domesticated*. In the '70s, feminists had railed against the notion that "a woman's place is in the home."

CHAPTER 4

HOW RANDAL AND T GOT THE IDEA TO HOP A TRAIN

Flashback of Detroit; July, 7, 1977.

THE DAYS FOLLOWING THE DAY OF RECKONING were sobering to say the least. My parents lowered the boom on me after my arrest for breaking-and-entering into a warehouse at the Tracks. Randal Stark similarly got his just desserts for committing a crime similar to mine. After "seeing the light," we started acting responsibly like the adults we were biologically becoming. At age seventeen, we walked and talked more like actual men. We held our heads up high and "put away childish things," as St. Paul said. Now it was upward and onward to the next stage of psychosocial development.

All that said, a different kind of rebellion simmered below the surface. It came from without rather than from within. To put it bluntly, much of the content on TV, in movies, and especially in rock music—prejudiced us against our parents and their belief system. It was an insidious process. Sometime around the year 1968, the mainstream culture began to side with the malcontents in the anti-war, civil rights, and feminist movements. Starting in '68, the news media, entertainment industry, and academia, acquiesced to what is called the "60s counterculture" or simply the "'60s."

Our parents bitterly complained about the devastating effects of this cultural revolution: the erosion of patriotism and respect for authority. Sexual mores were scorned. Conversely, our college-age siblings saw the '60s as the dawning of a new age of peace, love, and understanding," the Age of Aquarius, or the New Age.

Since '68—a year of unusual tumult, chaos, and anxiety much like '79 and 2020—there was a lot of talk about the "generation gap." I can attest to the Grand Canyon-like chasm that had existed between me and my parents. When my mother and I decided to attend a movie matinee in the winter of '77, it seemed we'd never agree on what flick to see together. But alas, we found one: *Bound for Glory* about folk music legend Woody Guthrie. Mom could relate to it because it takes place during the Great Depression of the 1930s, the era she grew up in and talked about a lot. Like John Steinbeck's *The Grapes of Wrath*, the film shows a farm family from Oklahoma struggling to survive. On top of worrying about starvation and other perils due to the dismal economy, the "Okies" had to contend with the Dust Bowl, monstrous black clouds of air-borne soot creeping across the land, snuffing out crops, livestock, and humans. They were forced to sell their property and move to California to find jobs picking fruit.

I could identify with *Bound for Glory* because, first, the actor who plays Woody, David Carradine, also starred in *Kung Fu*, one of my favorite TV shows. Second, I'd been impressed by what I read about Guthrie in *Rolling Stone* magazine, the "bible" of the rock music scene. The wise-cracking guitar player and political activist is most famous for his anthem "This Land is Your Land" and for inspiring a group of musicians called singer-songwriters, among them: (1) Bob Dylan, once dubbed the "spokesman of the '60s generation" and (2) Bruce Springsteen, the "new Dylan."

Woody at the height of his success turns his back on everything, including his job and family, to hop freight trains across the country. He becomes a hobo! Sure, it's a life of constant danger, privation, and poverty, but it's also one of fun, adventure, and, most important of all, *freedom*. Woody is no longer attached to anything! On watching this new phase of his life unfold on the silver screen, sixteen-year-old me sat there mesmerized. The figure of the hobo (or "migrant worker") was seen as the very symbol of freedom, liberty, and self-determination. For that very reason, he perfectly embodies the '60s notion of doing your own thing, being an individual, and shunning responsibility.

That's me! I almost shouted in the darkened Fairlane Mall movie theater. I too hated rules and people (especially family members) telling me what to do.

The dialogue that ensued after the movie perfectly illustrates the generation gap. When I said, "Wow, I want to be that guy!" (or something to that effect), my mom, visibly stunned, perplexed, and disgusted replied, "Who? That selfish deadbeat? A man who abandons his wife and kids just because he feels like it?"

ᴄ ᴄ ᴄ

FOR BETTER OR WORSE, THE MESSAGE of *Bound for Glory* stuck with me like glue. I became obsessed with it. The movie instantly renewed my interest in the Tracks. After a year-long hiatus, I returned there to walk my dog (or rather let him run loose), daydream, and sing to myself Dylan's "A Hard Rain's A-Gonna Fall" and other songs that capture the spirit of Woody Guthrie. The place now represented something more than just Hades. It was the Wild Frontier. I reminisced about simpler and more innocent times when my friends and I explored the Tracks like the pioneers explored the great American West. The new vision of the hobo made me relish its grungy atmosphere. Rusty, grimy, and filthy things appeared immaculate. Creosote smelled like perfume. Even loud train noises (if they stayed constant and rhythmic) were music to my ears.

I often wondered about the graffiti written on the old utility shed. Secret code? Are the burnt logs and empty wine bottles in the clearing of the thickets evidence of a "hobo jungle?" I imagined myself being before a campfire, in a circle of colorful and ragged characters playing harmonica, telling stories, and roasting wieners.

ᴄ ᴄ ᴄ

RANDAL NEVER GOT INTO THE HOBO THING. To this very day, he finds the idea as appealing as maggots on a rotting corpse. For that reason, he prefers to call his younger self a hitchhiker rather than a hobo. However, I *did* manage to turn him on to Dylan's then-highly popular album *Blood on the Tracks*. And of course Randal and I once conspired to stow away on a train together.

It all began one hot afternoon in July of '77, a time of hope and tedium. The hopeful part had to do with the expectation of entering 12th grade in the Fall. Randal and I looked forward to receiving special privileges as high school seniors. We would be allowed to goof off (to a certain extent), even skip classes. But it was a far bigger deal for Randal. He had savored the prospect of being the big cheese at our school.

The tedious aspect of the summer had to do with having to wait so long for school to begin in September—and being bored out of our minds. The conversation between us toggled back and forth between "What do you want to do?" and "I don't know, what do *you* want to do?" The usual ideas—biking, playing ping-pong, shooting hoops, etc.—were ceremoniously tossed out and shot down one-by-one like clay pigeons. It seemed like every activity had lost its allure. Finally, one of us came up with something that at least resembled a spark of inspiration.

"Hey, I know. . . Let's go to the *Tracks*."

"Hmmm, worth considering. . . yeah, let's do it." Our feet at once spring into action despite any reservations we might have. Given our history of malfeasance there, it's of course the worst idea imaginable. But we can't help ourselves. We feel so restless. And besides, it seems like half a decade has passed since our crime spree days (when it is probably not quite a year.)

We enter through the usual passage: the parking lot between two warehouses along Fitzpatrick Avenue, across the street from the baseball diamond in the neighborhood park. We stride on the main trail through the thick underbrush, up the embankment to the ballast where the rails rest on their designated bed of rocks. The creosote-soaked railroad ties smell particularly pungent combined with our sweat. The high humidity that day partly explains why we plod along the rails slowly and mechanically like a couple of sleepwalkers. Another reason is we are deeply engrossed in colloquy.

"I wish I could be with *Constance* right now!" Randal put forth.

Here we go again. I'm rolling my eyes as I kick a rusty Faygo can down the track.

HOW RANDAL AND I GOT THE IDEA TO HOP A TRAIN 27

Constance McGuire is the girl Randal met in Florida where he and his family spent Easter vacation. According to him, sparks began to fly at the swimming pool arcade. After having a wonderful time chit-chatting, Randal got her phone number. Ever since they parted ways, he thought about her and their potential romantic relationship day and night. But there's one problem. Constance lives 650 miles away! A drive from Detroit to her parents' place in Commack, New York (on Long Island) would take at least twelve hours. Without a car, money, and likely his parents' permission, the prospect of cultivating a love affair looked bleak. However, Randal refused to be deterred! In his mind, true love can't be hindered by trifling matters such as distance, logistics, and lack of resources. "Mark my word," he declares. "One day, Constance and I are going to be together at last!"

"Good luck," I reply patronizingly. My tone of voice reflects an annoyance at Randal's non-stop droning about the subject. In addition, I am physically drained from the ninety-degree heat and dispirited that even the Tracks had now become humdrum.

"There's got to be a way to get to New York!" Randal continues. His brilliant mind keeps actively cranking out ideas despite his lack of physical energy, though none of them appears even remotely desirable or feasible.

About six feet away from the steel rails, a couple hundred feet from the railway observation tower, there's a weird domed rock that's about four feet in diameter. In the past, my friends and I had stipulated that it's the tip of a gigantic meteor buried in the ground. When we are close to there, we hear a mighty roar getting louder by the second.

WWWHHHOOO-WWWHHHHOOOOOOOOO. HHHUUUM-MMMMMMMM!

A train is coming! Out of respect for our mortal frames, we ceremoniously step down from the ballast and distance ourselves about twenty feet away to let the diesel-powered monster pass. Despite the intense noise and sudden gust of hot air blasting into our faces, Randal looks at me intensely as I do him. Then one of us says to the other, "Are you thinking what I'm thinking?"

CHAPTER 5

THE MIRACLE

More flashbacks.

I HAD SPOKEN EARLIER ABOUT THE MIRACLE that occurred the day before we got picked up in Cheyenne. My partner Pete had an altogether different take of the supernatural than our driver Lucky.

I met Pete on a chilly Friday night in mid-to-late September 1978, about three weeks after Randal went away to college in Ann Arbor. Since Randal had been gone, I felt lonesome and alienated. Being surrounded by "shallow people" at U of M Dearborn felt like the zombie apocalypse. Fortunately, a weekend visit from Randal helped cure my blues to a certain extent. He and I decided to have some cold ones and shoot the breeze at some obscure location just like old times. We had in mind nearby Hines Park, a popular spot for partying, but settled on the empty parking lot of St. Bernard Seminary in Dearborn Heights. There, we came upon two strangers, a Pete and a Wally. They were out partying like us, except they were smoking weed instead of drinking beer. After everyone was properly introduced, the four of us chatted into the small hours.

Pete and I hit it off right away because we both liked Bob Dylan and Dylan just happened to be coming to Detroit in just three weeks.

Both Pete and I badly wanted to see him live, but to get a good seat, you had to stand in line all night outside of the Olympia Stadium box office. We agreed to meet up when tickets went on sale.

I was conceivably the only person in a twenty-mile radius who comprehended this guy. The secret to cracking the Pete LeBlanc code was to understand the singer-songwriter genre that had peaked in popularity around the year 1970, the music of Gordon Lightfoot, Cat Stevens, and of course Bob Dylan. One could imagine Pete as being the solitary figure in the Simon & Garfunkel song "I Am a Rock," the one who "feels no pain," "hiding in (his) room," etc. I would come into his pad "on a winter's day" (closing the door behind me) and he'd be sitting on his bed strumming his acoustic guitar, only half-noticing my presence. His demeanor initially came across as aloof and rude, but, after a few visits, I realized his mind is fixed on the dreams in his head. Like a moth ready to burst out of his cocoon, he longed to leave metro Detroit asap and never return. He said he hated school, work, and everything about our town.

The "books and poetry" on his shelf not only "protected" him (like in the S&G song), but they were also the keys to figuring him out. *The Catcher in the Rye* by J. D. Salinger captures him well. He was Holden Caulfield, the jaded teenager who criticizes practically everything in the so-called adult world. His library probably had every book written by early twentieth-century German author Hermann Hesse. *Siddhartha*, perhaps Hesse's most mainstream novel, was a best-seller in the '60s. In the book, a young man living in Buddha's time—who's disenchanted with normal middle-class life—decides to leave town forever and seek enlightenment and salvation by becoming a wandering ascetic monk. Hesse's *Steppenwolf*, also a '60s classic, inspired a rock band to adopt its name and whose signature song was "Born to Be Wild." When the book first came out, it was excoriated for its lack of morality, especially about sex and drugs.

Then there was Pete's favorite, Hesse's *Demian* (1919). It's a coming-of-age story about a young man named Emil Sinclair who learns a valuable life lesson: "Alongside serving God, we should also serve the devil." Raised in a religious home, Sinclair struggles between "the worlds of light and darkness." He befriends a classmate named Max Demian who doesn't quite fit in with the other kids. Mature for his age and street wise, Demian seems to know how to tap into some mysterious power or force which can strike fear in the heart of bullies, read minds, and perform extraordinary feats using mind-over-matter.

Demian becomes Sinclair's mentor. He bases his strange views on the story of Cain and Abel, except Cain, the first murderer, is actually the good guy—the hero! The ancient tale, reimagined in a twisted new way, is the central motif of *Demian*. The bit about serving both God and the devil probably isn't to be taken literally. It's likely a poetic rendering of a notion conceived by Friedrich Nietzsche called the *Übermensch*. (Hesse was heavily influenced by the German philosopher.) The term, translated "Overman" or "Super-human" is used for the superior person who operates in a godless universe "beyond good and evil."

Demian claims that after Cain kills his brother "he's awarded a special decoration for his cowardice: A mark that protects him and puts the fear of God into all the others". . . "Here is a man with something in his face that frightened the others. They didn't dare lay hands on him; he impressed them, he and his children." Cain and his "descendants" (followers of his philosophy) are too smart, courageous, and unique for ordinary folks to handle.

Cain is the person who stands out among the faceless crowd because he's decidedly different. He has the strength and fortitude to be himself.

In the story, the Lord sentences Cain for fratricide: "You will be a restless wanderer on the earth." This explained the wanderlust that had consumed me and my companions Randal Stark and Pete LeBlanc. We were sons of Cain! We of course didn't slay our male siblings, but we undoubtedly bore Cain's "mark of distinction" since we were so bright and "authentic" that we transcended even the categories of good and evil! In our eyes, we could do no wrong.

The Genesis story suggests the mark protected us supernaturally, so our concerned driver Lucky and our anxious parents could rest assured we were perfectly safe and secure hitchhiking across the country.

☾ ☾ ☾

BACK TO THE "MIRACLE." At Dorna's pad in Greeley, Rosie invites us to the kitchen table for some peanut-butter-and-jelly sandwiches, fresh cookies, and Celestial Seasonings herbal tea.

"So, tell me about your journey since we last met!" she urges.

"Rosie, this past week's been amazing," responds Pete.

The highlights could be presented chronologically or in order of importance. These include sleeping in a mansion in St. Paul, Minnesota one evening and staying overnight in a rest-stop outhouse two nights later, meeting fascinating people like t'non, a Native-American guy trapped in a white man's body. Then there's the big anti-nuke rally in the Black Hills of South Dakota. But one thing stood out since it just happened the day before.

"Yesterday we *lost everything*," says I.

"*What?!*" exclaims Rosie.

"Well, I should say *almost* everything," Pete puts matter-of-factly. "A train went off with our backpacks."

"A train?" asks a captivated Rosie.

"It all started in Sidney, Nebraska when a highway patrolman kicked us off the Interstate. We end up in the boondocks along the old service road next to some railroad tracks. And guess what? No traffic! But suddenly, we hear a loud noise from a distance. It's the sound of a train coming our way! We must make a snap decision, right? Either wait forever, or make a mad dash to . . ."

". . . An easy choice," I chime in. "We run over to the train, take off our backpacks, throw them on one of the flatcars and. . ."

"Goodbye backpacks! The train is going too fast for us to climb on board."

"You mean. . . ?"

"Yup. All our stuff, lost in the blackness of the abyss." Pete had a penchant for speaking poetically.

"Wow! What happened next?"

"Well, in a weird way, things just kind of worked out. Like karma. Another train comes by a short time later. Except this one is going just slow enough for us to grab and hoist ourselves on. We cling on for dear life for about an hour. We then find ourselves in this massive train yard in Cheyenne. . ."

"... Biggest train yard you'd ever see in your life. There must've been fifty or more trains next to each other, not to mention tracks! We desperately search for our backpacks among a gazillion freight cars. But it's no use. There are just too many of them! To find them would be like finding a needle in a haystack..."

"... And the plot thickens. We get cornered and arrested by a couple of railroad cops. Big, scary, and mean dudes, you understand, the kind that drink your blood like wine. And they're very, very pissed. They rough us up a bit and eventually haul us away for questioning. We wind up in some stuffy room, the office of the big railroad boss..."

"... The big boss yells at us for a while, inflicts us with horror stories about dismemberments and deaths of young people who tried to hop trains and failed. He even threatens to throw us in the slammer. Then, just when we start to sweat, he nonchalantly turns to his secretary and says, 'Call the Agent.' "

"The *Agent*?"

"Yeah, whatever, *whom*ever, that meant. A federal agent or something. *Secret* agent? I don't know. Anyway, a short time later, this tall, well-dressed dude in a cowboy hat and boots pulls up in his fancy jeep, comes in the office and says 'Gentlemen, I'll take you to your backpacks.'"

"... Yeah, then he drives us over to the exact same flat car where we had thrown our packs. Both are sitting right there, a little sooty, but unmoved, untouched!"

There is at least a five-second pause until a dumbfounded Rosie finally utters, "It just sounds too incredible. You guys aren't pulling my leg, are you?"

"Honest to God. Hope to die."

Wagging my head, I registered this remark: "Amazing luck, huh? The chances of something like this happening must be a million to one."

Without missing a beat, Pete answers with a glint in his eye, "Luck? Chance? No such things! The Mark of Cain protects us."

THE MIRACLE

CHAPTER 6

THE BATCAVE

Detroit flashback; July, 9, 1977.

RANDAL EXCLAIMS WITH GLEE, "*To the Batcave!*" With these words, we turn around and high tail it to his parents' house. To carry out the tricky business of jumping freights, we first needed to strategize and the place to do it was his basement. The fact my friend had named it after Batman's subterranean hideout shows how much he revered the "Dark Knight" (formerly known as "The Caped Crusader"). Randal's Batcave didn't have a supercomputer like the one on TV but Randal's brain sufficed! He used sound reasoning and solid data to solve problems. He had ruled out chasing moving trains early. "*Too dangerous!*" he decided after painstaking analysis. But Randal has another idea:

"Hey, why not get on a train when it's *not moving?*" he poses. "Ever notice there are a lot of trains just sitting there on the tracks waiting to be loaded or something? Why not sneak onto one of them and wait for the thing to start moving again?" Randal and I deliberate for hours about how this could be done the most efficiently.

The Batcave is the finished side of the basement, used occasionally as a guest bedroom, but it is most often Randal's place of solitude. He always kept the spot tidy and stocked with ample materials for any project that captured his fancy at any given time, nuts and bolts, office supplies, and such. Down there, we invented several board games together. We made posters during his ill-fated run for eighth-grade class president.

Then there's the "GBL." In ninth grade, when we were virtual nobodies in school, Randal concocted a plan to achieve popularity by starting a social club based on hedonism. After hours of deliberation, we named our new organization the "Gratification Bureau Limited" or "GBL" for short. However, our new outfit didn't last very long. When Randal's wise-cracking older sister suggested GBL stood for the "Gay Boys League," we scrapped the idea.

Another intricate scheme deserved to be quickly and completely expunged the moment it was conceived: The Great Kmart Heist. Randal thought himself a superhero, but he could be villainous when it suited him. He masterminded the whole nefarious plot—involving him, me, and another friend—to burgle the nearby retail-chain store. It involved careful coordination. One team member would inconspicuously crawl into a merchandise storage compartment shortly before closing time and then come out later at night to loot the store. Randal had detailed how to get the would-be robber in and out of the bin without being noticed during store hours and how to get the stolen goods out of the store without being detected by security. I naturally felt leery about getting involved, especially after recently getting busted at the Tracks. Fortunately, Randal's peer pressure stopped cold after he learned about motion detectors.

᠂ ᠂ ᠂

SLIPPING INTO AN UNATTENDED BOXCAR while it's not moving appeared as easy as crossing the street, especially if it was done under the cloak of darkness. However, a high degree of uncertainty plagued the endeavor from the start. The main obstacle would be of course not knowing when the train would start moving again. It could take hours, even days! Did we have the stamina to wait long periods in some dark, perhaps cramped, hiding place? What about having enough food and water to sustain ourselves during a potentially long wait. What about going to the bathroom? Moreover, we had surmised that the train was going in the general direction of East. But *where* East? Maine? Pennsylvania? Maryland?

On realizing we'd wasted our time on a colossal delusion, a disappointed Randal finally throws up his hands and mutters "Oh crap, this ain't gonna work!" Our hearts sink like marble slabs in the muck of the Rouge River. The complete despair we both feel necessitates a workable Plan B, so the Bat-computer of Randal's brain once again goes into overdrive until it (or my feeble mind) comes up with one: "Hey, why not *hitchhike*?"

"*Hmmm*. . . Yeah, a little more *predictable*. . ."

". . . and *safe*. . . er, well, sort of," I stammer. Young people thumbing around the country was not uncommon in 1977. It had been somewhat of a fad since the '60s, but, as of late, it was viewed less favorably considering publicized crimes involving hitchhikers.

Shifting our gaze from the Tracks to the Road, our plans became much more concrete. However, one last hurdle remained: concerned parents. What lie would we concoct explaining our absence? Of course, they would flip if they found out we were planning to hitchhike to Commack, New York.

"I know!" I speak, breaking a long silence. "I'll tell my mom and dad I'm going to your parents' cottage up north for a week or so."

"Yeah, and I'll tell my folks I'm going camping with your family. Perfect!" After this matter is addressed, the plan seems to come together in its completed form. We make our final decision to meet pre-dawn a week later at a bus stop along Joy Road. We'd first take the coach through our blighted city, walk across the Ambassador Bridge (over the Detroit River), and stick our thumbs out once we set foot in Canada. After our parents apparently bought our BS, we feel confident enough to start packing.

The night before our scheduled departure, I get a phone call.

"Ted! It's me." The shaky voice on the other end is a distraught Randal.

"What's wrong?!"

There is a long, tortured sigh before the dropping of the bomb: "My mom and dad *know*!"

"*What?!*"

"Todd told my parents." Randal explains that he'd stupidly divulged the secret to his older brother Todd so that "in case of an emergency" Todd could notify the proper authorities if necessary. Naturally, his sibling wanted no part of the conspiracy and immediately blabbed about the entire affair to Mr. and Mrs. Stark, ruining everything. This whole sorry episode reveals Randal Stark's fatal flaw: a tendency to take responsibility. That said, he was tempted to kill his brother like Cain slew Abel.

CHAPTER 7

CONVERSATION WITH ROSIE

Greeley, the afternoon of July 9, 1979.

SINCE WE ARRIVED AT DORNA'S, Rosie fussed over Pete's right elbow. During his musical performance at Poverty Gulch, he had seriously singed it being too close to the fire. The burn got so infected over the past week it resembled a red tree fungus. Thankfully, another one of Rosie's friends—a nursing student named Barb—lived close by. After our lengthy discussion about the miraculous train incident, Pete was sent over for some First Aid.

Before he left, I faced a predicament. Should I go with him or stay behind with Rosie? (As babysitter, she was obligated to remain with the kids.) You'd think this would be a no-brainer given my strong feelings for her, but this wasn't the case. To be honest, I was mortified. The idea of being practically alone with the "goddess" intimidated me as much as the thought of being stuck in an elevator with Pat Benatar, the hottest female rock star at the time.

With a deep breath, I pull myself together and then exhale.

"I'll stay here," I say resolutely.

Pete leaves and I am eyeball-to-eyeball with the woman of my dreams. I sit up straight at the kitchen table chair with a pasted-on smile, all the while nervously tapping my toes and wringing my hands under the table.

☾ ☾ ☾

"HEY KIDS, COME OVER HERE. I want to introduce you to Mr. Granger. He's from Detroit, Michigan. Do you know where Michigan is?" There is no globe or atlas map available in Dorna's trailer home, so I configure my hands to make them look like Michigan's Upper and Lower Peninsulas. When asked his age, Kenny makes us adults laugh out loud when he remarks "I'm glad I'm seven. This is the oldest I've ever been in my whole life."

"Oh, wow! I just *love* children!" Rosie bursts forth. "They blow me away. They're so innocent, spontaneous, and uninhibited. We need to be more like them. Y'know what I mean? We need to get in touch with our *inner child!*"

At one point, I finally get to the big question: "Rosie, do you remember recommending that book to me?"

Her blank expression signals that I needed to jog her memory. We spoke at Poverty Gulch in an old camping trailer with a leprechaun sticker on the door. Inside of it, there was the bookshelf that Rosie kept a paperback copy of *Ecstasy: The Forgotten Language* by Bhagwan Rajneesh. "Here you go, Ted," she had said, "This book changed my life. Check it out."

"Oh yeah! *Now* I remember," she finally responds. "Did you read it?"

I say something to the effect that the book gave me a "burning in my bosom," a reference to the Mormon expression for an intense stirring sensation in your heart when one encounters a vital truth.

"The stuff in there is right on target," I declare.

"Wonderful! I'm curious, what grabbed you the most about it?"

I promptly go over to my backpack leaning against the wall and pull out my green spiral notebook. It doubled as my travel journal and Truth Project.

What is the *Truth Project*? The hitchhiking trip gave me the chance to interact with virtually every belief system on the planet. I met liberals, conservatives, agnostics, atheists, Protestants, Baha'i's, Buddhists, Pagans, Hindus, Muslims, Jehovah's Witnesses,

Jews, Mormons, New Agers, Scientologists, Witches, and so on. I took notes on anything that piqued my interest and curiosity.

After flipping through this multi-purpose notepad, I turn to one of the inscribed Rajneesh passages. I clear my throat and begin reading:

> "A controlled man is a dead man... My sannyas (way of life) is spontaneity, living moment to moment without prefabricated discipline, living with the unknown, not exactly knowing where you are going... My sannyas is a radical revolution...I would like you to be totally uncontrolled. I would like you to be absolutely a chaos, with no order whatsoever."

"Be totally uncontrolled... No order whatsoever." This lines up with what Nietzsche said in *Thus Spoke Zarathustra*, "One must have chaos in oneself to give birth to the dancing star."

Being "absolutely a chaos" is apparently Rosie's life code. She denounces not only order but a preconceived life plan. Rajneesh is all about freedom in its purest form. Furthermore, he exhorts his reader to reject the conventional idea that a person achieves happiness and success through hard work and self-discipline. Happiness and success can only be reached through the exact opposite: *self-indulgence* (doing what feels good right now.) This line of reasoning is of course the flip side of what Mom and Dad taught me.

Rosie and I talk for about twenty minutes before Pete returns.

CHAPTER 8

THE APRON STRINGS SPEECH

Detroit flashback; July, 11, 1977.

WHEN RANDAL'S BROTHER TODD TATTLED on us, we were obviously devastated. My friend took it harder than me because his opportunity to see Constance McGuire was thwarted. But this doesn't fully explain why Randal got so unhinged. His frantic behavior was a total departure from his usual cool, calm, and collected self.

What was going on in that Bat-computer brain of his? Randal loved to strategize. What's more, he was obsessed with coming up with the "perfect plan." I think the fact ours came tumbling down like a house of cards drove him crazy.

Personally, I would've been okay with the new proposal to take a Greyhound bus to Commack. Sure, the trip would be far less fun, but it was better than not going at all. Besides, the compromise would likely make our parents happy. And us? Well, *sort of* happy. But this solution was totally unacceptable to Randal.

I must admit though, he was right about something.Taking the bus would lack something very vital and essential: adventure.

All this happened the summer *Star Wars* came out. The plot of the movie follows the Hero's Journey, a recurring pattern adopted by countless myths and legends that go back to the dawn of time. Randal and I thought of the hitchhiking trip in terms of a *romantic quest*. Like Luke Skywalker and Abraham in the Bible, we are minding our own business when a message (or more like a summons) from somewhere beyond (in our case, communicated via a passing train) suddenly interrupts our humdrum, ordinary existence. It's the call to adventure which urges Randal and me to leave our snug, safe harbor, to carry out a glorious mission. Toward the Journey's end, the Hero is expected to defeat some enemy, find the Promised Land, and/or bring home a treasure like the Holy Grail.

But there's one catch. A real adventure involves real danger. In this regard, going to Commack via Greyhound didn't quite cut it.

"If at first you don't succeed, *lie*, lie again." Randal didn't say that, but it captures his reasoning at the time. It fits him in terms of cleverness and audacity, but not if the ones being played were his own parents whom he still deeply respected. It was almost unthinkable to lie to them for a second time. No, instead you "keep them in the dark."

We would take the charter bus east through Ontario to New York. Note here that we'd be telling our parents the truth. However, we'd employ the Jedi mind trick in our use of language, specifically the definition of "New York." We wouldn't tell them that we meant the *State* of New York, not specifically Commack, New York. We'd conveniently "forget" to divulge one important detail. Once we set foot in Niagara Falls, New York, we'd hitchhike the rest of the way!

While Randal's folks granted their permission—we encountered the mother of all roadblocks: my mother. She dug her heels in deep, steadfastly refusing to give us her blessing. Either she thought the long bus ride was too much for us vulnerable teenage males, or else she smelled a rat. (I think it was the latter.) Randal and I had desperately hoped Randal's parents would persuade her with their reasonable acquiescence. But this was not the case. If there was going to be a trip, Randal would have to go alone. After *his* mom, in her usual good-natured way, tried but failed to sway *my* mom, an exasperated Randal comes to the phone. *"Ted, I'm coming over there right now!"* he barks into the receiver and abruptly hangs up. Afterwards, a frozen sensation seizes me like snake venom surging through my veins. It's as if the battle of the century is about to commence!

I have to say, it took some stones for Randal to decide to confront her face-to-face, but I'm not a hundred percent sure he knew what he was getting into. My mother was the female version of Dr. Jekyll and Mr. Hyde. While her usual self was warm and friendly, her alter ego was as vicious as a half-starved wolverine. Her words could tear you apart limb from limb.

Ever since we saw *Bound for Glory* together that one time, Mom and I got into a recurring argument over Woody Guthrie. To me, he was a larger-than-life heroic figure, a champion of individual freedom. To her, he was a total loser because of his incessant womanizing and the fact he neglected his family to save the world (with *communism* no less!) My explanation of Woody's appeal was as inconceivable to her as a round square.

As a staunch conservative, Mom believed in "conserving" the time-honored principles gleaned from the past, most notably the Ten Commandments, the Golden Rule, and Common Sense. She drilled into my brothers and me the need to study, work hard, and make the most of ourselves. But she was dogmatic and, hence, had a rough time adapting to change and new ideas, especially when they involved some element of risk.

She had a clear vision of what constitutes a hero. My maternal grandfather Marcus Radaskiewicz never served in the military, he was short in stature and blind in one eye, but, to Mom, he was a highly-decorated knight. His story parallels that of millions of immigrants who had come to America with hardly any material possessions, yet they managed to scrape by and work their way up the socio-economic ladder. However, his unassailable character, the way he conducted himself with people—especially with his wife and eight children—was always the best part of the story. Despite the incredible odds facing him during the Great Depression, Marcus stayed a faithful husband and father, a consistent breadwinner, and a true man of God to the end. He was Woody Guthrie's opposite.

THE SHOWDOWN OCCURRED AT SUNDOWN outside our side door. Randal comes peddling over on his bike wearing his typical olive green tank top and cut-off denim shorts. His head is held high like he'd just discovered his superpower. His eyes are cold and detached, his lips pressed together, and one side of his mouth went up. If he smiled, it wouldn't really be a smile, it would be a smirk. This quality of smugness was something he and I shared. It affected his entire body from head to toe, particularly the swagger in his step after he got off his bike.

I recoil when he strides toward us. His very presence brings Mom's long-festering anger to the boiling point. Our ill-fated plot revealed the extent of her son's deceitfulness and rebellion as well as his poor choice of friends. Her plump face reddens. Barely able to speak, she mutters, "The gall of him showing up here!"

"Mrs. Granger, with all due respect..."

"Save your breath, Randal! The answer is no, no, a hundred times no. You boys gotta stop coming up with cockamamie ideas like your stupid road trip. If you're so bored, I can find you something to do!"

"Look, Ted and I have just *got* to do this. Remember, we agreed to take a bus and not hitchhike."

"Why should I believe a word you say after what you two tried to pull? You're a damn liar, Randal Stark! Yet you have the audacity to come over here to argue with me. Who do you think you are? King S***! You should be ashamed of yourself!"

After that, the conversation swerves into a ditch. Mom goes off on three tangents: (1) "You kids are so ungrateful in spite of all we parents do." (2) "When I was your age..." and (3) "When you have your own kids, you'll understand."

Just when I think Randal will buckle under the pressure and succumb to her relentless verbal assault, he calmly eyes my mother and makes his final stand. Like a boxer who had absorbed vicious body blows from his opponent until the adversary's energy is spent, he deftly deflected her fury and went on the offensive. He then delivered what will turn out to be a historic speech:

"I may be totally out-of-line, Mrs. Granger, and I admit that we haven't been entirely forthcoming with you, but there didn't seem to be any other way. I've read what experts say about child-raising. Parents have to be, you know, *flexible*, or else their kids get messed up psychologically...They end up raising a robot or a puppet instead of a thinking individual...Mrs. Granger, you must listen to reason.

Let your kid be free to make his own decisions...If you want him to grow up to be a successful, healthy, and happy adult, you must let him learn through experience. Mrs. Granger, you must face facts. You have to *loosen the apron strings!*"

"You think you're so smart, Randal! It's so sad Ted listens to you more than me. Because of you, Ted's gonna get himself killed."

My mother obviously can't be reasoned with at this point, so Randal shifts to a new strategy, what salespeople call "creating a sense of urgency."

"Look, Mrs. Granger, it's *now or never*. If Ted doesn't go, I'm afraid I can't be friends with him anymore."

Stone silence. Randal paces back and forth, his gaze fixed on my mother.

I'll never forget the pained grimace on my father's face (Okay, I'd failed to mention his presence until now.) The-man-of-few-words like St. Joseph finally speaks just when Mom and I are rendered mute by Randal's shocking words.

"What did he say?" Dad asks.

"Mr. Granger, you heard me, *I don't see how I can remain friends with Ted* if he can't go with me to New York. I won't be able to look him straight in the eye anymore!"

At that moment, I must confess, I want to punch Randal's lights out. The nerve of him suggesting that our friendship is on the line because of a stupid trip! Besides, the very suggestion that I'll end up an unthinking momma's boy for the rest of my life is of course preposterous. How humiliating! I must remind myself that Randal was just BS-ing.

"Well, if that's how you feel, maybe Ted should find another friend!" Mom exclaims bitterly.

Then Randal, seizing the moral high ground, takes a deep breath and poses the question, "Why don't we ask Ted what *he* thinks?"

It's hard to imagine the atmosphere being more radioactive just minutes before. All eyes now turn and lock on a skinny, awkward seventeen-year-old me. I'm in the spotlight faced with one of the biggest choices I'd ever make.

"Well. . . I . . . I . . . *want to go*," I stammer with a lump in my throat. At that precise moment, I know nothing will ever be the same again.

Randal apparently had found Mom's weak spot, her Achilles heel. She is insecure about how others perceived her. The fact Randal's mom and dad had granted their permission probably gave him the edge the whole time. Not wanting to be a wet blanket or an "old fuddy-duddy," she finally surrenders.

"Weeellll, *okay*," she murmurs on the verge of tears, sounding utterly defeated.

Me? I should be relieved and full of joy. But it feels like Randal just took a meat cleaver and severed my umbilical cord.

CHAPTER 9

DORNA

Greeley, the afternoon of July 9, 1979.

WHEN THE MOTHER GRIZZLY COMES HOME, look out! I'm not talking about my mom but Dorna Platte. I had formed a mental picture of Dorna before she arrived. Her furnishings hint she is a person of taste in a tasteless era (the '70s). The shabby condition of her place shows she struggles to make ends meet. The absence of a husband/partner in family photos reveals she is either separated or divorced.

Dorna, a tall, slender blonde in a waitress uniform, enters the mobile home. Looking upset, she slams four loaded grocery bags on the Formica counter.

"Oh hi, Dorna," Rosie casually greets, "I want you to meet a couple of friends of mine..."

"ROSIE!"

Rosie is summoned into the kitchen for a "private talk." Minutes later, Pete and I are asked to step outside. The awkwardness in the air makes me more than happy to oblige.

Ten minutes later, Rosie comes charging out of the house like a raging bull, kicking over garbage cans on the porch deck. After she vents, she plops down into a lawn chair. "Look guys," she says with a groan. "Dorna is pissed that I let 'two strange men' into her house without her consent."

Pete and I eye each other perplexed. She slouches back and lets out a protracted sigh.

"The worst part is she thinks I'm endangering her kids!" As Rosie says this, her voice cracks. She's on the edge of tears.

"*Us* endangering her kids? How ridiculous!" remarks Pete.

"How insulting!" I exclaim.

"No, no, I gotta admit," she continues as she hangs her head. "I see where she's coming from."

"Rosie, really, I . . ."

"Oh, don't apologize, Pete. It's not your fault." She takes her time to inhale and exhale. "I'm afraid you guys can't spend the night here."

Silence.

"Oh well, no big deal," Pete finally responds with a shrug. Of course, he's lying. It *is* a big deal. A *very* big deal. What does this mean? Goodbye?

The three of us pace around the wooden deck a while until Rosie exclaims, "I got an idea!"

☾ ☾ ☾

IT IS NOT EXACTLY THE HYATT REGENCY DEARBORN, but it has four walls and a roof. We move our stuff into an abandoned pickup-truck camper found along Sunnybrook's gloopy western rim where the dirt-poor residents live. It rests on a dirt driveway supported by four metal rods instead of a vehicle. The exterior is white stainless steel accented with rust spots. The interior is decked with dark-wood paneling discolored by the sun. It has five grimy windows. The part that normally goes over the truck cab houses a moldy, foam mattress. As shabby as the place is, it beats being exposed to the elements outdoors by a long shot. My gladness over this turn of events is short-lived however.

"Ted," says Pete, "if you don't mind, Rosie and I are going to spend some time together." *What?! Time* alone *together?* I guess it could be worse. Pete and Rosie could have told me that they were spending their date *in the camper*, but they instead plan to take a stroll through town without me of course.

"Are you *sure* it's okay?" Rosie asks me empathetically.

"Oh, no problem at all," I reply. I am holding back my tears. The prospect of being all alone in the crummy section of Sunnybrook does not appeal to me. While the pair is away, I'll have to come up with something constructive to do or else I'll go nuts.

I read my Edgar Cayce book in the camper bunk bed until my feelings of jealousy, resentment, and self-pity get the best of me. At one point, I'm so agitated I must get up and pace around the trailer park. I stride over to the vending machine behind Sunnybrook's office building to buy myself a pop. There I meet an overweight woman in curlers yelling and threatening to call the cops on two skinny pre-teen boys who are kicking the daylights out of the machine. The young men keep insisting the thing "ate" their change. Fortunately, the sight of me standing there halts the uproar.

"A bunch of nonsense!" cries the woman. "I told their mama about those little s***s not once but three times. But of course she never listens. She's at work and these twerps think they run the place!" She goes on to rail against parents who shirk their sacred duty to watch their kids.

A short time later, as I'm heading back to the camper, I hear a voice calling over to me. It's none other than Dorna Platte, standing on her porch, minding her sizzling barbecue grill. She's wearing an apron and smoking a cigarette. "Hey, sweetheart, want a burger?" Maybe she felt sorry for me, this shaggy, gaunt teenage hobo. Perhaps her mothering instinct kicked in.

The charbroiled scent makes my mouth water.

"Why don't you come sit over here, hon?" asks Dorna.

Her generosity bowls me over. Along with two juicy cheeseburgers which I devour like a ravenous wolf, Dorna slaps down corn-on-the-cob and mac-and-cheese for extra measure. After the kids go inside, she and I engage in an adult conversation.

Dorna is a realist as opposed to a dreamer. How she and Rosie got to be friends is beyond me. Like my mother she speaks her mind. I don't appreciate her sharing unflattering private information about our mutual friend but I must admit, I find some of the details tantalizing. It all seems to revolve around Rosie's libertine lifestyle. One comment Dorna makes sends a shiver down my spine: "Rosie's day of reckoning is coming."

DORNA 49

☾ ☾ ☾

PETE AND ROSIE RETURN TO DORNA'S AROUND SIX in a jocular mood. Rosie brought a six pack of Coors in a brown paper bag, a testament to her perpetual party spirit. The possibility of it being a peace offering to Dorna also crosses my mind. She and my traveling partner seem pleasantly surprised to find me there on the couch watching the news.

After Pete and I do the dishes, we say good night and leave. On our way back to the camper, I clear my throat as if to release something pent-up.

"LeBlanc, you defeated me," I mutter without a hint of sarcasm. "I'm giving her up. I'm letting you have her. She's *yours*."

Pete shakes his head out of pity, disgust, or astonishment. It takes him a few seconds to process what I'd just said. He responds, "Ted, what's wrong with you? Look, Rosie doesn't belong to me or anyone else."

THE HOLY CITY

CHAPTER 10

THE NEW YORK TRIP

Detroit to Bridgeport, CT; July 12-14, 1977.

THE NEXT MORNING, RANDAL'S PARENTS drove us to the Greyhound terminal downtown where we boarded the bus to Niagara Falls, Canada. We would arrive at our destination around noon. During the four-hour ride, I mulled over the significance of what happened the night before. My thrill of adventure was tempered with grief of having to choose Randal over my parents, danger over security, manhood over boyhood — all in one fell swoop. I was crestfallen over how my choice deeply wounded them.

Walking over the falls via Rainbow Bridge invigorated me, I felt free. But once we got to the U.S. side, apprehension suddenly hit me. At last, I sensed the danger of what we were about to do.

With no luck hitchhiking that day, we ended up spending the night at the nearby KOA campground. We got our first ride the next day from Mario and Paul, a father and his adult son whom we befriended at the camp. Their affable nature, their light-hearted humor felt reassuring. Subsequent rides from apparently normal people also put our minds at ease.

At the end of Day Two, we got dropped off in Albany where we checked in at a motel. That evening, disaster strikes: the 1977 Blackout, one of New York City's worst-ever crises. What caused America's largest city to go dark for 24 hours? Investigators figured out that lightning had struck a Consolidated Edison substation setting off a massive chain reaction across the power grid. To get a sense of the scale, the damage caused by the looting and vandalism in the '67 Detroit riots cost about $60 million. Well, New York City's blackout mayhem was five times that—a whopping $300 million! The ninety-degree heat, hard economic times—even the public's paranoia of the infamous serial killer Son of Sam—were blamed for the chaos.

While all this is going on, Randal and I are safe-and-sound in our air-conditioned motel room three hours away from the area of devastation. Our only problem is *Charlie's Angels* keeps getting interrupted by news. Though we can't grasp the enormity of the situation, Randal has the inclination to call home to tell his parents that we're okay. Sometime later, he reflects aloud, "Man, I'm really glad I called. Everyone's freaking out over us. They all assumed we were right smack dab in the middle of the chaos." That's precisely what bugs me about Randal. He is Gallant (the wise, sensible cartoon character in *Highlights* magazine) and I'm Goofus (his opposite). My buddy intellectually does the right thing while it's not even on my radar. That's just how Randal is—Mr. Responsibility.

☾ ☾ ☾

THE NEXT DAY, A TV REPAIRMAN picks us up folllowed by a family from Detroit. We accidentally end up in Massachusetts missing an important turn, so we decide to take a different route: to Bridgeport, Connecticut where we can take the ferry across the Long Island Sound. After that, we have a driver named Kathy, then a French-Canadian dude who could hardly speak English, then "Joe" who takes us straight to the ferry dock. And so on and so on . . .

Most details of the trip are now an amorphous blur in my memory. It's funny how you end up forgetting the bad times and recalling the good. The worst part of hitchhiking is of course the long waits for rides. Truth be told, 95% of the time, you're stuck in some crummy place feeling as stir-crazy as a caged monkey.

CHAPTER 11

JOHN HANCOCK

Greeley, the morning of July 10, 1979.

THE NEXT MORNING, ROSIE URGES US to join her on a day trip to the mountains, an invitation we can't pass up. Since we have time to kill before we leave, we hang out with another one of her cohorts who happens to live in a single-wide mobile home two rows down from Dorna. Rosie says he's a short-order cook.

Three knocks bring a tall, gangly dude about thirty to the door. He sports a crop of gristly brown hair that hangs down to his shoulders, long sideburns, and a droopy horseshoe mustache. He has half-inch long fingernails and a prominent Adam's Apple. The backwards letters of "Save the Whales" across his chest show that his pale blue t-shirt is inside out.

"Hey, John!" Rosie greets heartily.

"Come on in," he replies with a western drawl and cinematic arm gesture. He receives us warmly, but he seems to be a little preoccupied. In a barely audible mumble, he says, "I had just dropped some acid," prompting Pete and me to look at each other with loaded smirks. John however shows no signs of being on LSD,

"Oh. . . We'll come back later," asserts Rosie.

"No, no, no, no, no, no. Really, it's alright," he replies, flinging the door wide. "Stay a while. Have a seat."

Once we enter, Rosie says, "Guys, this is John. . ."

"John Hancock," the host chimes in, nodding and extending his right hand.

"Interesting name," I remark. My noting it activates a beaming face which reflects a deep-seated pride. "No, I don't head up an insurance company," he laughs. "But I'm a direct descendant of one of the signers of the Declaration of Independence."

Once Rosie, Pete, and I get situated around John's dining room table, our gaze promptly turns to a pair of black vinyl over-the-ear headphones resting on a couch pillow on the floor. They resemble the ones I got from Radio Shack. Apparently, John had been laying on the floor before we showed up. Next to the headphones is a ballpoint pen and an open spiral notebook with some handwriting in it. Next to that is a paperback copy of *Thus Spoke Zarathustra* by Friedrich Nietzsche. Rajneesh calls it "the Bible of the future."

"I've just been meditating on Nietzsche and Handal's *Messiah*. Great combo!" John says as he skulks across the room to turn off the stereo receiver.

As he serves us fresh coffee and scones from the local bakery, I survey the room. The books on his shelves seem to touch every alternative spiritual topic imaginable: astrology, tarot divination, scrying, astral travel, alchemy, and so on. There's a statuette of the Hindu god Shiva on the lamp table and assorted wall hangings, knickknacks featuring pentacles, triple moons, and eyes of Horus. All these—plus framed degrees on the wall.

I notice and pick up a book on his coffee table entitled *The Points of Solomon*.

"It's a translation of the scrolls discovered in Egypt that date back to the eighth century B.C.," our friendly host remarks. "They're a bunch of magic spells that King Solomon entrusted to the Queen of Sheba. She, in turn, passed them down to her descendants who preserved them through the centuries. Do you know anything about Solomon?"

"Of course, he's the great Hebrew king in the Bible," says I, "the richest man in his time."

"Wisest man ever, next to Jesus of course," Pete adds. "He regarded wisdom far more precious than any earthly treasure. Using his wealth, he set out to know everything and do everything to achieve it."

"*Do everything Turn! Turn! Turn!*" Rosie starts singing and dancing to the familiar Byrds classic.

"The lyrics say, '*to* everything,' not '*do* everything,'" John asserts. "Common mistake. But, hey, not at all inconsistent. I mean, Solomon engaged in virtually every experience imaginable. He did it all. He built architectural wonders, vast libraries chock-full of the best literature of the time and he read it all. . ."

"And he also had hundreds of wives and concubines," Pete quips.

"What a love life!" Rosie exclaims.

"I'm sure he did all kinds of drugs, too."

"The Grand Experiment!" I put forth.

The Grand Experiment was a concept inexplicable to those outside of our social circle. It had been my modus operandi all summer. I identified with King Solomon hurling himself into the realm of the senses with reckless abandon to gain knowledge about everything. This recalls the discussion Randal and I had when we were first introduced to marijuana: "Look, Ted, maybe we need to take the plunge," Randal challenged. "How can you really know something is good or bad unless you try it first?"

These words stuck with me. The sentiment behind them inspired me to pursue every conceivable experience—however novel, strange, unconventional, nontraditional, or even criminal. This method of finding truth, the empirical approach, was believed to be the surest means to reach a comprehensive understanding of myself and the world. When I express this opinion, John praises me left-and-right, up-and-down, and diagonally. "Yeah! Yeah! That's right!" he replies. "Like Ralph Waldo Emerson said, 'All life is an experiment. The more experiments you make, the better.'"

From then on, John takes a shine to me. Little does he know that Randal Stark came up with the insight in the first place, not me. I basically plagiarized Randal who maybe ripped it off from Emerson and now I am taking credit for it. However, my puffed-up head will be quickly deflated. A dissenting voice blurts out, "Hey, didn't Solomon say 'Vanity, vanity, all is vanity'?" It was Pete.

"That means Solomon realized all the different stuff he did was BS," he says. "Look guys, you don't have to eat crap to know that it doesn't taste good."

☾ ☾ ☾

AUTHOR TOM WOLFE ONCE SAID, "Somebody has to be the pioneer and leave the marks for others to follow." Believe it or not, John Hancock would assume that role in my life, though I only met with him twice and both encounters were not that long. It seemed like we were destined to meet. Besides teaching me new things, he reinforced what I already knew. He approved of my to-do list:

First, seek knowledge from *alternative* sources, particularly Eastern mysticism and philosophy, paganism, and the occult. Reject all Western ideas and norms.

Second, try LSD to achieve a higher state of consciousness.

Third, hitchhike around the world. Why stop at the United States? Check out "The Overland Trail." Also known as the "Hippie Trail" and simply the "Overland," it was quite revered at the time. It extended as far west as London and as far east as Bangkok, a span of roughly 7,000 miles. Young, thrill-seeking Westerners could travel the Overland for dirt-cheap, meet interesting people, and smoke quality hash with friendly locals. Of course, the top draw was the beautiful scenery, but the goal was to experience the "Mystic East" which usually meant India. The fantasy—like the one in Hermann Hesse's *Siddhartha*—was to find spiritual enlightenment through asceticism and hedonism (both!) until you end up at the feet of your very own guru. This spiritual guide would teach you everything you need to know about life. As the Beatles conferred with Maharishi Yogi, I'd check out Bhagwan Shree Rajneesh.

CHAPTER 12

COMMACK, NY

Long Island; July 15-16, 1977.

I T'S SHORTLY BEFORE DAWN. I feel a kick in the ribs through the thick padding of my sleeping bag. I open my eyes to a flashlight in my face. A security guard is standing there and he's not happy. "C'mon, you guys, get a move on!" he hollers at Randal and me like a drill sergeant. Before the rude interruption, we had been comfortably snoozing away on the front lawn of a Holiday Inn. The hotel is located along Long Island's Highway 347, just twenty minutes east from our destination, Commack, New York.

Most people visit New York to see the Statue of Liberty, the Empire State Building, and Central Park; we have our sights on a quite unremarkable suburb. Commack isn't known for anything except Rosie O'Donnell and the island's sleaziest motel. At the time, we didn't know anything about the notorious Commack Motor Inn. Since we badly needed a shower to be presentable for Constance and her family, we decide to check into a room there. (The old man at the front desk looks at us kind of funny when we request the special two-hour rate.) Unfortunately, our clean-up effort comes to naught. Randal and I end up looking and smelling like two homeless guys after walking from the motel to her house.

When we finally arrive at Constance's parents' modest ranch home, her mom and dad welcome us warmly, but Constance herself, I have to say, is stand-offish. In her defense, it's likely that the unexpected arrival of Randal—some guy whom she hardly knew and much less cared about—overwhelmed her (or else *under*whelmed her) with his sudden arrival. At least the pretty, strawberry blonde is polite. Randal will get to spend plenty of time with her—but never alone. Her boyfriend Duane will seldom leave her side the whole time we are there. To add insult to injury, Duane is only Constance's *temporary* boyfriend. Her real beau is a military man stationed in Japan.

Disappointment doesn't come near to describing how Randal must feel. It is like a scene from a nightmare. We spend most of our time sitting around in the McGuire living room engaging in small talk. After we had exhausted the topic of the blackout, we discuss movies, sports, and Billy Joel (who once lived in a neighboring town). When we come perilously close to running out of things to say, we talk about running out of things to say. Worst yet, for the entire period, poor Randal must endure looking at Constance cuddled up next to Duane on the couch! To get a much-needed break, Randal and I decide to go to the beach. (Constance and Duane opt out thankfully.) Which beach? Following Duane's advice, we choose North Beach. We should've picked South Beach, the one along the ocean where there's real sand and waves. The water at North Beach (along the Long Island Sound) is so still it breeds mosquitoes.

Boredom. Stagnation. Humiliation. These are the words that first pop into my head when I think of Commack, New York. We had to get out of there as quickly as possible or else succumb to the doldrums! We need something extraordinary to occur on our trip—something positive and uplifting.

CHAPTER 13

MOON GULCH

The Rocky Mountains 50+ miles west of Greeley; the afternoon of July 10, 1979.

OUR CONVERSATION WITH JOHN HANCOCK made me realize that History reigns supreme in Greeley like it does in Dearborn. I noticed Rosie and her friends have a love/hate relationship with their town. On the one hand, they complained about Greeley being too conservative. On the other hand, they are proud of its heritage.

"It's named after Horace Greeley," John Hancock had explained. "He was the New York editor who coined the popular phrase 'Go West, young man!'" John went on to say that the city was founded in 1870 by Nathan Meeker, one of Mr. Greeley's colleagues.

Meeker was inspired by one of the founders of socialism, Charles Fourier. Convinced that mankind is perfectible, Fourier set out to build the world's first workable utopia. In it, collective humanity would come before the interests of individuals. Everyone shares everything to benefit everybody. Meeker's settlement in northeast Colorado was originally called "Union Colony No. 1" which implied that—once all the bugs were worked out of it—there would be a "Union Colony No. 2," then a "No. 3," and so on, until the *whole world* is one big Union Colony.

I had dreamed of a worldwide utopia at age seven when my family and I went to Expo 67, the World's Fair in Montreal, Canada. Dignitaries from all over the planet showed up, including Queen Elizabeth, President Johnson, and even Tiny Tim. The theme was mankind's expected bright future, world peace. The expo featured "the World in miniature," a village of pavilions standing for different countries: France, Germany, India, Japan, and so on. Visitors got a taste of what each nation had to offer to the global community. By far, the most impressive pavilion was that of the United States of America, a twenty-story geodesic dome made of clear acrylic.

Sadly, world events that summer would put a damper on the heady optimism. One was the Six-Day War in the Middle East. The other was the Detroit riots. At some point during our family vacation, my mother stopped dead in her tracks. Looking mortified, she said, "I don't remember locking the doors before we left!"

A couple years later, an article in *LIFE* magazine caught my attention. Entitled "America and the Utopian Dream," the pictorial essay profiled a few hippie communes that had proliferated across the U.S. at the time. I was intrigued by the weird clothes and unkempt appearance of commune members, but more so by the beautiful babes prancing around naked. I read that the reason for joining one of these groups is to create the perfect society. Everyone is equal and shares everything. Each member does his or her part to benefit the whole. All for one and one for all!

☾ ☾ ☾

AFTER VISITING JOHN HANCOCK, WE SET OUT for Moon Gulch, an alleged enchanted place in the nearby Rockies. The trip is a religious experience. It's a resplendent day, sunny with the temperature around eighty. Somewhere past the town of Loveland, I am sitting comfortably in the back seat of a red '72 Pontiac Firebird, when *WHOOSH*, I'm engrossed by the sound of an electric rhythm guitar blaring out of the car speakers. The chord progression sluggishly creeps along in the key of E Major.

DAH DAH da-dum-dum. . . DAH DAH da-dum-dum

Then a second guitar player joins in.

DUM DUM DUM duh-duh . . . *DUM DUM DUM duh-duh*

As the two riffs blend like converging rivers, my mind recognizes the bluesy rock-and-roll song "Rocky Mountain Way" by Joe Walsh. Before me, occupying most of the windshield, are the snow-capped Rockies reaching up to the cobalt sky! As the sight takes my breath away, Walsh injects his reedy voice:

"Spent the last year / Rocky Mountain Way / Couldn't get much higher. . ."

The anticipation that everything is getting "higher" overtakes me. I'm teary-eyed with intense feelings of bliss. I'm gripped with an extraordinary sense of hope and optimism.

☾ ☾ ☾

JUST ONE MORE TURN AROUND THE BEND and there's Moon Gulch! We made it! The site's austere serenity charms us at once. Mother Nature makes her own music with the rushing water of the creek, her light show being the sparkling surface co-mingling with the brilliant colors of the earth and sky. The house at Moon Gulch is a typical shotgun ranch except it has a friggin' 40-foot diameter dome attached to it. It's a geodesic dome—flat triangles assembled into a nifty half-sphere. The bottom sides are made out of wood; the top ones are sheets of glass which let the sunlight in.

One might characterize the interior décor as Boho Chic, which includes lots of paisley, mystical Asian art, and hanging plants. It has an Alice-in-Wonderland feel. Our generous hosts, one of Rosie's college friends and her partner, overwhelm us with their warm hospitality, carefree disposition, and open-minded attitudes. I particularly admire their determination to live the simple life in harmony with nature. They appear to be happy and content being self-sufficient, growing their own food, raising chickens and children.

"It's another Poverty Gulch!" Pete exclaims. He is right in the sense that the residents at Wisconsin's Poverty Gulch and Colorado's Moon Gulch are true hippies who pride themselves for entirely dropping out of society, practicing a lifestyle in line with their high-minded ideals, most notably peace and love.

☾ ☾ ☾

MOON GULCH AND POVERTY GULCH HAD IN COMMON their isolation from the outside world. Yet, in this regard, Moon Gulch had one big advantage over Poverty Gulch: mountains. World War III could break out at any minute! When the s*** hits the fan, Moon Gulch's residents would be protected on all sides. Natural ramparts would shield them from devastating blasts and hopefully fallout.

Being secluded in the mountains has other benefits as well. You're completely hidden from and beyond the reach of foreign attackers. You're insulated from the rest of the world's moral corruption. You can start a new civilization to replace the old one. While humanity is busy annihilating itself, your little mountain community can bide its time in a safe environment, creating, and modeling a new-and-improved mankind. All negative elements of the old order—such as hatred, selfishness, and greed—can be forever banished and replaced by peace and love.

That's the main idea behind James Hilton's *Lost Horizon*, the 1933 novel that was adapted into a movie, the one I would see on my last night with the Moonies. The humble, gentle, and wise inhabitants of a city in a remote mountain valley, Shangri-La, would take over the world once the evil warmongers killed each other off. The meek inherit the earth.

Was Moon Gulch as wonderful as I had imagined?

No, I found it boring. All I did was sip tea and read books in the study while the others talked in the other room. The wind chimes outside sounded nice though.

CHAPTER 14

ASBURY PARK, NJ

Flashback; July 17-18, 1977.

ON THE COMMUTER TRAIN PLATFORM next morning, Randal gives Constance a chilly goodbye hug and a tepid peck on the cheek. He then reaches into his shirt pocket and hands her a folded-up scrap of paper containing some verse. They're lyrics of the Bob Dylan song "Shelter from the Storm." In my opinion, "Don't Think Twice, It's Alright" would have been a better choice.

After talking with Constance's parents over breakfast, we had decided to shelve the idea of sightseeing in New York City. (If the metropolis is a scary place even in normal circumstances, picture what it would be like after a catastrophic blackout!) Our new plan is to pass through the metro area with no stops except Grand Central Station. From Commack to Asbury Park, I would watch my heartbroken buddy mentally shake the Long Island dust off his feet and gradually assume a more upbeat attitude. It helps thinking about the good times we are going to have in Asbury Park, a cool resort town along the Jersey shore which happens to be the adopted hometown of Bruce Springsteen.

Springsteen's music had had an uncanny effect on me during that time in my life. Prior to leaving Detroit, I spun his *Born to Run* album one more time for the road. It was so apropos for the moment. How do Rock & Roll and other art forms touch the human soul? It's a mystery to be sure. Somehow musical notes arranged in a pattern, accompanied by thought-provoking lyrics, can produce extraordinary interior responses: a sense of well-being, melancholy, transcendence. Wittgenstein, a noted 20th century philosopher, once lamented how it's impossible to communicate to others what music had meant to him. "How can I hope to be understood?" he concluded.

With Springsteen, it wasn't just the music, it was the image. The so-called rock media had depicted him as the promised messiah. After seeing Bruce and his band perform live in concert, *Rolling Stone* writer Jon Landau wrote auspiciously. "I saw Rock & Roll's future and its name is Bruce Springsteen." This intrigued me. I found a number of things appealing about Bruce once I listened to the new album. The cover of *Born to Run* features a black-and-white photograph of him, a scruffy, bearded beatnik in a cool black-leather jacket holding his electric guitar. He looks jubilant as he leans on the shoulder of his sax player, Clarence Clemons, an African American. For me, the photo was emblematic of the racial and ethnic harmony I'd earnestly yearned to see. The Detroit I grew up in was never the same after the '67 race riot. Even before that, relations between Blacks and Whites had never been that great.

We take a train to Asbury Park. Once we get there, we book a room at the dingy Pink Flamingo Motel and then spend all day enjoying the beach along the Atlantic Ocean, casing joints along the boardwalk and the Circuit, humming Springsteen songs. It's a delight to see people having a good time, particularly the girls. We go on rides like the Tilt-a-Whirl, the Fun House, and Bumper Cars. We eat Coneys and French fries. One notable spot is the Palace Amusements where we play pinball under "Tillie," a mural depicting a sinister-looking face.

It seems so incongruous that Randal and I will end up calling Asbury Park the "Holy City." This once-opulent town had seen better days. It is now dusty, broken-down, and downright grungy.

Its faded glory and decay are not only due to the elements but a decades-long economic downturn.

How could such a place inspire us so deeply? Asbury Park has in its favor the ocean. It's like what Ishmael said in *Moby Dick*: Whenever you get depressed, you hightail it to the sea. Watching and listening to the rhythmic waves, feeling the wind on your face, and breathing in the salty air is the surest way to clear your head.

A marine biologist named Wallace J. Nichols even formulated a theory called Blue Mind that suggests simply being close to the water has wonderful psychological effects.

The classic carnival atmosphere of Asbury Park brings out the child in you. Moreover, its vintage carousels, arcades, and rides make you feel like you're a kid back in the late-nineteenth century. Mark Twain's Gilded Age! The Beaux-Art and neoclassical-style buildings give the town a distinguished European ambiance. At the same time, the fancy facades with mermaids, old Spanish ships, and other fantastic nautical images enchant the soul.

Springsteen helped us to appreciate Asbury Park. His first three albums romanticize the place. Bruce's early songs make you want to lose yourself in the grand, colorful, and shabby fantasy. In my daydream, I serenade a girl named Sandy watching the Fourth-of-July fireworks on the beach. I have Madame Marie tell my fortune. I attend Wild Billy's Circus which is haunted by the "great greasepaint ghost on the wind."

Most significant of all, the town is racially integrated. People of all races live together in perfect harmony like in Martin Luther King's dream.

CHAPTER 15

THE END OF THE LINE

On the way back to Greeley from Moon Gulch.

AS WE'RE GOING EAST ON HIGHWAY 34, another familiar song comes on our driver's car radio. It starts with a galloping cymbal and then the raspy-voiced Bruce Springsteen speaks: "In Candy's room, there are pictures of heroes on the wall / But to get to Candy's room you gotta walk the darkness of Candy's hall." Who is Candy? She's none other than Rosie who is in the El Camino with Pete, me, and our driver Jake. She is sitting in the front passenger seat with the wind blowing in her hair.

Bruce, the rock-star "prophet," starts to sing: "There's a sadness in that pretty face. . ." She isn't her usual sunny self and is uncharacteristically quiet, pensive, even agitated like something is weighing on her mind. *What's up?* I wonder.

While waiting outside a farm supply store where we got dropped off, Rosie gives her confession.

"I'm going back to Madison," she speaks like a character in a Western. "There's a guy I gotta see." She is of course talking about Madison, Wisconsin, where we met, but who's the dude?

"Look, guys, I can't do this anymore," she continues. "I had enough!"

Dumbfounded doesn't begin to describe my reaction. It almost sounds like she's contemplating suicide or murder.

"For one thing," Rosie goes on, "hitchhiking is dangerous!"

What?! Ten days ago in Wisconsin, she pooh-poohed the element of risk. Granted, her entering strange motor vehicles on a regular basis was exponentially more perilous for women than it was for us men, especially young attractive females like her traveling alone. How she managed to avoid harm could only be explained as divine protection. She had the Mark of Cain like us!

Now this? Why the attitudinal U-turn?

"The truth is I had a close call. Back in Minnesota, a truck driver tried to rape me at a rest stop. And, if not for a stroke of luck, the situation would've been a lot worse."

"Whoa!"

"Look guys, things have changed. Now I'm not just responsible for myself, but for another precious life."

"You mean. . ." While I choke on these words, I lift my hands out as if to shield myself from oncoming traffic. LeBlanc's forehead furrows like an accordion.

"Yes, I'm *pregnant*."

CHAPTER 16

RETURN WITH ELIXIR

Asbury Park, NJ to Detroit; July 19-21, 1977.

WITH ASBURY PARK BEHIND US, Randal and I head back to the Motor City. We had entered a new phase of our romantic quest called the "Return with Elixir" where the Hero—or heroes in our case—bring home the precious treasure: a vial containing "Elixir," a magic potion. It is a miracle cure that makes the spiritually sick healthy again. It's a symbol for our message of hope—our gospel. We name it "Karma™" which I'll explain in a bit.

After we left New Jersey, Philadelphia was a big deal. Staying overnight at the home of Randal's Uncle Alfred and Aunt Carol turned out to be a welcome respite from the rigors of the road. They lived in a colonial house in one of Philly's posh suburbs. From there, we took the commuter train downtown to check out Independence Hall where the Founding Fathers signed the Declaration of Independence and the Constitution. Being at the exact spot that these historic events occurred incited patriotic sentiments.

After Philly, we get stopped by the highway patrol somewhere in rural Pennsylvania. Like some geeky tourist who'd just discovered an Amish albino, Randal pulls out his camera and asks the cop if he'd like to pose for a photo. The police officer, wearing a brown wide-brim hat and dark sunglasses, seems taken aback by my buddy's odd request but he reluctantly agrees! (A smile however is too much to ask.) After checking our ID's and verifying we're not runaways, the lawman lets us go, spurring simultaneous sighs of relief.

Pop culture in the 1970s had shaped our view of law enforcement. We recount our cop story to an ex-Marine named Jim who picked us up a short time later in his Chevy truck. Laughing heartily, Jim points to his citizen's band (CB) radio that he says is used to evade "smokies" (highway patrolmen). He then asks us if we'd seen the latest hit movie *Smokey and the Bandit*, starring Jackie Gleason and Burt Reynolds. The movie cop (Gleason) is a fat, cantankerous buffoon, and the criminal on the run (Reynolds) is a fun-loving wiseacre who always manages to evade justice. The message isn't lost on us. Police officers are dummies like Jackie Gleason and guys like Randal and me are smart like the Bandit.

We would reach Detroit the next day. We hit pay dirt with our final ride along an entrance ramp along I-75 North. The driver, a retired teacher named Elmer Lee, took us through much of Ohio and Michigan. He even let Randal drive, but my partner paid a heavy price for the privilege. He had to endure Elmer's non-stop talking for four hours. (Thankfully, I got to snooze in the back seat.) The old man was so boring that Randal would later dub him "The Mayor of Commack." I'm sure my friend zoned out frequently, but he magnanimously forced himself to nod occasionally out of the kindness of his heart.

CHAPTER 17

BREAKFAST AT SAMBO'S

Greeley; the morning of July 11, 1979.

THIS MORNING, SKYLAB, THE ORBITING SPACE STATION (what was left of it) finally crashed somewhere in the Australian outback, evoking a collective sigh of relief. Many had laid awake at night worrying that the 77-ton chunk of burning metal would come crashing down on them at any given moment. During the days leading up to the event, journalists had fun evoking the familiar children's fable Chicken Little which is about a chick who kept saying "The sky is falling."

July 11th was also the day Pete and I would leave Greeley for good. Before we head out, Rosie manages to round up a few of her cohorts to give us the proper send-off. It would take place at their home-away-from-home, a Sambo's restaurant. The well-wishers at our booth include Rosie, Barb the nurse, and John Hancock.

Jubilant words overpower the noisy din.

"I want to build a living cathedral here!" All eyes turn to a long-haired freak standing there holding his chest like Sir Lawrence Olivier's Hamlet. Friends snicker; strangers glare at my new role model John Hancock as if he's a pink fairy armadillo. "Hey everyone, breakfast is on me!" he says with verve to those of us sitting at the table. After thanking John copiously, we'd hear his astonishing news.

But what about *Rosie's* astonishing news? For whatever reason, she barely mentions it all morning. Her telling us the day before that she is pregnant still felt strange. Why was I so floored? It wasn't so much the idea of her keeping the child as much as her *settling down*. I guess I naively thought she would remain a hobo the rest of her life (like what I intended to do). I asked myself, "Why in the world would someone of her caliber want to give up *freedom*, the ultimate sacred thing, to do something so ordinary and enslaving as raising a child?" It seemed so off-kilter for the ultimate free spirit.

ᒪ ᒪ ᒪ

NOTHING EVER STAYS THE SAME! Rosie's life would change dramatically. The stunning announcement John Hancock is about to make would suggest that he too is at a major crossroads.

"Hey guys, I just spoke with my lawyer. He says there's been a breakthrough in my case. Things are moving in my favor. It's practically a done deal."

"Congratulations!" utters all practically in unison. I'm thinking, "What case?"

Barb turns to Pete and me to fill us in. "He is talking about the business of the Will. He sued family members over cutting him out of the inheritance." On hearing this, the others chime in to supply us details. To make a long story short, John had been branded the "black sheep of the family" because of his bad decisions.

"What do you plan to do with all that money?" I inquire. I learned earlier that his family had millions.

"First off, I'm *givin' it away*."

"Giving it away?!"

"That's right, Ted. Do you see these people sitting around you?" John eyes his friends like they're his disciples. "They saved my life. When I hit rock bottom, they pulled me out of the gutter. They were the only ones willing to lend me a helping hand. Sooo, now I'm paying 'em all back. I'm setting up a bank account where these precious friends of mine can tap into it whenever the need arises." Everyone present is of course bug-eyed, and speechless on hearing this.

"You're my *real* family," he declares on the verge of tears, a response that's contagious.

"The second thing I want to do with the money is travel the Overland to India," John says as if he's already packed and ready to go. The excursion, he notes, will begin in Afghanistan.

"Why start *there*? Afghanistan is a landlocked country." I have my sixth-grade teacher, Sister Mary Walter to thank for my mastery of Geography.

"Good question. Well, you see, Ted, it's this *Iran* thing. . ." John doesn't have to explain. Images of the Islamic revolution in Persia appear daily in the newspaper and on TV, particularly those of delirious mobs in the streets screaming and holding up fists and pictures of Ayatollah Khomeini. The fall of Iran's Shah (King) and the Ayatollah's rise to power was the top story for months. The year before, it was inconceivable that one religious leader could take over an entire country and impose a strict religious code (sharia) on all its citizens. Even more scary was the fact that Iran's people were perfectly okay with an old cleric with a black turban and angry eyebrows micro-managing every aspect of their lives.

"It's a baaaaad trip, man!" John put forth wagging his head. "People are chanting 'Death to America' and s***!"

Barb the nurse, who knew a thing or two about the Overland, lamented the fact that Tehran, Iran's capital, used to be a friendly, hospitable place. Americans felt at home there because the city was thoroughly modern with its shopping malls, fast food joints, and hotels. But the Shah of Iran, pushed his country too hard to be like the West, technologically and culturally. The Persian people—seeing modernization as a threat to their traditions and cultural identity—finally got fed up and rebelled.

Long story short, the Overland going through Tehran had to be closed down. The hippies were no longer welcome there because they represented American imperialism, sexual depravity, and moral decay.

"Don't worry, John," assured Rosie. "This will be over in a year. Mark my words."

"Well, at least Afghanistan and everywhere east of there is peaceful," John reassures himself. "I'm not going to let some uptight religious fanatic spoil my good time!"

Famous last words. On Christmas Eve of '79, the Russians would invade Afghanistan. The country would become a war zone. The entire Hippie Trail would be shut down for good. This event seemed to make it official: The hippies had gone out of style.

CHAPTER 18

KARMA™

70 miles northwest of Detroit; Fall, 1977.

I N SEPTEMBER OF '77, RANDAL AND I BEGAN our senior year at Bishop Borgess High School in Redford Township. Gaining some level of popularity in high school had proved to be a long, arduous climb, but now it seemed we were close to reaching the summit. The news of our New York odyssey quickly spread. The story even appeared in the school newspaper. Even though it just happened two months prior, it had already become the stuff of legend. And it would continue to develop with each retelling and become more polished over time. We originally told it to brag, entertain and, most of all, boost our social status. But then—as philosophical and spiritual themes began to appear—we used it to spread our "gospel."

All the attention from our peers naturally made our heads swell. Randal Stark had finally accomplished his dream of establishing himself as a man of high importance at our school (at least he thought he did). When sharing about the trip with others, he fancied himself being a paragon of human understanding. He went around quoting all the enlightened rock stars like Springsteen, Dylan, or

Keith Reid, the lyricist of the rock band Procol Harum. At parties, Randal would make himself the center of attention philosophizing about the meaning of life.

The religious version of our story made its official debut at a weekend retreat in October—at a place called Camp Tekakwitha.

Tekakwitha is near Webberville, an hour's drive west of Detroit. The main building, tucked away amongst towering evergreens, has an austere post-and-beam construction made up of white pine timbers. The smoky aroma inside comes from a large rock fireplace in the main room. Windows looking out at the trees, the log furniture, and nature-inspired rugs make the interior feel cozy and serene. A humongous moose head mounted on the balcony makes the scene complete.

Fifteen of us high schoolers and three teachers had car-pooled there. The formal retreat activities began in earnest on a Friday evening and would end the following Sunday afternoon.

Catholics love retreats. These special events give you the chance to escape the distractions of modern life, commune with nature, and rekindle your relationship with God.

Sitting on cushy chairs and sofas arranged in a circle, each of us 11th- and 12th-grade students take turns answering questions posed by Ms. Eileen Frey, one of the Religion teachers.

"If you were a kitchen appliance, which one would you be and why?"

Nervous laughter fills the room, followed by silence, as did most silly ice-breaker questions designed to get people out of their comfort zones. Randal says he'd be a refrigerator; I say an electric can opener.

Then comes the question of the night—the quintessential deep question—the one that makes you shudder and cringe because you must open up and share your innermost thoughts with others:

"Do you have a relationship with God?"

Unlike most of our classmates, Randal and I don't mind getting deep. We had done it so many times amongst ourselves. And we see "sharing time" at the retreat as a golden opportunity to present our profundities to others.

"First off, what do we know about God? . . . Eric?"

"The all-powerful eternal being."

"Mora?"

"The creator of everything."

"Randal?"

"I don't see God as some old man in the sky, but like the 'Force' in *Star Wars*. When you trust in the Force like Obi-Wan Kenobi told Luke Skywalker, it gives you the power to do the unimaginable..."

I jump in since my turn comes after Randal.

"Yeah, it's *scientific* like the law of gravity. When Randal and I went to New York, we experienced that power up close and personal," I say enthusiastically.

"'Tell us more,'" an intrigued Ms. Frey beseeches.

"During the New York trip, we found ourselves utterly blown away by the reality of . . . *people*. We were amazed at how kind and generous they were—especially total strangers who went out of their way to help us out."

"You always hear about how people are selfish, nasty, and evil," Randal continues. "But Ted and I discovered most folks are pretty cool."

"But how does that relate to your idea that God is the Force in *Star Wars*?"

"Well, the force I'm talking about is the power of *love*. I mean, the love for your fellow man. It's like an invisible energy field that draws and binds all humans together. Love is God and God is Love, in the most literal sense."

"When Randal and I got back from New York, we concluded that 99% of what religion has to offer is pointless."

"Yeah, dogmas like the Trinity, the Immaculate Conception, and Transubstantiation. Who needs 'em? The only important thing is, 'Love your neighbor as yourself.'"

"Then there's the *Law of Reciprocity*, the idea 'you reap what you sow.' When you do good to others, goodness will sooner or later befall you. It's built into nature. And bad people get what they deserve too. Justice, I mean."

"Sounds like you guys really thought this through."

"Yeah, you might say we invented our *own religion*," Randal responds with a wry smile.

"We're religious founders just like, you know, Buddha, Muhammed, Jesus, and all the rest of 'em."

There is a stunned silence. We are obviously joking around, but deep down we think we have made a breakthrough akin to Fleming discovering penicillin or Einstein coming up with $E=MC^2$. Of course, in the old days, we would have been accused of heresy and burned at the stake. But, despite our blatant disrespect of organized religion, teachers at our Catholic school would not only tolerate us but congratulate us!

"There is one other thing. Every religion has a holy city, right? A Mecca, a Jerusalem. Well, ours is Asbury Park, New Jersey."

"*Asbury Park, New Jersey?*"

"And we also have an unholy city," I said.

"Yeah, what's that?"

"Commack, New York."

"Hmmm."

"Does your religion have a name?"

"Yes. We call it *Karma*™."

The religion of Karma™ makes a startling claim which I admit we stole from Christianity. Every human being should be treated with the utmost respect, because he or she is *Imago Dei*. Our brand new belief system prompted us to push out stranded motorists during the Great Blizzard of '78 asking for nothing in return. We raised money for Detroit's inner-city poor through the Focus Hope walk along Eight Mile. We were kinder than before.

CHAPTER 19

RANDAL'S REPUBLIC

Dearborn, Michigan; Spring of 1978.

HIGH SCHOOL GRADUATION WAS IMMINENT. Randal Stark and I went to our favorite place to study—Dearborn's Henry Ford Centennial Library—but we couldn't keep our minds on the books. The Centennial is a sprawling modern structure at Michigan Avenue and Mercury Drive. The building is kitty corner from the Ford Motor Company World Headquarters and just east of UM-D where I would attend college in the Fall. I always thought the library was a bit of a humbug. From the outside, it appears large enough to hold as many books as the Library of Congress, but then you discover that only the second-floor houses books and the aisles there are super wide.

"Ted, what branch of Psychology are you going into?" asks Randal out of the blue. He is referring to the three theoretical models presented in Psych 101, our college prep class: Psychoanalytic, Behaviorist, and Humanist/Existentialist.

"Definitely Humanist/Existentialism."

"I pick Behaviorism."

My choice, the Humanist/Existentialist school, was co-founded by theorists Abraham Maslow and Carl Rogers. Among other things, it's all about helping individuals make "meaningful choices" and get "in touch with their feelings." In the popular imagination of the '70s, the therapist in this theoretical school wears a poncho, jeans, and sandals to work. He has people sit in bean-bag chairs and stare at lava lamps in his office. He models being closely connected to people, nature, and the here-and-now.

Randal's selection—the Behaviorist school started by John B. Watson—sharply contrasted mine. It's all about tracking people's behavior on spreadsheets to help them develop good habits and eliminate bad ones. Reward and punishment is used to elicit desired responses. He had been interested in Behavior Modification and a method called Aversion Therapy since eighth grade, but his aha moment came while seeing *A Clockwork Orange*, a film we saw together recently in Ann Arbor.

"Sorry, Randal, I don't get it. That movie shows Behaviorism in a bad light. Brainwashing—er, sorry, Aversion Therapy—is shown as something terrifying. I'm thinking about what the lab-coat people did to Alex in that one scene."

"Hey, I'm not denying that Aversion Therapy can be used the wrong way. But just imagine its incredible potential!"

"To reprogram the entire human race to automatically do the right thing?"

"I was talking about it in terms of helping people in my own private practice, but now that you mention it, let's explore this a bit, Ted. How would *you* go about designing a global utopia?"

"Hmmm. Well, I would create an environment where people love one another and the government would force everyone to share like in socialism."

"I used to believe in socialism, but not anymore."

"Huh?"

"Look, Ted, the entire basis of socialism is wrong. People are not equal—and that's a good thing."

"Whoa!" Indignation wells up inside, Then I catch myself. There he goes again. Randal the provocateur, putting me on. "Come on Randal, that's downright un-American. It says right there in the Declaration of Independence that men are created equal."

"Well, they are in one sense. But, in another sense, they are not. From Day One, each person is different. Some are more physically fit than others, right? Some are more intelligent. Some are more talkative, and so on. That's why people usually end up with the jobs they're cut out for. That's why you and I are the philosopher-kings."

"*Philosopher-kings?* Now I know Randal is putting me on!"

"Yeah. You know, the rulers of Plato's *Republic*, the so-called Guardians. We're in that exulted class of people, the smart ones, the elite."

"Okay, then, what's your plan?"

"It's quite simple. We split everyone up into three groups, the Jocks, Freaks, and Geeks." What did Randal mean by "Jocks, Freaks, and Geeks"? As everyone knows, teenagers tend to classify themselves into distinct crowds—jocks, brains, hipsters, punks, preps, skinheads, nerds, etc. Randal had conveniently narrowed them down to three.

"You see, Ted, each group would have its own job in the perfect society. The Jocks would be the auxiliaries, the military class to keep order. They are up to the task because they're strong and ruthless, qualities our government would need to keep people in line. Also, they're motivated by popularity. They like others to admire them for their physical prowess and brave exploits."

"Okay, what about the Freaks?"

"Freaks are the producers. They're the ones who work after school so they can afford drugs and record albums. They make things so they can *buy* things. And they're perfectly happy with that."

"Geeks?"

"The Geeks are the geniuses who run the whole thing. They're the nerds and dorks (whatever you want to call them) who know all the right things. They also have the smarts to teach and direct others on how to best live their lives."

"Does that make *us* Geeks?"

"Well no, we're above even them of course. Geeks don't understand the concept of cool like we do. We stand alone at the top."

Due to homework, we couldn't go much further in this discussion that day, but we would return to it months later. That June, we graduated from Borgess. I worked that summer as a sales clerk at the Montgomery Ward department store in Livonia. Meanwhile, Randal worked on the Ford factory assembly-line.

A TALE OF TWO COLLEGE TOWNS

CHAPTER 20

WELCOME TO BOULDER

Boulder, Colorado; the afternoon of July 12, 1979.

ROSIE DENOUNCING THE ROAD for the sake of her safety and unborn child had initially evoked consternation. But, upon further reflection, I came to realize she was doing the right thing. I figured—if humanity is to survive—the next generation needed to be raised by free-thinkers like her. Maybe, just maybe, her offspring would be the "dancing star" Nietzsche spoke of. As for John Hancock and his rags-to-riches story, his winning a long legal battle with estranged family members over inheritance money struck a chord in me. I'm ashamed to admit this now, but I wanted to cheer, "Yeah! Yeah! *Screw your family.* Family is nothing more than a tool used by the corrupt establishment to control you." I was intrigued by the fact John replaced his biological kin with a new "family"—namely Rosie and the gang.

Fresh in my mind, John's New Age philosophy would serve as a template while I was in Boulder, the home of the University of Colorado. The progressive town had a lot going for it: books and drugs and people practicing non-traditional lifestyles and countercultural forms of spirituality. So much diversity! So many ways to grow and expand your consciousness! I had never been to Boulder before, but I knew it was just like Ann Arbor, Michigan.

Ann Arbor—along with most other college towns—is so distinctive that people often say, "It's a different world" (usually while shaking their heads). That's because it revolves around an institution of higher learning. Businesses there typically cater to those who have their heads in the clouds. High ideals permeate, dominate, and intoxicate. There are bookstores galore as well as record shops, gaming parlors, bars, coffee shops, and so on, directed to every taste and whim of those in their late teens and early twenties. In a college town, you can sample practically everything new under the sun. It has a vibrant cultural scene where you can see all kinds of movies, concerts, etc. for very reasonable prices. (Considering the sky-high cost of tuition, you deserve a break!)

☾ ☾ ☾

THE CITY OF BOULDER IS 50 MILES SOUTHWEST of Greeley and 25 miles northwest of Denver. It was fitting that Buford, our last ride, would be the official greeter. Wearing a marijuana leaf t-shirt and tattered blue jeans, the scraggly young man kept raving...

"Man, you dudes are gonna *love* Boulder... all kinds of stuff to do... parties everywhere... street musicians... people from all over... nice babes... good dope... What else could you ask for?"

"Where are the best spots?"

"If there's only one place you gotta go, it's the Pearl Street Mall."

"Pearl Street *Mall*?"

When he said "mall," I pictured *Fairlane* Mall, the new enclosed shopping center in Dearborn anchored by JC Penney's, Hudson's, and Sears. I recalled its shimmering terrazzo-tiled floors, its hexagon-shaped skylights, and its three-floor courtyard area that make you feel like you're stuck in an M.C. Escher drawing. Randal Stark works there in a sporting goods store. The mall happens to be across the street (Evergreen Road) from my school, U of M Dearborn. It's funny to think, all year long, I was jealous of Randal living the good life on his own in fabulous Ann Arbor. Meanwhile, I was stuck living with my mom and dad on Detroit's west side, working and going to school in dull, uninspiring Dearborn. Now in the summertime,

Randal and I had switched roles! Poor Randal had to endure living in his parents' house and working long hours in Dearborn while I'm footloose-and-fancy-free in Boulder!

☾ ☾ ☾

WHEN BUFORD DROPS US OFF, Pete and I discover that the "mall" in downtown Boulder is actually an *outdoor* public space, four blocks of Pearl Street sectioned off from 11th Street to 15th Street for pedestrian traffic only. It's lined with small trees, flower gardens, and meticulously preserved old buildings. The brick-paved street appears old-fashioned. If you look west, you can see the magnificent Flatirons hovering along the horizon. This relatively small mountain range—featuring five brown sandstone formations—lives up to its name. The mountains resemble flat irons like the ones the pioneers used.

The Pearl Street Mall, for all practical purposes, is Boulder's town square, a conglomerate of various shops and restaurants plus the grounds of the county courthouse. Most of the stores are upscale, trendy, and edgy to accommodate diverse tastes of an educated, creative, and free-thinking crowd. Cylinder-shaped kiosks display handbills that direct people to interesting spots throughout the city, for example, live-music shows in taverns, yoga-exercise meets, and political events.

Paradise! Not a utopia by any stretch, but perhaps the closest thing to it in this world. Disbursed among the distinguished-looking and fashionable walkers are a significant number of homeless people. Strung out on drugs and alcohol, often panhandling, these haggard-looking souls look like they're straight out of a Charles Dickens novel.

CHAPTER 21

DEARBORN, MI

Flashback; September, 1978.

DEARBORN IS NOT A COLLEGE TOWN in the usual sense. You might instead call it a company town since it revolves around the Ford Motor Company. Tiny compared to U of M's main campus in Ann Arbor, the University of Michigan Dearborn is only two miles west of Ford Motor World Headquarters and just east of Henry Ford's Fair Lane Estate. U of M Dearborn, Henry Ford College, and a nature reserve presently stand on what used to be Mr. Ford's private property.

My first semester was traumatic. The level of difficulty of my classes blindsided me. Being surrounded by strangers made me feel isolated and lonely. I detested UM-D because it was too small to accommodate the number of students enrolled. Between classes, I felt like a lone dogie in a Texas cattle run. Since much of the college was under construction, students spent most of their time in temporary structures called modules which were often poorly ventilated and insulated. Being in one of them too long, you risked freezing or baking to death.

My biggest disappointment however was Dearborn wasn't radical like Ann Arbor. Sure, there were tattooed punk rockers showing off their ediginess and political activists giving speeches in the commons area, but the college's counter-culture lacked vigor. Most students lived with their parents and treated school like a nine-to-five job. Prepping for a career was more important to them than saving the planet. UM-D specialized in Mechanical Engineering which deals with the real world rather than an imaginary one. It wasn't big on Philosophy, Art, and Psychology which I considered the real meat-and-potatoes subjects.

☾ ☾ ☾

RESIDENTS OF HENRY FORD'S HOMETOWN are gaga about history, hi-tech (as it relates to cars), and religion. To them, family is first, foremost, and always. They're ethnically diverse. Polish, Irish, and Italian families had lived there since the nineteenth century which means Catholicism is huge. But here's the unique thing about Dearborn: It has the highest concentration of Arab Americans in the whole United States! They had come from countries like Yemen, Iraq, and Syria but mostly Lebanon. Most of them are Muslims, so our city is considered "the Muslim capital of the West." In the 1970's, the already huge Muslim population climbed exponentially because of war refugees pouring in from Beirut and southern Lebanon. (For more information about this religio-ethnic group, read Afterword A.) Long-time metro Detroiters were taken aback by the emigrants' fervent religious devotion and distinctive attire, especially the women who wear burqas, chadors, and hijabs.

When I first spotted a pair of chador-wearing women on Dearborn's east side, I thought they were old-school Catholic nuns! After I saw more of them on other occasions, I learned who they were and realized they were part of a growing population. My friends and I viewed them with curiosity, pity, and condescension, considering them culturally backward and insular. We thought they needed to get with the times, especially regarding women's rights.

Most of the Dearborn Muslims are Shia as opposed to Sunni. It took me years to tell the difference. To understand the two groups, you have to learn about Islam's early days. The bitter conflict goes back to when the Prophet Mohammed died in AD 632. It was concerning who should succeed him. The Sunnis believe the leader should be chosen by consensus. The Shias claim that only

Mohammed's male blood relatives (Ahl al-Bayt) starting with Ali ibn Abi Talib (600-661)—the Prophet's cousin and son-in-law—are qualified to fill the spot. The term "Twelvers" refers to those who believe in the twelve Imams—Ali and his direct descendants who ruled the Shia for eleven consecutive generations—plus the twelfth Imam, Muhammad Ibn al-Hassan, who "vanished from the eyes of ordinary men" in 873 or 874 but is expected to gloriously return in the future. This messianic figure is supposed to usher in a golden age of Islam, one that will last for a thousand years. The belief in the return of the Twelfth Imam (aka the Mahdi) parallels that of the Second Coming of Christ in Christianity.

The Shias' emphasis on the Prophet's bloodline highlights the importance of family in both branches of Islam. True, we Polish also believe in family first, but, in my opinion, the Muslims run circles around us in this area. Even my college friend Zainab who described herself as a "cultural Muslim" said to me one time, "I have God and I have family—what else do I need?"

CHAPTER 22

VANITY FAIR

Boulder, Colorado; the afternoon of July 12, 1979.

THE PEARL STREET MALL WAS the best people-watching place I've ever seen. Besides promenading about on a fair-weather day, folks young and old (mostly young) sit on park benches to read, engage in conversations, and play board games. Like Vanity Fair in John Bunyan's *Pilgrim's Progress*, there is always something going on. From noon to late evening, jugglers, mimes, clowns, magicians, and storytellers perform in the open. Musicians however dominate. From formally dressed string quartets on the Boulder Courthouse lawn to the scrappy guitarists in doorways and on street corners, they enchant one and all with their wondrous sounds, particularly one audience member: an aspiring singer-songwriter named Pete LeBlanc.

It's hard to believe Pete and I had known each other for only ten months. Having been through so much together, especially on this trip, we had become like brothers. Our relationship even featured a bright, shiny *kill switch*. The radical individualists we were, we had agreed that our freedom as individuals comes first. It certainly should never be compromised by the will of the other partner (or anyone else for that matter). With this principle in mind, we decided before leaving Detroit that when one of us feels imposed upon by the other—we would immediately separate and do so amiably. The imagined scenario played over and over in my head. I say, "Pete, I think it's *time*." With his hand on his chin, he would reply without hesitation, "Sure, no problem, Adiós Amigo!" We'd shake hands and part ways like Abraham and Lot did in the Bible.

No offense to Randal, but Pete was a better traveling companion than him. Pete was much more spontaneous. Since hardly anything works out as planned when you're hitchhiking, detours and even dead ends must be treated with equal enthusiasm as highways that take you to your destination. Of course, not all diverted paths lead to where you want to be (Being stranded at a grungy rest stop on a rainy Fourth-of-July evening wasn't exactly fun.). But, often, unexpected settings and circumstances translate into meaningful memories.

Randal was too cautious and anxious that something might go disastrously wrong. In retrospect, he was right.

Pete, unlike Randal, "got" the hobo concept. An avid reader of *Rolling Stone*, he esteemed Blues and Country music which sentimentalized trains, railroad tracks, and hobos in their lyrics. And naturally an avid Bob Dylan fan like LeBlanc would fully appreciate the archetypal hobo Woody Guthrie as a matter of course.

☾ ☾ ☾

YOU'D THINK IN A PLACE LIKE BOULDER, diverse people would mix and mingle. But they tended to stick to their own kind. Like the proverbial birds of a feather, Whites flocked together, as did the Blacks, Asians, and so on. Pete and I gravitated toward college students and the homeless.

In '79, Boulder was a relatively friendly and accommodating place for vagrants like us. If you found an acceptable place to sleep at night, the law left you alone. In years past, local businesses had encouraged police to aggressively crack down on bums, tramps, and hobos. However, ordinances were eventually relaxed. Tolerance, acceptance, and inclusion would rule the day. Hollywood must've taken note when they made Boulder the setting for a new TV sitcom called *Mork and Mindy* (which premiered on ABC-TV in September of '78). The show celebrates an eccentric transient guy (played by Robin Williams) who just happens to be from another planet.

This open attitude was apparently driven by a city population dominated by the Baby Boom generation, then still only in their twenties and early thirties. The idealistic Boomers tended to see the spark of humanity in the unwashed transients. They perhaps even recognized their younger hippie selves having a great time despite being poverty-stricken. Indeed, many of the drifters were actual hippies still living out the narratives of Jack Kerouac's *On the Road* and Hermann Hesse's *Siddhartha*.

Pete and I of course weren't derelicts down on their luck. We were just two adventurous teens who decided to be hobos for fun.

☾ ☾ ☾

OTHER SOCIAL GROUPS IN THE MALL differentiated themselves along the lines of musical tastes. They included heavy-metal enthusiasts, punk rockers, and Deadheads. After surveying the Mall and surrounding areas, we rested our weary frames on the grass by the Courthouse. There, a young man with a Fedora hat and ungroomed facial hair approaches us. He has on a t-shirt featuring a human skull with a bouquet of roses for hair. His two female companions sport tie-dye clothes, face paint, and exotic jewelry that scream "HIPPIE." They have a mascot: a rambunctious black Labrador Retriever with a red bandanna for a collar.

"Hey, dudes, we just came from Seattle. Do you know where we can find some *drugs*?"

"Dunno," I reply. "I was going to ask you the same thing."

Our new acquaintances have interesting nicknames: "Horse," "Star," and "Ganja." They call themselves "Deadheads," devotees of the San Francisco band, the Grateful Dead. Since LeBlanc and I had attended a "Dead" concert in Detroit back in January, I marvel at how fans *worship* the group. The intensity of their adoration surely rivals that found in religion. (Indeed, some would attest The Dead *is* a religion.) I should talk: My friends and I had practically deified the Beatles, Bob Dylan, and Bruce Springsteen.

The trio with the canine talk nonstop about the Dead and individual band members (most notably the band's front-man Jerry Garcia) framing their personal accounts of concerts in terms of the supernatural. The "strange things" they report include mysteriously recovering lost concert tickets, suddenly experiencing déjà vu, and having "visions' induced by hallucinogenic mushrooms and LSD. Most of all, Horse, Star, and Ganja show their devotion by the way they "follow" the group quite literally, attending every Dead show slated that year—all seventy-plus!

Here's another thing pertaining to the Dead and religion. One of the rock band's all-time greatest hits had this one line: "A friend of the devil is a friend of mine." This fit right in with LeBlanc's serve-both-God-and-the-devil philosophy based on *Demian* by Hesse.

During my week stay in Boulder, I would get a chance to see a number of these Deadheads up-close. I concluded that most of them were not real hippies. Fresh in my memory were the real Mc-Coys: Rosie Smith, John Hancock, and the inhabitants of Poverty Gulch and Moon Gulch. Disappointingly, people like our threesome didn't come close to what I considered the gold standard. Sure, they used all the right buzzwords, but they obviously didn't know the code. They seemed to be shallow and pretentious, inferior carbon copies. Whenever I brought up Existentialism, Transcendentalism, and Individualism, the three main ingredients of "Hippie-ism," their eyes glazed over like I was talking gibberish.

CHAPTER 23

GO BLUE!

Ann Arbor, Michigan flashback; October, 1978.

SPEAKING OF "ISMS," RANDAL AND I couldn't wait to take Philosophy 101. We had assumed the college course would illuminate each of us like the sun beaming on the awe-struck prisoner freed from Plato's dingy Cave. It seemed self-evident. The more you ponder the meaning of life, the wiser (and therefore happier) you'll be as a person—just as Socrates taught. In our minds, the term "philosophy" was synonymous with "wisdom." However, this didn't turn out to be the case.

As I said before, Randal and I had invented our own religion called Karma™ (not to be confused with Hinduism, in whole or in part). It was also our philosophy of life. Aside from our kidding around that Asbury Park is "the Holy City," we took Karma™ itself a little more seriously. In sum, it combined "the Law of Reciprocity" (The moral universe we inhabit ultimately rewards people for doing good and punishes those who do bad.) and "the Golden Rule" ("Love your neighbor as yourself."). But even though it appeared to be very durable, fixed, and axiomatic, our higher learning required us to scrutinize it. It got "deconstructed," to use the current term.

☽ ☽ ☽

ONE DAY, MY PHILOSOPHY INSTRUCTOR, Dr. Paul Thagard, did something out-of-the-ordinary in class. He sketched a human brain on the chalkboard with wires coming out of it.

"Imagine at this very moment," he says pointedly, "some evil scientist on another planet keeps your brain in a glass jar. Your gray matter is connected to a computer, so everything you're experiencing right now is an illusion."

This classic thought-experiment—called Brain in a Vat—is designed to make you question everything you perceive to be true and real, including the hand in front of your face. It's part of a branch of Philosophy called *epistemology*, a fifty-dollar word that means the study of knowledge. Mulling over deductions made by eighteenth-century philosophers John Locke and Bishop Berkeley, Thagard explained that a certain David Hume and his reluctant disciple, Immanuel Kant (and *his* followers), would lead the Western mind to a shocking conclusion: Most, if not *all*, human knowledge is *impossible*. It's all constructed in your brain! Everything you claim to "know" is subjective!

Professor Thagard—a lean, blond-haired, thirty-year-old man from Saskatoon, Saskatchewan—didn't take this extreme position. Or perhaps he just applied it to religion. In any case, he maintained that authoritative knowledge can be learned through science and reason. Thagard specialized in the area where the science of cognition and philosophy converge. On the first day of class, he briefly told his life story. Like Randal and me, he was raised Catholic and was an altar boy, but he said he had changed his views on religion at age fifteen by reading Bertrand Russell's *Why I Am Not a Christian*. It was precisely Thagard's easygoing, amiable nature that made him so unnerving. He didn't fit my preconceived mental image of a surly atheist with an ax to grind. He was actually a nice guy. The recurring theme of his lectures was the notion that God can't be taken seriously since there's no evidence for his existence. As far as we know, the mind is nothing more than a brain, an organic "machine" that has resulted from random collisions of atoms over the course of billions of years.

True, evolution had been taught in Catholic school, but only in the context of an intelligent Creator guiding the process (theistic evolution). Thagard argued, (1) Only matter exists and it consists of atoms. (2) Matter has no intrinsic purpose and meaning. (3) Humans have no intrinsic purpose and meaning since they're made of nothing but matter. The soul doesn't exist either.

On hearing these truth claims, I lost my enthusiasm for Philosophy. Thagard and my other professors—whose words I considered practically infallible—seriously undermined everything my parents taught me about God, immortality, and morality.

Here's some inspiring words to tape on your bathroom mirror: *Life is meaningless.*

"Why don't you kill yourself?" Thagard asked rhetorically one time (though he said it in a nice way). After inviting his students to contemplate the idea of absolute nothingness—that humans had appeared out of nothing and will eventually end up nothing—he offered this consolation: According to recent findings in neuroscience and psychology, our brains are hardwired (via evolution) to "love, work, and play." Sooo, students. *enjoy life!* But, with all due respect to the professor, I found this answer to "Why don't you kill yourself?" unsatisfying.

ᓬ ᓬ ᓬ

THE MUCH-ANTICIPATED FOOTBALL GAME between Michigan and Michigan State took place in Ann Arbor on Saturday, October 14, 1978, a sunny but cool day when the autumn colors had reached their zenith. The Michigan Wolverines humiliating 24-15 defeat did not spoil the party afterwards at Randal's college dormitory Bursley Hall. Boisterous laughter ensued, music played, and alcohol flowed as if our team won. Each dorm room had been given the charge to administer its own mixed drink. The bathrooms housed beer kegs. Awards were bestowed to those who were stupid enough to down every concoction on the floor. There were invisible lines that people dared each other to cross. Who would take the drinking game challenge? Who would try hash or LSD? Who would throw food around and act like John Belushi in the then-popular movie *Animal House*? Overused phrases like "go for the gusto" aptly characterize this mind trip. Pete LeBlanc—the guy who Randal had invited the night before as we drove to the Bob Dylan concert—would make all this posturing and brinkmanship seem as lame as the antics of a house cat.

It all began around midnight when people congregated around the TV. It was the world premiere of a New Wave Rock group called Devo on *Saturday Night Live*. The members of the band, wearing yellow radioactivity-protection suits and dark safety goggles, gyrated robotically on stage as they delivered a quirky version of the Rolling Stones classic "Satisfaction."

From the ridiculous to the sublime, a Channel 4 newsflash came on during the commercial break. Newscaster Mort Crim said, "Cardinals in the Vatican have reconvened to select a new pope." This was significant because the last time this historical event took place was just seven weeks ago. A man named Albino Luciani, who had become Pope John Paul I, died under strange circumstances after serving as St. Peter's successor for only a month!

"It's a hit job, I tell ya. Someone wanted the Pope dead," opined one of Randal's dorm friends.

"Yeah, how does a guy die from a heart attack in his *sleep*?" replied another, inspiring the unveiling of a few conspiracy theories in the room.

Some dude slouched in a beanbag had an altogether different take: "Maybe, it's a *sign from God*." Several people within earshot immediately weighed in. Emotions flared as what typically happens when the subject of religion is brought up. The dominant thread was the quandary of the ages: Does God exist?

"I'm in Jehovah's corner!" Pete LeBlanc spouted out assuredly. "I believe in every word in the Old and New Testaments!"

There was nervous laughter. Eyes rolled. Those present—presumably those who'd been recently convinced by their professors that religious faith is intellectually untenable—seemed irritated, amused, and even stunned by the supposed simpleton's words. Some girl blurted out in a drunken stupor, "Three cheers for JEHOVAH!" but she had no takers.

"But," Pete continued his sentence, "I also pay equal homage to *the devil*."

There was an awkward pause. Then, "Let's hear it for SATAN!" shrieked the confused, sloshed girl. Eyebrows raised and jaws dropped. Pandemonium ensued. In such a party atmosphere, jocularity almost always trumps seriousness. Offensive utterances can be easily construed as tongue-in-cheek humor or a put-on. If all else fails, Jim Beam could be blamed. But Pete sounded so off key and off-putting that attaining pardon was probably futile. Besides, he didn't seem to care if he was forgiven. His smugness was apparent. He appeared to enjoy the brouhaha he had caused. During a relatively brief ruckus, I heard someone murmur, "Who *is* that guy anyway?" followed by the reply, "Oh, he's one of *Randal's* friends."

This incident may have triggered Randal to pull me aside later. "Ted," he said, "I'll be honest with you. Pete's kind of an ass****."

STILL REELING FROM THE UNTIMELY DEATH of Pope John Paul I—Catholics in my neighborhood suddenly found themselves in a state of ecstasy. A certain Cardinal Karol Józef Wojtyła (1920-2005) was elected Supreme Pontiff. Much rejoicing ensued over the fact that the new pope was a son of Poland. (Back then, about a third of Cody Rouge residents were Polish, another third were Irish.)

When I watched the newly ordained Pope John Paul II on TV deliver his first sermon on a Vatican balcony, I had no idea who he was. The local news media divulged that Wojtyła—once the archbishop of Kraków, Poland—had visited Hamtramck, metro Detroit's biggest Polish enclave. Besides being the first non-Italian pope in 450 years, he didn't seem to fit the mold of the head of the Catholic Church. He wasn't old and frail like previous popes. He was a poet and actor who loved outdoor sports like skiing, camping, and fishing. His main message "Do not be afraid" was not empty talk. It came from a man who had conducted underground resistance meetings in defiance of two bloody totalitarian regimes: the Nazis and the Soviets. Beside the salient fact John Paul II was Polish, my mother surprisingly zeroed in on another exemplary attribute: "Ted, do you know he's a *philosopher*?" Recognizing her stratagem (of course to get me back to church), I reflexively held up my lead shield of resistance by changing the subject. But I must admit I was pleasantly surprised to find out that Poland produced a genius. You see, the 1970s was the heyday of "dumb Polack" jokes. (For more information about John Paul II, see Afterword B.)

☾ ☾ ☾

THANKFULLY, RANDAL DIDN'T FORGET about me after moving to Ann Arbor. He invited me to visit him regularly, mostly to take part in parties like the one just described. There, I inwardly ached on seeing what I was missing out on: the "college experience" which Randal had spoken so glowingly about. He made great strides winning friends and even becoming popular with the good-looking girls on his floor. I envied him for having such a blast. He and his new peers had so much freedom.

The winning formula he used to gain social approval in high school apparently worked with this new set of peers. I noticed that the New-York-trip narrative greatly enhanced his public image. Because of it, his dorm-mates treated him like a rock star. When I came to visit, I, his former traveling partner, got the red-carpet treatment.

One Sunday morning, I woke up on the floor of his dorm room which had been trashed from the hall party the night before. His desk, normally used for studying, was littered with bottles of rum, overripe banana peels, and slices of coconut, orange, and pineapple. In the middle was a blender used to mash up the tropical ingredients into a beverage called a Rock Lobster, in honor of the hit song by a new musical group called the B-52s.

Then there was the *bong*, the water pipe used to cool cannabis smoke. Its very presence highlighted how far Randal had come in just a month-and-a-half. The night we tried marijuana for the first time (two years before), we swore we'd never get too familiar with it lest we get hooked to harder stuff. But now look at my friend! He's accustomed to drug paraphernalia like a handyman is to his tools. He can quickly rattle off the different varieties of hemp. He even graduated to hash, which has much more THC than pot. He may have tried other mind-altering chemicals.

By October, I noticed that the drugs had taken their toll. Randal had red eyes most of the time. He carried around an uncharacteristic stupid grin. His overall movements were clumsy. The most disturbing thing was he allowed his carefully chosen threads to get disheveled. That said, Randal wasn't nearly as pathetic as his roommate, Finch, who smoked weed around the clock. Finch even did it during school hours. "I study better when I'm high," he said with a shrug and smile. Three months later, the results of this innovative learning strategy were in. Finch flunked out of U of M Ann Arbor.

Anyway, Randal's foul mood that morning could easily be blamed on his throbbing headache and his dread of having to clean his place up. Nonetheless, his comments hinted at something else altogether.

"You know, Ted," he uttered pensively. "Pot is a lot like soma."

"*Soma?* What's that?"

"It's the happiness pill everyone takes in *Brave New World* to ward off the misery of existence."

CHAPTER 24

THE PEOPLE'S REPUBLIC OF BOULDER

Boulder, July 14, 1979.

THEN THERE'S THE MARXIST VISION of Utopia. I was close to hitting the kill switch even before entering Boulder. Pete's presence was starting to annoy me. Besides my still-festering resentment of him over Rosie, we were hopelessly at odds over politics. Our conflict was not liberal versus conservative, but political versus apolitical. I was itching to join some social movement to change the world, but Pete dodged getting involved in activism for whatever reason. (Perhaps joining *any* group went against his independent nature.) Though we both agreed that the end of the world was nigh, he seemed downright indifferent to any effort to try to stop it.

A week earlier, Pete and I had attended an anti-nuke demonstration in the Black Hills of South Dakota (one of many held that summer in the aftermath of the Three Mile Island incident). On Sunday, protesters embarked on a political march from Rapid City, South Dakota to a uranium mine. While I was all revved up to take part, Pete piped in and belittled the whole enterprise, calling it a "big waste of time." Irritated and disappointed, I almost pulled the kill switch, but I let Pete talk me into leaving the "phony" activist scene behind. Though I regretted my decision at that time, I wound up glad, realizing the time wasn't right.

☾ ☾ ☾

"THE PEOPLE'S REPUBLIC OF BOULDER!" I blurted jokingly when we first arrived. This of course is a reference to the town's presumed romance with socialism, a sentiment that it shares with its ideological sibling Ann Arbor. Occasionally, political rallies took place in the Mall. Boulder, founded during the gold rush of the mid-1800s, eventually adopted the grandiose dream that Greeley had once embraced but quickly abandoned—that of a socialist utopia. But the brand of socialism Boulder now espouses, thanks largely to the eggheads at the University, is based on the theories of Karl Marx, not Charles Fourier.

Ironically, Boulder isn't socialist in practice. Capitalism dictates practically everything that goes on there. The demand for housing far supersedes the supply, so real estate prices are astronomically high. Only the wealthy can afford to live there permanently. What makes Boulder so appealing to the upper crust? Beside the fact it's a college town, it has mountains and great weather. Since it's sunny in Boulder three hundred days of the year, people are inclined to stay outdoors most of the time. With a health and physical fitness culture second to none, citizens are always walking, biking, and climbing. It's no wonder the big corporations headquartered there, IBM and Ball Aerospace, routinely pitch the town's "good life" to potential employees. Even the University uses this savvy marketing strategy to attract cream-of-the-crop, elite-class students.

Free enterprise's strong showing in Boulder doesn't deter the hardcore Marxists though. On Pearl Street, where a crisp handbill posted on kiosks everywhere calls for the complete overthrow of the capitalist system, I meet a man peddling socialist newspapers. He reminds me of a young Fidel Castro with his army hat and stubbly face. He wears a flashy button with the image of Leon Trotsky, a noted Socialist. Unlike most passers-by who avoid him like the plague, I stop and ask for a copy.

"That will be 25¢ please."

Begrudgingly, I reach deep into my pocket and hand it to the guy. (The nerve of him asking a "hobo" for money!) In exchange, he hands me one of his papers. The headlines use slogans like "JOIN THE REVOLUTION!" "WORKERS OF THE WORLD UNITE!" etc. It of course has pictures of clenched fists and cartoons of fat cats stepping on people's sternums. It features articles about the current insurgency in Nicaragua, a country in the news a lot.

Despite my buyer's remorse, I feel a certain kinship with this guy whose name is Morris, because he too is concerned about the fate of the planet and its inhabitants. I am a left-wing-radical *wannabe* in the same way I'm a hippie wannabe.

"Morris, people have been trying to spark a revolution for years, but the conservatives seem to keep getting in the way. Did you hear Ronald Reagan is running for President again?"

"Yeah, I heard about that." Morris responds with rolled eyes and a groan.

"You have half the country against you," I continued. "How do you plan to tame that beast? These people are angry. They're not gonna lay down and die and say, 'Here's my money, go ahead and redistribute it.'"

Morris lets out a long sigh. "That's where it gets a little dicey. Yeeeaaah, it's gonna take some militancy. Like in any war, when you encounter those who won't abide, you have to, uh, you know..."

"Kill the bastards?"

"Wwweeeeellllllll..." He smiles nervously and starts scratching what appears to be an insatiable itch on the back of his neck. "To be perfectly honest, the very thought of that scares me. But I suppose, when push comes to shove, you gotta do what you gotta do. But look, Ted, armed struggle isn't necessarily inevitable."

"No?"

"You can abolish landlords, but you don't have to *kill* them. I know, I know this sounds like a cop-out but, for me, it goes back to *labor*. That's a big source of power for us. We can achieve a lot of things by going on strike, wrecking property, and stuff like that."

"Good to hear."

"Look, fascists are motivated by *fear*. If we comrades concentrate on mobilizing our people—you know, grow our movement—we must have a show of *force*. When that's achieved, the opposition will be so scared, they'll have no choice but to back down."

"In other words, intimidation. Great strategy, man!"

CHAPTER 25

BRAVE NEW WORLD

Dearborn and Ann Arbor; October, 1978.

TO RELIEVE MENTAL DISTRESS, I would hike around the nature reserve at the Henry Ford Estate. I've spent countless hours there on the trails. One forest path wraps around a small lake called Fair Lane Pond. The lily pads and the mirror-like reflection of the trees on the water conjure up Henry David Thoreau's Walden Pond.

I can picture Mr. Ford strolling about these grounds with his old pal Thomas Edison discussing underground water sprinklers. (Fair Lane had the world's first.) It's mind-boggling to think how much both men had transformed the world. Without Edison, there would be no incandescent light bulbs or record players. Without Ford, regular people wouldn't own cars and be able to travel to far-away places. Thanks to Ford's assembly-line idea, practically anything from jumbo jets to microchips can be produced on a massive scale.

And it would be only a matter of time before his mass-production techniques would be applied to human beings. Every person could be made perfect like designer jeans! Maybe that's what Huxley was driving at.

I knew it was daft at the time, but I thought just being in the densely forested area of the Ford Estate would help alleviate the grief I was going through in the Fall of '78. The idea was to get "off the grid," find inner peace by going off the beaten path to the wildest, loneliest, most desolate spot I could find and remain there for a while. Sadly, I found none there. Sure, there were no humans around, but I could still hear the rumble of the traffic along Ford Road and Evergreen and the smell of the sewage coming from the Rouge River.

As always in October, the scene was enhanced by the red, orange, and yellow leaves so brilliant in the sunlight that your eyes hurt. Instead of marveling at how beautiful the scene is, I'm thinking that bright orange is the color of the fire engulfing the entire world. Such was the effect of the news media and Philosophy 101 on my fragile psyche at the time.

I have no hard feelings toward Professor Thagard. He did me a great service teaching me how to think objectively and rationally. Believe it or not, his stance on the human condition was actually *biblical*. He asked the same big questions and gave the same gloomy answer as Solomon in the Book of Ecclesiastes. (What's the meaning of life? Answer: There is none—well, apparently.) This sent my mind into a tailspin. I felt depressed yet, at the same time, liberated. It was like a weight was lifted off my shoulders. It's now okay for me to sin since there's no final judgment. Another prevailing thought: I, Ted Granger—equipped with this new information—am immeasurably superior to most of the world's population who are religious. As a result, I was critical of faith and found pleasure in antagonizing the faithful.

"Time to get up for church, dear," my mother entreats through my bedroom door one Sunday morning.

"But ma," I groan. "I'm an *atheist* now."

"WHAT DID YOU SAY?!" These words echo through our Detroit bungalow on Piedmont and Elmira. I'm sure she already knew where I was at religiously but was in denial up to that point. She slips into a purple fit of rage. "We spend all that money on college, and they turn our kids against God!"

☾ ☾ ☾

RANDAL STARK WOULD LATER ADMIT GOING through the same godless stage. And, come to find out, it began when *his* professor also sketched a human brain on the chalkboard with wires coming out of it.

Until that conversation in his dorm room regarding soma (the happiness pill in Aldous Huxley's *Brave New World*), I got the impression Randal was living it up. The grass is always greener on the other side, as they say. The trouble was, over in Ann Arbor, the grass was more plentiful than in Detroit/Dearborn. He smoked a lot of it with his new friends at Bursley Hall and, for a time, his mental faculties were probably a little skewed. He yielded to the idea that his version of soma was the cure for his woes. Using it, Randal had tried to escape reality and distract himself from the existential despair evoked by Philosophy 101.

Sometime during that period, Randal the Mastermind revisited the topic of ruling the world. (It was his hobby, I guess.) He had fancied himself being the head philosopher-king of the entire planet.

"In light of the new information," he reflects out loud. "It's up to *us* to keep all our subjects happy and content. The Jocks, Freaks, and Geeks—*everyone*—must believe the 'Noble Lie' that they're doing 'God's work.'"

"God being *Henry Ford?*" I squawk. "Honestly, Randal, the whole idea is preposterous!"

"But Ted, Mr. Ford is only a symbol in the book. He stands for modern technology. Stuff is produced in factories to meet every conceivable human want and need. Instant gratification, including the sexual kind, is available 24/7. Pain and suffering is eliminated. The bottom line is we, the Guardians, give people what they want, so they, in turn, do what *we* want. Get it?"

"That's brilliant, Randal!"

Next, Randal brings up conditioning ("hypnopaedia" in *Brave New World*), a whole other topic. Suffice to say, it's a *Behaviorist* word. Again, Randal Stark chose Behaviorism as his academic field of study. The Behaviorist school of Psychology proposes that all our actions are determined solely by the environment and free will doesn't exist.

CHAPTER 26

THE GYPSY

Boulder, the afternoon of July 16, 1979.

GOOD MOVIES ALWAYS HAVE THAT dramatic ending, one that's intense, nerve-wracking, and breathtaking. When mapped out on the classroom white board, every story has a plot resembling a path going up a mountain. Like sex, the "rising action" moves toward the summit or peak until the "climax" is reached. My life back then was like that by design. Being a work of art, it had to follow the familiar literary scheme which meant my time in Boulder had to end on a high note.

I want to try LSD. Maybe Paradise can be found inside my head!

Pedestrians trod the Gilded-Age brick pavement still puddled up from a thunderstorm a half-hour ago. The sweet, after-the-rain smell combines with the aroma of charbroiled chicken from a sidewalk cafe. It's one of those moments frozen in time like your graduation or wedding day but this was serendipitous. Brilliant sunlight pierces the shadowy clouds hovering over the rust-colored Flatirons in the west. A rainbow, one of the most vivid ones I've ever seen, extends across the sky like overstretched arms from heaven. A sign of hope, no doubt, and it comes not a moment too soon. I desperately need a large dose of optimism after wallowing in self-pity all day. People congregate around a kilted gentleman standing in the commons as he performs "Amazing Grace" on his bagpipes. It seems like the perfect time to make my big move.

A gal with black hair catches my attention. About five feet three with plump cheeks, she sports a red scarf around her head and large earrings obviously going for the carnival-gypsy look. On seeing that she is telling people's fortunes with tarot cards for free, I get in line.

"What's your sign?" she asks me when it's my turn.

"Taurus."

"Wow, I guessed that right away!" she exclaims with a broad grin. The "gypsy," who had introduced herself as Lucinda, has a child-like disposition. She's giddy, and garrulous. She emits "positive energy" (a term she used once or twice). She describes everyone and everything as "beautiful" much like the way Rosie and the people at Poverty Gulch and Moon Gulch do. It's as if she is on another plane, or else "on something" (or both).

She shuffles the deck and has me touch it with my palm. Then Lucinda places several cards in a line on the folding table, some face down and others up. I don't recall the exact order, but they contain symbols or suits of medieval lore: "Wands," "Swords," "Cups," and archetypal somebodies such as "The Fool" and "The Empress." Each card has its own meaning, so Lucinda keenly examines them and interprets what they all mean individually and in unison.

"I see you're on a trip a long way from home. . ." she prefaces her oracle. I'm sitting there gobsmacked thinking, *My Lord, how did she know that!* I am carrying a backpack? "The cards also indicate you're on another kind of journey. . . a spiritual one. . ." Then she takes a long dramatic pause and beams warmly. "Whoa, you'll be happy to know this—you'll soon find what you're looking for!" Could Lucinda be right? Could she be confirming what I was setting out to do—to undergo the ultimate drug-induced experience "soon" . . . possibly that very night?

"How soon?"

"Whenever you will it to be."

"Tonight?"

She just laughs, refusing to give any definitive answer. "YOU fill in the blanks."

My heart soars at the thought of the *planned acid trip.*

"When it comes to spiritual things you never compromise," Lucinda continues. "You're a stubborn son-of-a-gun. You never stop at one answer, do you? Ha, ha, ha. Not everyone likes a truth-seeker because of that—but *she* does."

"The Empress?" I query, staring at one of the cards which bears the image of a woman wearing a purple royal robe and a crown.

"That's right. She's the Goddess, Mother of All the Living, the Earth Mother. I like to call her 'Mom' for short, just 'Mom.' Ha, ha, ha. Isn't that funny? Well anyway, Mom sees everything you're doing and smiles."

"I think she smiles down on everyone."

"No! Ha, ha, ha. You're wrong. She favors YOU, silly. Oh God, you're really something! You're all heart. That's exactly why you're so special to Mom."

Unfortunately, Lucinda's accuracy level will go downhill from there, but it doesn't matter at this point. Her charm and high estimation of me had won me over, so I ignore the inconsistencies. Besides, when you're trying to orchestrate the flow of events to fit a predetermined "movie script," truth gets edited out. Like Don Quixote seeing windmills as giants, I perceive Lucinda as a spot-on accurate fortune-teller.

When she finishes telling my fortune, I ask her, "Do you know where I can get some acid?"

"Okay, I'll fix you up," she replies confidently.

Lucinda and I then proceed to search for her drug-dealer friend up and down Pearl. The crowded street made it difficult. During the afternoon rush hour, scores of people had come to eat out and watch street musicians and other entertainers perform. At one point, we stop to watch a belly dancer do her stuff. As the young dervish gracefully sways her exquisitely curved form across the sidewalk to the exotic music, Lucinda cannot contain herself. "SHE'S MOM! SHE'S MOM!" she shouts. Then the gypsy herself stands up and jumps up and down playfully, yelling, "See her aura! Hey, check it out! She's turning into snakes!" (I realize *she* must have been on acid.) On seeing the well-endowed dancer hand-signal her to come up and dance with her, Lucinda exclaims, "Wow! I could never refuse Mom!"

CHAPTER 27
SISTER MARY FISHER

Dearborn flashback, Fall of 1978.

A S PRACTICALLY EVERY COLLEGE STUDENT knows, a dystopia is the opposite of a utopia. It's a society characterized by human misery. The typical dystopian novel like George Orwell's *1984* or Ray Bradbury's *Fahrenheit 451* is about a utopia gone wrong. Usually set in the future, it takes place in a civilization that uses technology on a global scale. Machines, electronics, and advanced scientific know-how are all expertly coordinated to create an earthly paradise but end up doing the exact opposite. A common theme of dystopian fiction is the "collective will" tries to erase the identity of each individual person. Freedom to think for yourself is strongly discouraged. An elite class, usually led by one totalitarian leader, turns the individual into a faceless, obedient slave. There is almost always a pervasive ideology behind a dystopia, one in which everyone is forced to follow whether they like it or not. It almost always resembles Marxism, fascism, or some other form of autocratic statism.

Brave New World (BNW) is generally considered dystopian. The funny thing is I'm not sure if Randal Stark thought it was dystopian or utopian. For instance, his tacit approval of the hookup culture (the current term) in his dormitory—which resembled the free-for-all sexual norms in BNW—suggested the latter. And, like his own views, the fictitious government in Huxley's book organizes people according to a rigid caste system—but instead of the three categories he prescribed (Jocks, Freaks, and Geeks), BNW uses five (Alphas, Betas, Gammas, Deltas, and Epsilons). As he explained, the citizens in Huxley's vision-of-the-future genuflect before pictures of Henry Ford and do the "sign-of-the-T" to pay tribute to Mr. Ford's game-changing Model T car.

In BNW, Dearborn's favorite son is considered the lord and savior of the universe (quite literally)! That's because his mass production system has made the ideal world possible. Everything runs smoothly and efficiently and will continue to do so forevermore! The absolute best consumer goods are available to everyone all the time, satisfaction guaranteed! Technology promises perpetual happiness from womb to tomb. As the old slogan goes, "Ford has a better idea."

☾ ☾ ☾

I NEARLY FELL OUT OF MY CHAIR on my first day of Composition 101. I found out my new professor at U of M-Dearborn is a Dominican nun! As you might imagine, women of the cloth are as common at a secular university as wild parrots are in Michigan. And, by the way, her head and face kind of resembled the tropical bird. To me, her presence there was a sure sign of how backward the college was at the time, in stark contrast to its uber-progressive parent, U of M Ann Arbor. *Nuns teaching college? Are you kidding me?* I thought to myself. *Are we living back in the Dark Ages?* The heavyset, fortysomething woman introduced herself to the class as Sister Mary Fisher.

Sister Mary (who did not wear the traditional habit) came across pleasant enough. I didn't get to know her that well since she rarely engaged in small talk. It wouldn't have mattered anyway since her individual identity and personality traits were eclipsed by my preconceived image of nuns in general. Memories of twelve years of Catholic school came flooding back. I tended to caricature nuns as crabby, over-punitive, and mildly deranged (though many in fact weren't like that). But since I leaned left politically, it was okay for me to judge, stereotype, and even misrepresent others if they belonged to some oppressor group. And, indeed, the Roman Catholic Church fit the bill. As any wise woke person understands, the Church is public enemy number one, because it advocates patriarchy, pro-life, and marriage only between a man and a woman.

Two things worth noting happened in Sister Mary's class. First, I wrote my research paper on how Rock & Roll is changing the world for the better. I reasoned that this genre of music, being played on radios and stereos everywhere, will eventually sway the masses with its '60s-inspired lyrics (a reasonable premise considering how John Lennon turned me on to communism and George Harrison to Eastern religion). My paper's most-used reference was a book called *The Greening of America* by Christopher A. Reich (1970) which claims that "Consciousness III" (the '60s counterculture) will transform society into a utopia.

The second notable thing was my confrontation with Sister Mary.

"Listen up, students, I want you to clear off your desks except for a pen and paper," she instructs at the beginning of class one morning. "Today, we are going to write a timed essay. Within a thirty-minute time frame, I want you to brainstorm, organize your thoughts, and write a composition on the subject of your choice... Okay? *Ready, set, go.*"

I become totally discombobulated. My mind freezes, my heart races, my stomach has butterflies. I'm fixated on the clock on the wall, my blank paper, and the large amounts of writing my classmates had been able to produce. Time fritters away as beads of sweat drip down my forehead. O, the humiliation! Then anger wells up inside of me like a tsunami wave. *The nerve of Sister Mary putting me through this! My rights had been violated!*

After the words "your time is up" are spoken and my empty sheet with only my name on it is handed in, I approach my crucifix-wearing tormentor with clenched fists, "Sister, this is outrageous! Assignments like this cramp my style. Creative people like me need time to express themselves." The way I said this bordered on disrespectful, rude and, yes, *smug*, especially the "creative people" part. To her credit, Sister Mary doesn't respond to my outburst in kind, but she doesn't turn the other cheek either. Preoccupied with other students, she blows me off like some pesky gnat buzzing around her head. To get her attention, I say something which is designed to incite fear, and I also fancy myself being a warrior for justice. "Sister, who is your supervisor? I need to talk to that person right *now*!" As I utter these words, Sister Mary shakes her head at the sight of me, this delicate snowflake standing before her, acting like an irate customer complaining about bad service in a restaurant.

"Oh, okay. His name is Dr. Grewe," she responds glibly. "He's the head of the English department."

So, I storm over to the main office of CASL (College of Arts, Sciences and Letters), to tattle on Sister Mary for her discriminatory practices. Marxism 2.0 taught me that comrades can win more followers by not focusing so much on working-class concerns like the old-style Marxists. They must branch out to champion the causes of every conceivable victim group: non-whites, women, gays, etc. Since I felt I was disabled, I could confidently say that I am a oppressed victim of the *abled*! I'm a victim—not of racism, sexism, classism, etc.—but of *ableism*!

Dr. Grewe graciously welcomes me into his office found in one of the lousy modules I spoke of before. Warmth and kindness shine from his face. He is all ears figuratively and literally. His beard suggests that I might get somewhere with him. It reminds me of the one sported by Vladimir Lenin. On second thought, it was more like a goatee like the kind beatniks wore.

"Hmmm, I noticed that the nameplate on the door says 'Eugene Grewe.' Any relation to the Eugene Grewe who teaches over at Bishop Borgess High School?"

"Oh yes, that's my son!"

I feel my brow crinkle on realizing I'm sitting across the desk from the father of the man students called the "Vernors Gnome" because he looked like the ginger-ale mascot. I never had Gene Junior as a teacher but I had seen him around. He taught English and Mythology. Though amused by the fact Gene Senior and I share the same small world, I suddenly realize my one-man protest march is doomed from the start. The chances seem slimmer than slim that he'd take my side over Sister Mary's. Presuming he's a Catholic, he probably was the one who hired her in the first place!

I tell Grewe I'm being oppressed and that the University should be more inclusive to creative disabled individuals like me. Then he, in a nice way, pooh-poohs my personal grievances and admonishes me to "bury the hatchet with Sister."

Ugh!

CHAPTER 28

THE SHADOW OF DEATH

Detroit and Dearborn; November, 1978.

PAULINE GRANGER (FORMERLY PAULINA Grzegorzewski), my paternal grandmother, died at age 80. As my relatives and I grieved her loss, we realized we had come to a crossroads in our family history. She was not only the last surviving grandparent, but the last of the storied immigrant generation. I'll never forget seeing the joy on her face a month before she passed. It was provoked by her fellow countryman Karol Wojtyla assuming St. Peter's chair in Rome. Like Simeon beholding the Christ Child in the temple, she now knew she could die happy. What's more, seven years later, the Polish pope will deliver a stirring homily in person just a stone-throw away from her front porch!

It was sad clearing out her possessions from her house in Hamtramck. Besides furniture, clothes, and jewelry, we removed many articles that had reminded her of her eternal home—sacred icons, statues, crucifixes, candles, holy water founts, pictures of saints, and biblical scenes, you name it. Her pad was a virtual church, typical of homes back in the old country. It's a shame most of that stuff ended up in the trash.

The act of purging those religious items was emblematic of my attitude toward religion at the time. What I once viewed with wonderment as a child was now seen with contempt. For instance, she had a 3 x 5 icon of Our Lady of Częstochowa on the wall of her enclosed back porch. No Polish residence was complete without some reproduction of the Black Madonna, the holy image housed at Poland's Jasna Góra Monastery. Hailed as the Queen of Poland, she's the Polish counterpart to Our Lady of Guadalupe, the Queen of Mexico (or, as many Mexicans prefer, the Queen of the Americas). She's the one Poles turn to in hard times.

Once I got into a flap with my 22-year-old brother Bart over it. The altercation started innocently enough.

"I always wondered why the faces of Mary and the Christ Child look so dark," says I.

"Candle soot is what I heard, Bart replies. "Carbon residue built up over the centuries."

"What about the two scars on her right cheek?"

"Those are from the time some dumb-ass criminals tried to steal it. When the goons made what they thought was a clean getaway in their wagon, their horses strangely refused to move. In frustration, one of the thieves throws the icon down and stabs Mary twice in the face with his sword. Bad move! As the crook gets ready to strike her again, God himself knocks him down. Poor dude! Before he kicks the bucket, he must squirm in agony for a while before facing far worse torments in hell!"

I rolled my eyes and said something to the effect of "Oh brother. *Grown* people actually believe that nonsense?" Unfortunately, when I said this, Grandma was standing right there. She didn't utter a word but looked displeased. Later, Bart pulls me aside and exclaims, "You idiot, why did you say that in front of her! Can't you show some respect?"

"But her religion is ridiculous! Look, maybe I did Grandma a favor by calling it out."

"Moron!" Bart retorted.

☾ ☾ ☾

MASS SUICIDES IN GUYANA CULT... 914 DIE IN JONESTOWN DISASTER... CULT OF DEATH... screamed the headlines on the

THE SHADOW OF DEATH

morning of November 19th. Come to find out, almost a thousand members of a religious cult called the People's Temple were either murdered or committed suicide in less than three hours in a South American jungle. I wasn't fully impacted until I saw the pictures. The aerial shot of the crowd surrounding a metal-roof pavilion reminded me of ones taken during an outdoor rock concert, except everyone in the Jonestown photo is dead! Close-ups showing decaying corpses of men, women, children, and even babies huddled close to each other saddened and horrified me. The story is that most of them drank from a vat of cyanide-laced fruit punch. Survivors said the victims were following the orders of a black-haired, pasty-skinned preacher in aviator shades named Jim Jones.

They had spent months trying to build a socialist utopia, but things went disastrously wrong.

My first thoughts are "Where is Gehenna? West Africa, right?" I consulted a global map. "No, that's Ghana and Guinea." Then the light bulb goes off. "Oh yes, *Guyana*, a northern South American country east of Venezuela." The next question is "What are the macabre and salacious details?" I'd spend hours in the periodical section of the Ford Centennial Library investigating.

The Jonestown massacre will cast a long shadow on the American psyche. Even today, progressives say Donald Trump is Jim Jones; conservatives say the whole Democrat Party is a "death cult." Everyone claims their political opponents are fatally brainwashed by politicians and the media (while they themselves are totally objective, rational, and know all the facts.). The phrase "drink the Kool-Aid" widely circulates.

CHAPTER 29

A SIGN FROM HEAVEN

Dearborn flashback: the evening of November 27, 1978.

ZAINAB WAS ONE OF THE FEW FRIENDS I made during the Fall of '78. We had a class together and shared the same lunch period. She looked out for me. When I was sitting alone in the cafeteria, she invited me to sit at her table with her and her friends. She had large almond-shaped eyes, prominent arched eyebrows, and long black hair. She could be bossy at times. People in the '70s would label her a "women's libber" because she was always talking about male oppression. Zainab was big on social justice in general. She called anyone who walks all over people a "Yazid" (yuh-ZEED), whatever that means. A Yazid could be an abusive husband, a power-hungry cop, or an unreasonable landlord. At one point, she called the Shah of Iran a Yazid.

It's nightfall in Dearborn. I enter my gold '71 Plymouth Duster parked on the fourth floor of the UM-D parking structure. I turn the ignition key only to find the car won't start! I need a jump. So I run over to the nearest stairwell and go up a flight to catch Zainab and her cousin Hussain before they drive off. Along the way, I encounter twenty or so people, peering into the night sky. Judging by their appearance, they're all Muslims.

Fortunately, I'm able to flag Zainab and Hussain down. Hussain is able to jump start my car with his Chevy Nova. After completing the process, I thanked the pair repeatedly and then asked, "Do you guys know what those people are doing over there?"

Zainab causally replies, "Oh, they're looking at the Moon to see Ayatollah Khomeini's face." She goes on to explain that they think it's a sign from heaven that Khomeini is the Twelfth Imam!

CHAPTER 30

THE RED DRAGON

Boulder, the evening of July 16, 1979.

LIKE A SINKING SHIP, THE TANGERINE SUN descends behind the craggy horizon as I plod up Walnut Street toward the rust-colored Flatirons. The thought of what I am about to do stirs mixed emotions, mostly anticipation and apprehension. Will the Red Dragon that Lucinda got me whisk me away to Nırvana, a place of perfect bliss as the drug dealer promised? Or will it result in a bad trip? I know the risks involved but choose not to think about them. I expected dropping acid to be a culmination of all the Maslowian peak experiences during my road trip and indeed my entire life. It would be the *ultimate* experience.

Walnut turns into Kayak Run Road as it comes up into the mountains. It then snakes along Boulder Canyon. The rock formations on either side of me cast an imposing shadow. Since the thought of scaling one of these seems preposterous, I am now tempted to turn back to town until I see some loopy teenagers ahead turn down a path off the main road at a place called Pioneer Park. After tracking them for a while, I discover a sign marking a spot designated for climbers. The trail is made up of a series of adjacent ledges along a massive cliff. It goes in a sweeping zig-zag pattern along the southside of the rocky bluff. It is said to offer the view I'm looking for.

But the immediate concern is of course to not slip and fall to my death. I ascend with relative ease until I get to the point where there's little or no vegetation. I must be extremely cautious about where I plant my feet. A more-than-adequate sense of balance is essential, especially when lugging a heavy backpack. The higher I rise, the more challenging it gets in terms of physical strength and vigor. Add to that the difficulty of having limited sunlight to guide my path

I keep hearing chatter and laughter in the background. Like me, many folks are here to appreciate the panoramic vista. Once you look past their foolhardiness, you have to admire their courage, risking life and limb to attend a party in a place that's not even safe for a mountain goat. At the same time, I resent them. Like Nietzsche's Zarathustra, I came here to get away from such rabble.

A familiar voice! That of a person I'd seen many times with the Deadheads. He has a memorable name: Crazy. I first observed him up close while waiting in line in front of the Boulder Plasma Center where Pete and I donated for extra cash. Crazy is a hulk of a man with a thick Southern accent and a cowboy hat. True to his moniker, he had a perpetually glazed expression, zombie-like gestures, and often incoherent speech. Despite being hard-to-see in the dark, I recognize him immediately by his idiosyncratic rant, "TIMOTHY LEARY IS DEAD! TIMOTHY LEARY IS DEAD!" (I think he is quoting a Moody Blues song.) His cry now has a haunting quality as it echoes against the surrounding cliffs.

A few hundred feet from the summit, I roll out my sleeping bag and rest. The vantage point at my chosen spot is grander than a scene on a postcard. The city lights of course outdazzle the gazillion stars seen above.

Ommmmmmmm.

My fingers gingerly reach into my shirt pocket, pinch and pull out the Red Dragon. I stare at it, or better yet, meditate on it for a minute like it's the Holy Eucharist. Here is the higher, deeper, or new consciousness encapsulated into a minuscule square of purple-red blotter paper! Think of it: What took ancient holy men years to achieve through rigorous ascetic practices and contemplation can be delivered at once. It's just too easy! Finally, I place the paper in my mouth, slowly suck and swallow the juices and eventually scarf down the whole thing and wait patiently for the results.

Regrettably, a voice from below distracts me like a fly buzzing around my ear.

"HEY, YOU OVER THERE," it calls to me with slurred speech.

"WHO ARE YOU?"

"I'm a mountain man," I reply resolutely.

"HEY, MOUNTAIN MAN, DO YOU HAVE SOMETHING FOR THE HEAD?"

"Boy, do I have something for the head. Come down here!"

There is a long pause. Five, six, seven seconds go by.

"*I-I . . . CAN'T!*" the male vocal sound says huffing and puffing, a sure sign of a Herculean struggle. The corners of my eyes begin to tear up with sorrow and compassion.

"It's easy if you put your mind to it," I say positively. "I'm supposed to be hallucinating. I made it."

"AWWWRIGHT, YOU M***** F***ER, I'LL PUSH YOU OFF THE F***ING CLIFF!"

"You have to come up."

Silence. "ALRIGHT, I'M COMING DOWN."

"You mean *up*."

"YEAH."

Silence again. One Mississippi, Two Mississippi, Three Mississippi. "Are you still out there?!"

"HELLO? DO YOU GOT ANY DRUGS?"

"No. . . sorry, I don't have any," I reply.

"OH S***, I AM SOOOOO F****D UP!"

CHAPTER 31

CHRISTMAS OF '78

Detroit; the evening of December, 16, 1978.

D ECEMBER 11 WAS THE DATE OF the infamous Lufthansa Heist in New York City, the largest cash robbery in United States history up to that time. About 20 million (in today's dollars) was stolen at JFK Airport. Since then, the reputed mastermind, Jimmy Burke, has been immortalized in movies such as *Goodfellas* (1990). This event recalls Randal Stark's mind-child, the Great Kmart Heist, which thankfully never got off the ground.

It's a frosty mid-December evening at my friend Ron's place on Piedmont Street in the old neighborhood. Randal arrives about 10:45 p.m. As soon as he comes through the front door, a lit reefer dangling at the end of an outstretched arm greets him.

"No thanks, I've given up pot."

"Hmmm... Okay... that's cool. How come?"

"I just decided to quit, okay?"

Everyone treated Randal respectfully until the THC kicked in. Amidst the lively conversation, innuendo disguised as teasing begins to rear its ugly head. Speaking for myself, it arises from a deep-seated resentment. I was jealous of him living in Ann Arbor while I was stuck living with my parents in Detroit. His aloof manner was beginning to bug me, especially when he said he hated the Bob Dylan concert and disliked my new friend LeBlanc. Randal giving up drugs added yet another bone of contention between him and me. It was ironic given the fact that only weeks before, he had preached about marijuana's remarkable health benefits and its potential for political change based on his take on *Brave New World*.

Randal in his black leather jacket over a plain white t-shirt (part of the quasi-New Wave/Punk look he'd been cultivating as of late), sits slouched back in Ron's La-Z Boy recliner with his arms folded. His right foot nervously taps on the beige carpet. After ten minutes of being subject to ever-so-subtle ridicule, Randal, the paragon of self-control, finally loses it. "SHUT, THE HELL UP, MAN!" he explodes, sending shock waves in the room. His rage is undoubtedly directed at *me* (since the others are almost perfect strangers to him.) Silence ensues until the vacuum is filled by the start of *Saturday Night Live*. It's the episode with reggae musician Peter Tosh.

At an inconspicuous moment after the show, Randal moves over to me. His face is pale, his affect flat, his voice heavy as he speaks earnestly and gravely, "Ted, it's time for me to face the music." When he utters this, I immediately think of the ELO album *Face the Music*—the one with the electric chair on the front cover. This seemingly irrelevant mental image turns out to be an apt metaphor: He's been in the hot seat as of late, in a drama I call "Face the Parents." While Christmas had supplied him a much-needed break, it also forced him to give his mom and dad a full account of what he'd accomplished (or not accomplished) over the past four months. It was not a pretty picture. Just imagining him sitting there at the kitchen table squirming, trying to answer their pointed questions makes me cringe even now. As excruciating as it is, explaining your dismal grades to your folks is a cakewalk compared to the dance that poor Randal had to perform concerning another pressing matter...

"Ted, I got *arrested*." Randal blurts out solemnly.

"What?" My eyebrows go up and my jaw practically falls to the floor. I'm simultaneously shocked and strangely fascinated. I am reminded of Randal the Criminal Mastermind who had painstakingly planned the Great Kmart Heist.

"I got busted for vandalism," says Randal.

"*Vandalism*? Of what, where?"

"A rock."

"A *rock*? You vandalized a rock?"

"Not just any rock, *The* Rock, the one in East Lansing. My friends and I were caught spray-painting graffiti on it."

Huh? He was put in the slammer for nothing more than a silly college prank (done to embarrass Michigan State, U of M's chief rival football team). What a letdown! Worse yet, as I discovered later, practically everyone in East Lansing had painted the Rock at some time or other. It's sort of a popular tradition. Residents had used the hundred-year-old landmark to tout their graduation, pop the marriage question, and express their political views. Randal and his cohorts just happened to get caught during the moment in East Lansing history when the practice was outlawed. Local citizens had voted to have it banned because they were fed up with constantly seeing profanity.

One would think that committing a misdemeanor on par with littering and jaywalking could easily be shrugged off. But not by Randal. A man of high standards, he was probably more disgusted with himself than his parents were of him. In any case, the latest arrest was seen as the last straw. Being a self-disciplined and self-determined person, Randal required little or no external prodding to change his ways.

It should come as no surprise that Randal's turning-over-a-new-leaf coincided with the holidays—a time of recollection, epiphanies, and resolutions. The notion of starting 1979 right with a shiny new goal had apparently inspired my other close friend sitting across the room.

"I decided to hitchhike to California," Pete LeBlanc casually reveals.

CHAPTER 32

MA PREM NANDO

Boulder, the morning of July 17, 1979.

THE SKY IS OVERCAST. A VEIL OF MIST fills the air. Like Zarathustra in Nietzsche's *Thus Spoke Zarathustra*, I descend from the mountain to face the crowd in the marketplace. I'm ready to lie to people about how great LSD was. But my immediate concern is finding Pete LeBlanc to tell him I'm leaving town immediately. In the process, I come across several individuals I'd met during the past week, most of whom seem to have a hard time differentiating between fantasy and reality. There is Lance whose outlandish stories make you doubt every word he says, his biggest whopper being that he's "best buddies" with Jerry Garcia of the Grateful Dead. There is Buck who dreams about dying a glorious death at the ripe old age of 27 like his idol Jim Morrison.

As I comb through every nook and cranny along the Pearl Street Mall to find Pete, I come upon a woman, probably in her mid-twenties, wearing a bright orange robe and sandals. She has Nordic features, notably her pale complexion and blonde hair. Judging by her uncommon garb, she's obviously a follower of some religious sect. I notice a black-and-white portrait of a bald, bearded man in an oval locket dangling from a red-beaded necklace. I recognize the man's face at once.

"Excuse me, are you a follower of Bhagwan Rajneesh?"

"Yes, I am a Sannyasin," she answers. "Are you?"

"No, but I'm so glad to meet you. I never met a real Rajneesh follower before. Mind if I ask you a few questions?"

"Sure, my name is Ma Prem Nando. . ." Noticing my blank expression, she promptly admits it's not the name given to her by her parents. Once this clicks in my mind, I go ahead to tell her about how my friend Rosie turned me on to Bhagwan back in Wisconsin. Before responding, Ma Prem and I introduced ourselves. I tell her I'm on a trip from Detroit to California and had just had another kind of trip the night before:

"I experienced oceanic bliss. . . It was very powerful. . . It made me feel at one with the universe!" I was BS-ing her.

Ma Prem shares she'd been through a messy divorce and that she is planning to go to Rajneesh's ashram in Pune, India soon to study under her new spiritual master. I mentioned that I too had intended to check out Bhagwan at some point and travel to that part of the world via the Overland Trail.

"Do you know where I can get a copy of *Ecstasy: The Forgotten Language*?"

"Ummm. . . let me think. . ." Ma Prem responds pensively. Then, after a five-second pause, she stops dead in her tracks. "Ted, I have an idea! Would you like to have lunch with me?"

"Yeah, sure!"

About ten minutes later, I find myself sitting across from the affable Ma Prem at a small table at a local diner, a health food restaurant. The meatless establishment smells like cardamom and cloves. Plants in ceramic bowls hanging along the front window gives the place a homey atmosphere. Books on New Age spirituality are available on a rack next to the cash register, but we're told they are out of Rajneesh for the moment. My disappointment is offset by the delight of getting into a deep conversation and being treated to two scrumptious vegetarian tacos. At one point, I pull out my notebook containing the Truth Project and start going through some of the most salient Rajneesh passages I had inscribed. I quoted this before, but it bears repeating:

"A controlled man is a dead man... My sannyas (way of life) is spontaneity, living moment to moment without prefabricated discipline, living with the unknown, not exactly knowing where you are going... My sannyas is a radical revolution... I would like you to be totally uncontrolled. I would like you to be absolutely a chaos, with no order whatsoever."

"When I read this, I was blown away," I reflected with my hand over my chin. "It made me think that everything my parents taught me about resisting temptation, having self-control, and taking responsibility is all bullcrap! Reading the part about 'being a chaos' felt so liberating. He's spot-on. You just gotta do what feels good in the present moment and not feel guilty about it."

"That's right. Life is all about being spontaneous, losing your inhibitions, living in the here-and-now, not dwelling on the past, not worrying about the future."

"Easier said than done," I remark with a tell-tale sigh.

"If you don't mind me asking, is there something weighing on you, Ted? I sense a heavy heart."

"I-I don't know..."

"Look, it's okay to be sad. Sadness is inevitable in life. Bhagwan says you need to relish it.'"

"I suppose my problem is... just-just... *other people* telling me what to do and not allowing me to be who I am. Parents especially. But even my traveling buddy keeps me from being a hundred-percent myself. That's why I have to split."

"Believe me, I can relate. Breaking up with my husband was no picnic. At one point, I concluded that the main source of my misery is *roles*."

"Rules?"

"No, ROLES. I mean my *role* as a wife, my motherly *role*, my daughterly *role*, and so on. They really get in the way of a person trying to discover her true self." Ma Prem then augments with a chuckle, "But, come to think of it, *rules* are bad too!"

Like a priest, shrink, or bartender, my new friend asks me more questions and patiently listens as she tries to unearth *my* truth in light of Bhagwan's wise teachings.

"To be an individual is the hardest thing in the world... Everybody wants to kill your individuality and to make a sheep out of you... I am basically an individualist, because only the individual has a soul. No group can claim a soul—they are all dead arrangements."

After swallowing a mouthful of tofu salad with Italian dressing, Ma Prem adds, "Listen to me, Ted. ALL groups—every single one of them—is bad for the soul. The worst group of all is husband and wife. The second worst is *family*. Do you know what I mean?"

"Oh, yeah. All too well unfortunately."

"One of the things I love about Bhagwan is he goes right to the jugular..."

I'm nodding the whole time she's talking, but I must confess, I am shaken by Rajneesh's broadside attack on the *very concept* of family. I remembered what Zainab said back in Dearborn: "I have God and I have family—what else do I need?" At the time, I balked, but was I ready for Rajneesh?!

໒ ໒ ໒

AFTER A WARM HUG, MA PREM AND I go our separate ways. I continue my search for Pete but still can't find him anywhere, so I end up leaving Boulder without saying goodbye. With the Colorado college town behind me, the realization sinks in. I'm no longer part of a twosome. I'm a *one*-some. I naturally feel apprehensive and nervous about traveling alone. Not having a partner will obviously make me more vulnerable physically and less safe. Then there's the loneliness factor.

That said, I'm absolutely free! There's a spring in my step. I realize going solo opens up incredible opportunities. With no one around (except strangers) to judge me and make me feel embarrassed, I can do whatever the heck I please. I can try things I never dreamed of trying before. I can even impersonate other people, taking on false identities. I can reinvent myself over and over like Bob Dylan does—just for the experience.

CHAPTER 33

NEW YEARS

Detroit and Dearborn flashback; January, 1979.

ON TV, DICK CLARK SHOUTS AT THE stroke of midnight, "3...2...1...and a Happy New Year!" The crowd celebrates a new beginning at New York City's Times Square. Who would've guessed that historians will regard the upcoming year as not only terrible but uniquely terrible? They have a special Latin term for such years: *Annus Horribilis*. There have been only three since my birth in 1960—'68, '79 and 2020.

True, '68 was the year our beloved baseball team, the Detroit Tigers, won the championship, but it was awful in most other ways. For starters, Martin Luther King and Bobby Kennedy were assassinated. It was the year the Vietnam war escalated and violent protests broke out. In 2020, we had to endure the COVID-19 pandemic, social upheaval, and a contentious presidential election.

Annus Horribilis 1979 was bad for a lot of people. Disco died. The musical genre my friends and I loved to hate: gone, finished, extinct like the dinosaurs! On July 12, 1979, radio personality Steve Dahl blew up a huge bin of Disco records at Chicago's Comiskey Park after a baseball game. The massive explosion pulverized albums by artists such as Donna Summer, Chic, and of course the Bee Gees. Moments later, ecstatic Rock fans stormed the cratered field like our troops on the beaches of Normandy, chanting at the top of their lungs, "DISCO SUCKS!" This insurrection had long-lasting consequences. A seemingly unstoppable parade of top-ten hits in the Disco category came to a grinding halt.

Despite the tragic end of Disco, that was not the worst of it. On January 31, 1979, China, a hardcore communist country with global ambitions, suddenly "goes capitalist," prompting the U.S. and other countries to normalize trade relations there. Now, oddly enough, our major trading partner is also our biggest threat.

On April 1, 1979, The Islamic Republic of Iran was established. The Shah, Mohammad Reza Pahlavi, a staunch ally of the United States, was overthrown and replaced by Ayatollah Khomeini, a charismatic Shia Muslim cleric. Khomeini introduced to the world a new political doctrine called the *wilayat al-faqih* (the Guardianship of the Jurist). Since the revolution, Iran has been one of America's biggest adversaries.

On July 16, 1979, Saddam Hussein became Iraq's president. In upcoming years, this tyrant will incite three major wars, one with Iran and two with the United States.

The world would never be the same again. A new age has begun!

CHAPTER 34

WHO IS THE ANTICHRIST?

Dearborn; January, 1979.

IN THE NEW YEAR, I STARTED A NEW PHILOSOPHY class—
"Nature of Man." The professor, Denis Dutton, took over where
Thagard left off. In his mid-thirties, Dutton sported a droopy
mustache and wore a sweater with leather patches on the elbows.
He had a golden voice and a way with words. In contrast to the
earnest, amiable Thagard, Dutton was a cocksure provocateur who
presented his material with a snarky irreverence and droll sense-
of-humor.

At one point during the semester, Dutton asks us pointedly.
"Who do you suppose the antichrist is?"

Laughter ensues. Everyone in the class knows they're being
played. (Dutton is actually a proud agnostic or atheist.) Several of
my peers nominate figures like the Pope, Henry Kissinger, and even
John Travolta.

"I say *Friedrich Nietzsche*," Dutton puts forth. I'm picturing the
sickly, cranky German philosopher with his beady eyes and monstrous mustache.

"But he's in his grave," someone retorts.

"Yes, but, in a sense, he's very much alive. Here's why I think Nietzsche is the antichrist. Ready? Number one, *he said so...*" Dutton then supports his claim with several quotes from Nietzsche's book *The Antichrist*.

"Number two, he not only attacks Christians and Christianity, but he also dares to take on the Man from Nazareth himself. He goes right to the source." More quotes.

"Number three, he's a prophet. Nietzsche foresaw today's crisis. 'GOD IS DEAD!' By that phrase, he meant the massive decline in the belief in God will result in the massive decline in the binding, transcendent values that are based on God. Justice? Morality? Truth? Now just empty words. As Dostoevsky says, 'If there is no God, everything is permitted.'"

"Nietzsche is Mr. 666, I tell you. He's coming down from his mountain to teach us the Übermensch, the new type of human being who can create new values and meaning *from scratch*. He wills his own versions of 'goodness' and 'truth' into existence, ex nihilo, literally out of nothing, like God once did."

GOLDEN GATE CITY

CHAPTER 35

CALIPH-ORNIA

Downtown San Francisco; the morning of July 20, 1979.

WEST OF RENO, I GET A RIDE from Mel from Wichita. He's a middle-aged man in a black Mercury Marquis. Obviously tanked, Mel hands me the car keys. I nervously get behind the wheel and start driving. I would've been okay with it, except for the fact we're in the Sierra Nevada Mountains and my aptitude as a motorist isn't quite up to the altitude.

Fortunately, after five long minutes, the next hitchhiker can replace me at the helm. His name is Moccasin Kelly, a thirtyish man with dark hair, a beard, and a red bandanna used as a hat. He's a breath of fresh air, a man of the world. He claims to have crisscrossed the entire U.S. twenty-or-so times and says that he is a "professional gunfighter." (He explained he's a stunt man who specializes in gun-related stunts.) A feeling of optimism sweeps over me as we pass the "WELCOME TO CALIFORNIA" sign. The sky seems to miraculously clear up. Captivated by the radiance of our visually stunning alpine location, Kelly pulls over to take in the beauty. A little while later, Mel, craving another drink, asks Kelly to stop at the bar in the nearest town. Once the three of us are seated and served, Kelly raises his chilled mug of Coors.

"Gentlemen, we have two things to be thankful for. We're alive and we're free!"

At these words, we clink glasses.

☽ ☽ ☽

CALIFORNIA, THE GOLDEN STATE! LAND OF hopes and dreams! Apparently, this idea existed long before the surfing craze, the song "California Dreaming," and even the 1849 Gold Rush. Spanish explorers supposedly named it after an island paradise featured in a 16th Century romance novel. This island is populated by Amazonian warriors. And they all happen to be Muslims (which accounts for "California" being derived from the Arabic word, *caliphate*). Their queen, Calafia, rallies her troops to fight the Christians at Constantinople with a flock of griffins (creatures that are half-lion and half-eagle).

In our own time, the State of California has become the go-to place for people to start a new life, reinvent themselves, and hopefully find fame and fortune. Mark Twain earned his chops as a writer here. Woody Guthrie made a name for himself here, not to mention countless movie legends and rock stars. To paraphrase Horace Greeley, if you're bored or frustrated or discouraged with your life, go to California, where you can begin again with a clean slate. The narrative has been repeated in countless ways, but it doesn't always have a happy ending.

☽ ☽ ☽

TO MANY, SAN FRANCISCO'S MYSTIQUE is captured in Tony Bennet's sappy song, "I Left My Heart in San Francisco." On the northern tip of a peninsula, it's surrounded by the Pacific Ocean, the Golden Gate strait, and the San Francisco Bay. Its most beloved vista is obviously that of the Golden Gate Bridge along Marine Drive. Cool, gentle breezes, and often fog sweep through the hilly metropolis. Crooked and steep streets feature Victorian-style homes with flower decks and pastel-colored stucco facades. Cable cars evoke a childlike wonder like toy trains under the Christmas tree. Then there's Coit Tower, Chinatown, and Fisherman's Wharf.

In other ways, San Francisco is like any other big city. It's a bustling town with heavy traffic. It has skyscrapers like the

Transamerica Pyramid, and of course blighted areas. One-hit-wonder Scott McKenzie once said to expect to meet "gentle people there," but I had no illusions concerning the city's hoodlum population, mostly from watching *Dirty Harry* movies and the ABC cop show, *The Streets of San Francisco*. Author Eric Hoffer observed in Annus Horribilis 1968, "the young (are) beset and preyed upon by (human) vultures, wolves, and parasites." The news coming out of San Francisco seemed uniquely strange. There, you had scary radicals like the Black Panthers, Satan-worshipers like Anton McVey, and psychopaths like the Zodiac Killer. Most notably, it's widely known as a hotbed for cults. Eight months after the fact, the city is still reeling from the Jonestown massacre. As it turned out, San Francisco was the home base of the People's Temple and Jim Jones had close ties with high-ranking city politicians including Harvey Milk, the gay rights icon who was assassinated only nine days after the tragedy in Guyana.

Before we left Greeley, Rosie gravely warned us, "When you get to San Francisco, watch out for the Moonies."

"*Moonies*, who are they?"

"They're a cult that kidnaps and brainwashes people."

"Oh, okay." Her sensationalist depiction of the group sounded like something out of a supermarket tabloid.

"Not to worry" was the knee-jerk response, accompanied with an eye roll which implied "Of course I'll be careful. What do you take me for?"

ᘡ ᘡ ᘡ

I SET FOOT IN DOWNTOWN SAN FRANCISCO exactly a month to the day after I left Detroit. It's a luminous Sunday afternoon in the upper 60s. My latest driver had recommended I make Fisherman's Wharf my first destination. Once I get off the Bay Bridge, I take the Market Street bus to Fourth Street where I catch the northbound bus.

The Wharf is found along San Francisco's north shore at Jefferson Street between Powell and Hyde. It is what you'd expect from the city's top tourist attraction, lots of people milling around shopping, eating, and sightseeing. On the one hand, it's overly glitzy and commercialized. Like Niagara Falls, Ontario, it has a Ripley's-Believe-It-Or-Not Museum, arcades, tacky T-shirt stands, and kitschy souvenir shops. On the other hand, the Wharf has an appealing aesthetic. This has much to do with it being so close to the water where you can relish the panoramic view of the bay. the Golden Gate and Bay Bridges, Alcatraz and Angel Island, the piers, the boats. In weather-beaten vessels docked along the shore, seamen haul nets full of their latest catch—crabs, scallops, and other seafood—just in time for dinner.

As I venture around, I feel something jiggle behind me. I turn around and there standing before me are two beaming young men.

"Oh, sorry about that," says the short one with the curly-brown mullet haircut, wearing an army jacket like the kind you find at Harry's in Dearborn. "Just wanted to fix the sleeping bag on your backpack. I noticed it was kinda sagging."

"Oh... thanks."

"By the way, where are you from?" he inquires.

"Detroit, Michigan," I answer and continue to tell them about myself and my trip, glad someone finally noticed me. I seem to hit it off with Jim, the curly-haired one, but I feel a little uneasy about his blond-haired companion named Mark. While Jim and I do all the talking, Mark (whom I am told is from Denmark) is standing there with a silly grin plastered on his face. He's too clean-shaven and clean-cut. He comes across overly affected and la-di-da. His frequent nods, hearty laughter, and other over-the-top reactions seem a bit unnatural and contrived.

"Well, nice meeting you, guys. Gotta go." I cut short the conversation like I'm late for a doctor's appointment.

"Likewise, Ted," Jim responds with a warm smile and a firm handshake (as does Mark). "Oh, by the way, if you are not doing anything later, I'd like to invite you to dinner. We and a bunch of friends are getting together at six o'clock sharp. Here's the address." He reaches into his coat pocket and hands me a slip of paper about twice the size of a business card. Printed on resume-quality stock, it has an ink drawing of an open gate. The gate is the kind you'd expect to find in front of one of the local Victorian-style homes, the ones made from wrought iron. Being highly decorative with swirly designs often made to look like flowers, these gates add a certain

beauty to a house as well as supply security. Below is the address.
"Thanks, guys. I'll definitely keep that in mind. Bye."

CHAPTER 36

NORTH BEACH CROSSROADS

Downtown San Francisco, the afternoon of July 20, 1979 (same day).

REMEMBER SAYYID QUTB WHO RAILED against America's sexual immorality after attending a church-sponsored dance in Greeley, CO? (His beef? Couples slow-dancing to "Baby, It's Cold Outside.") In an anonymously written booklet, we are told he later "went on top of a mountain, and he could see the whole of creation in front of him, and he realized the beauty and harmony that existed amongst the creation as a whole. He said that the sweetness of iman (belief in Allah) hit him."

As a result of the experience, the future thought leader decided to ditch his secularist self and revert to the Islam of his youth. He was reborn!

Where did this earth-shattering event occur?

San Francisco of all places!

HUFF, HUFF, HUFF! I'M PANTING like a sled dog at the finish line. My leg and abdominal muscles are aching. Sweat is streaming down my forehead. That's because every other city block in San Francisco has a steep hill to climb.

At Columbia and Broadway, I'm breathing heavily for a different reason. Before me is a strip club on the northeast corner called the Condor. The three-story building, which dates back to the '20s, has a towering red and white sign that screams CAROL DODA TOPLESS. The sign also contains a picture of a cute blonde in a black bikini. A flickering neon-light arrow points to the main entrance. Today, on the brick wall, there's an official California historic marker: "THE CONDOR. WHERE IT ALL BEGAN. THE BIRTHPLACE OF THE WORLD'S FIRST TOPLESS AND BOTTOMLESS ENTERTAINMENT." This incredible claim is all the more salient when you consider that the Bay Area—which includes San Francisco to the north and Silicon Valley to the south—is the *porn capital of the world*. It will soon lose this lofty title to Los Angeles, but it will eventually reclaim it with a machine that even H.G. Wells or Jules Verne could not have imagined. It's called the Internet.

Golden Gate City is the place to be! It has been the epicenter of "free love" even before the '60s. For over a century, prostitution flourished because San Francisco is a sea port. Kitty corner from the Condor is the City Lights Bookstore where Kerouac and Ginsburg read aloud their literary works which glorify promiscuous sex. The fact I'm a lone stranger in the most progressive metropolis in the world is not lost on me. No one from back home is around to judge me or make me feel ashamed about doing certain things.

Rosie Smith had introduced me to the religion of the future! Bhagwan Rajneesh is superior to the other religious leaders because he's the *"sex guru."* With him, you attain spiritual enlightenment through being indiscriminately sexually active!

Exploring San Francisco, I mull over my next move but have mixed emotions. I'm thinking it would be fun and life-changing to try out Rajneesh's hedonistic spirituality as well as Randal Stark's experience-everything theory, but my conscience is saying not so fast. (A good thing, an *excellent* thing considering that the general public didn't yet know that AIDS, the deadly sexually-transmitted disease, is spreading like wildfire in San Francisco!)

Later that afternoon however, sex is the last thing on my mind. While sightseeing, I work up an appetite for food. My tour guide, a bum named Uncle Jack, had shoplifted a three-pound filet of Alaskan salmon by stuffing it under his shirt at a grocery store. We were planning to roast it of course, but the idea of the raw meat marinated with the sweat of Jack's hairy chest made me lose my appetite. I split up with Jack at around 5:30 p.m. to search for a more palatable food source. Naturally, it was near the time of the aforesaid dinner meeting. My growling stomach had overruled my earlier apprehension, so I decide to go to the house Jim and Mark had invited me to. As I head in that direction, I encounter two young men.

"You seem to be looking for something. Need any help?" asks one of them.

"Yeah, this house on Bush Street." I show him the piece of paper with the address.

"What a coincidence! That's where *we're* going! Just follow us!"

The three of us cross Bush at the light, turn right, and walk over to a red-brick, three-story building with a fancy iron-grill gate like the one in the picture. Crossing the threshold of the door into the vestibule, I notice a pile of backpacks and bedrolls to my right and a massive collection of shoes to my left. One of the two guys named Dale tells me it's customary to remove these articles before going up the stairs. This concerns me because separating myself from these items puts me in a vulnerable position.

Part of me says, "What the heck! Throw caution to the wind."

The other part is asking, "Crap, what am I getting myself into?"

CHAPTER 37

THE DINNER MEETING

Downtown San Francisco, the evening of July 20, 1979 (same day).

AFTER STICKING ON MY NAME TAG AND going up the elegant staircase, I find myself before a throng of sixty or so young men and women. Many of the people here are very *collegiate* in terms of physical appearance, age, and likely social status. Though it's a diverse mix racially and ethnically, most are of European descent. Many are East Asian.

A cute blonde in a maxi-length denim jumper greets me.

"Hhheelllooo, Ted, I'm Natalie. Who are you with?"

"Uh..."

"I mean, who invited you here?"

"Oh, some dude I met at the Wharf named Jim Corner."

"Oh, James is not here yet, but don't worry. You'll meet some really cool people here before he shows up. So make yourself at home!"

The décor is homey. The ornate interior matches the Victorian theme of the exterior. But the thing to behold here is the people. They're abnormally happy. The gleeful, gregarious, and lively way they interact, often smiling and laughing, makes me think of an over-caffeinated cheerleading squad. This type of behavior is very much at odds with the Polish in me. (My people have a demeanor quite the opposite.) Here, you can easily distinguish the newcomers from the regulars. The former look disheveled, scruffy, and bewildered. The latter look clean-cut, wholesome-looking, and well-groomed.

There is something weird about the eyes of the regulars. They're glazy with a faraway look. They're wide (suggesting the term "wide-eyed innocent" which is consistent with their childlike behavior). Staring at me with her baby blues, Natalie grills me about my trip, my background, and my personal interests. With her sweet disposition and radiant smile, she casts a spell on me. For a fleeting moment at least, I entertain the notion that she likes me in a romantic way. But, when I reveal that I attend the University of Michigan and plan to go into Psychology (if the hobo thing doesn't pan out), she grabs me by the arm and says, "Oh, I just *have* to introduce you to somebody!" So, I'm dragged across the crowded room to a brunette woman with a stylish wedge haircut standing next to the buffet table. She's probably in her early thirties. The self-possessed, stern, and commanding way she carries herself gives me the impression she's one of the ringleaders. "Ted, this is Kristina, Kristina Morrison," Natalie says before she disappears into the crowd.

Despite my hopes being suddenly dashed with Natalie, I'm delighted Kristina and I have so much in common. She attended U of M, she majored in Psychology, and she's from West Bloomfield, a suburb of Detroit. Small world! However, the topic that really blows me away is her recollection of all the exciting things happening in Ann Arbor in the late '60s when she was living there. The town at the time was widely considered an epicenter of many anti-war demonstrations and marches for minority and women's rights. It had a mythical status.

"Oh, yeah!" Kristina remarks. "I was very involved with those protests. In fact, I was one of the organizers." As she speaks, her intense eyes flash like solar flares. They express a certain mischief.

I am not only impressed. I'm starstruck. Standing before me is a real live '60s radical! She goes on to list famous activists she claims to have personally known in Ann Arbor (Tom Hayden, for instance)—and later at U of C Berkeley, another militant hotspot.

"How did you end up in California?" I ask Kristina.

"At first, I came here to earn my master's at Berkeley, but I got sidetracked: I discovered this movement. Ted, what you're seeing here tonight is part of that."

"A *movement*? What kind of movement?"

"Stay tuned. You'll learn more about it tonight. We call ourselves the Creative Community Projects, an organization kind of like the Peace Corps. We help the poor and needy around the world and advance the cause of social justice. Our goal is to create a society based on the ideals of peace and love, not just talking about it. Y'know what I mean?"

"Yeah, yeah, of course!" I answer by nodding my head emphatically. "Talk is cheap! People always complain about how messed-up the world is, but no one ever *does* anything about it. John Lennon said it best: 'Love is the answer.' Loving your neighbor is the solution to all the world's problems. If people would just 'give peace a chance' and love each other—I mean, deeply from the heart, self-sacrificially like Christ did—we'd have a perfect world."

There's a pause. Kristina, this electrifying, mischievous-looking person stares at me with her penetrating eyes like she's plumbing the width, length, height, and depth of my soul. She shakes her head as if in wonderment and gives me an approving expression. "You have a lot of wisdom, Ted!" she utters with a cool, piercing smile. "There may be a place for you here."

I'm floored. The revolutionary appreciates me!

She then introduces me to her "kid brother" Matthew, also a U of M grad, but sadly our talk is cut short by people vying for his attention. I have to say, meeting the Morrisons would prove to be pivotal. Beside them giving me a hearty thumbs up, the fact we see eye-to-eye politically boosts the credibility of the group in my estimation.

Immediately after talking to Kristina and Matthew Morrison, I spot Dale and Bruce, the guys I came in with across the room, and make my way over to them. It seems that Bruce, the one with the English accent, has a captive audience gathered around him as he tells his travel stories. I'm jealous he's so popular. However, when I chime in with tales of my own, all the attention diverts to me. About six or seven people lock into what I have to say. Practically every other word I utter evokes resounding laughter, even in spots that aren't meant to be funny. Occasionally, someone interjects with something like "That's great!" or "You must have had a wonderful time!" I'm the life of the party.

The dinner bell rings. Everyone gets situated in steel folding chairs speedily arranged into neat rows. Someone hands me a paper plate of salad with French dressing and zucchini with tomato sauce. *Cool, vegetarians!*

"Are you a religious group?"

"Wwweeellllll, yes and no. We study the principles behind the different religions, but we don't follow one in particular." *How refreshing! They're open minded.*

After dinner, a young woman holding an acoustic guitar stands up in front. She's joined by two male singers. They remind me of Peter, Paul, and Mary.

"How is everybody doing tonight? Are you all feeling JOYFUL?" the "Mary Travers" of the group shouts vigorously.

"YYYYYEEEESSSSSS!" the crowd belts out with thunderous applause. Once song books are distributed, the threesome launches into the familiar tunes "Down by the Riverside," "You Are My Sunshine," and "Blowin' in the Wind." I notice some of the words had been changed. The answer isn't blowin' in the wind, but "in the hearts of men." And John Denver's country road leads to the "Heavenly Kingdom" not West Virginia.

The vocalists intermittently make silly remarks throughout the sing-a-long. They pretend to be a trio of lounge lizards in their final song, "I Left My Heart in San Francisco." Outwardly, I smile and clap. Inwardly, I cringe, feeling embarrassed for them. I'm wondering, *how did the radical Morrisons get mixed up with these goons?*

Next, the guitar girl makes a special announcement: "I'm pleased to introduce to you a very special guest. . ."

"YYYYYEEEEAAAAAYYYYY!"

". . . the very distinguished Dr. Mose Durst, an English professor from the prestigious Laney College. Dr. Durst has studied Psychology under the renowned theorist Abraham Maslow, and he is a founder of a business consulting firm. Our charity work has greatly benefited from his involvement. He is now going to give us a short talk about the principles we live by. . ."

People at once rise to their feet and fervently applaud a man with thinning hair and wire-rim glasses. After rising from his front-row seat, the broad-grinning academic steps up to the podium. Dr. Durst is an odd kind of "rock star." An archetypal nerd, he seems overdressed for the occasion in his light blue three-piece suit. His demeanor however is very engaging. He comes across warm, upbeat, and even fatherly. His scholarly credentials give him an air of authority.

"Why are we so skeptical?" he opens. He delivers this question with zest and verve. "Because we see things from a partial viewpoint." He points to a cartoon on a poster perched on an easel. It's of an elephant surrounded by five blind men. He says something to the effect that every human is a "blind man" perceiving the beast differently since he is touching a different limb or part. The whole truth can be known if we are "open to new ideas."

His speaking and rhetorical skills are so impeccable that he could put Dale Carnegie to shame. Buttressing his points with easy-to-understand examples and humorous (albeit corny) anecdotes, Durst flips through a series of visually stunning charts and diagrams which help support his case. His voice is clear and well-modulated. He's dramatic. There are no awkward pauses, yawns, or "ums." He never refers to notes and always looks the audience straight in the eye. In a word, he's *perfect*.

"The universe is governed by certain spiritual laws just as it's ruled by physical laws like $E=MC^2$ and gravity. Why don't we see it? Because we are paralyzed by fear and ignorance. The most important of these spiritual laws, if you will, is the principle of giving-and-receiving action, or what we call Love. Quite simply, Love is the universal force that holds everything together."

WHOOOSH! Durst had just nailed it: *KARMA*^{TM}! If Randal was here now, he'd flip.

The charismatic professor goes on to expound on several fundamental truths that most, if not all, people would agree with, concerning life's purpose, the problems of society, and the need to "create a better world." He ends his presentation with a challenge: "You heard it said that there is gold in California. All you have to do is find it!" Of course, the collective response to Dr. Durst's final words are cheers like you'd hear at a football game.

As Durst winds down, I notice Dale, who had been sitting next to me on my right, has been replaced by Jim Corner! The changing of the guard.

"Hi, Ted. Sorry I'm late. I'm so glad you could make it tonight," Jim whispers with a sheepish smile and firm handshake. "Did you enjoy the lecture?"

"It was interesting. Though I'd just like to ask. . ."

Just then, a young man requests everyone's attention, "I want to share with you some slides from our farm up north near the town of Boonville." The room goes dark and a series of images appear on a projector screen. The speaker explains each slide like a travel agent giving a sales pitch. One shows a group of cheerful young adults holding hands in a circle before a campfire, another shows them having a wonderful time shucking corn together, still another shows them playing volleyball, and so on. "We have such a blast in Boonville," the man boasts. "We're one big happy family, bringing out the best in each other!"

When the lights come on again, Jim and I get more acquainted. He asks, "Would you be interested in going on a weekend retreat?"

"Sure." I'm thinking this would be a great side adventure.

"That will be $20 please," Jim says with his hand out.

Oh. . . . this thing costs money. Pause. *Oh well.* I reach into my pocket and fork over the cash.

❃ ❃ ❃

NEXT, I AND DOZENS OF OTHER DINNER attendees pile into an old school bus due north. It has the image of an elephant painted on the side (no doubt a reference to the cartoon beast in Dr. Durst's lecture). The two-and-a-half-hour ride will remind me of the field trips I went on back in grade school when everybody sang fun songs most of the way. At one point, I overhear people talking about the "Family," how great it is and how their lives had been changed forever because of it.

PART II: THE CULT

THE GREENHOUSE EFFECT

CHAPTER 38

THE RIDE TO BOONVILLE

On the way to a farm near Boonville, California, 115 miles northwest of downtown San Francisco.

THE FAMILY? SO THAT'S WHAT they call themselves! I'm amused in a gallows-humor kind of way. *Isn't that what Jim Jones followers called themselves?*

I catnap part of the way and chat with Jim Corner part of the way. I do most of the talking. He keeps asking about my all-time favorite subject: me, which I'm more than happy to oblige. Oddly enough, it doesn't bother me that he politely and skillfully evades the questions I have regarding him, the nature of the group, and our destination. At around ten, we arrive at the gate of a very imposing barbed-wire fence. The headlights reveal a sign that says "WELCOME TO IDEAL CITY RANCH." After the vehicle enters and the gate is securely shut behind it, we grab our belongings and exit the Elephant Bus in single file. We are instructed to be as quiet as possible so that no one sleeping is disturbed. The chill in the air adds to my unease. It's too dark to make out anything except a utility-pole light in the distance illuminating two adjacent house trailers. The smell of hay, manure, and campfire smoke along with the loud chirping of crickets emphasizes the ranch aspect of the place. The group is then divided up by gender. The gals follow their designated leader to the trailers; us men follow the dude with a flashlight to our sleeping quarters, a building called the "Chicken Palace" because it used to be a chicken coop. The scant light reveals a much larger space than anticipated. We had been told to carefully tread around a good number of bodies sacked-out on the floor. The whole process felt weird but I was too exhausted to think about it much. Jim, with his own flashlight, finds an open spot where we can lay our stuff down, spread out our sleeping bags and crash.

CHAPTER 39

(DIS)ORIENTATION

Boonville, the next day.

THE NEXT MORNING, MY SOUND SLEEP IS interrupted by the sounds of the rooster crowing, then an acoustic guitar, and then a baritone voice singing a familiar children's song: *"When the red, red robin comes bob, bob, bobbin' along, alonggg..."* "WAKE UP, SLEEPY HEADS!" rings the voice. "RISE AND SHINE!"

After I practically pry my eyelids open, I scrutinize the roving songster, a black-haired twenty-year-old man with a chubby frame, rosy cheeks, and a silly grin. Along with him, the morning light fully reveals the inside of the Chicken Palace. It looks like it was hastefully built, out of necessity with little or no regard for aesthetics. But it has solid walls and glass windows. There was no evidence of chickens ever being there. I'm surrounded by forty or so young men who are, like me, camped out on the cement floor. The moment the music is heard, I witness a rare phenomenon: Two-thirds of the room's occupants bust out of their sleeping bags and leap into the air like rockets from their launch pads. They promptly get dressed and dash out. The remaining third however slowly struggle to lift and drag their heavy torsos outside.

Jim, who was at my side all night, gives me a gentle nudge. "C'mon, Ted, it's time to get up," he entreats. "We have a big day ahead of us." It takes some time, but I manage to get out to where a human circle has already formed. It includes the "sisters."

"GGGOODD, MMMOORRNNING, EVERYBODY!" greets the guitar man. "My name is Joshua! It's now time for some calisthenics."

"YYYYYYYYAAAAAAAAYYYYYYYY!"

As we all do sit-ups, jumping jacks, and toe-touchers together in the cool, dewy air, I notice the enthusiasm gap. The acclimated perform the exercises with relish, gusto, and high energy while guests like me plod along, seeming to merely go through the motions. There's apprehension, hesitancy, and awkwardness.

After the workout, Joshua says with a booming voice, "I'm glad to see so many new faces! You've probably noticed by now that things are done a little *differently* around here."

"HA-HA-HA-HA-HA-HA-HA-HA!"

"For one thing, the people here are happy, I mean *really* happy. What's our secret? Well, look around you, isn't it awesome?! It's the Promised Land." Revolving my head 360-degrees, I see an old barn and farm equipment: tractors, planters, harvesters, farm trucks, wagons, irrigation system parts. The lawn we're standing on is bordered by a hedge of cottonwood trees to the west and grain fields to the north. The Chicken Palace with its featureless exterior is immediately to the south. Behind that are the trailers where the women slept. Behind the trailers is an upward slope that becomes a cliff. Trees along the slope and cliff indicate the presence of a creek. To the east, there are humongous rolling hills under the light-soaked clouds. Their golden cast, caused by the sun's effect on the dry grass, recalls what Dr. Durst had said the night before about "secret treasure" waiting to be found.

"This place may seem a bit crazy to you at first but hear me out: If you open your mind and heart, I guarantee you, you'll appreciate what's going on here. Here at Ideal City Ranch, we put principles into practice. The most important thing we do here is love each other. We generate so much love that it actually makes the crops grow better!"

"HA-HA-HA-HA-HA-HA-HA-HA!"

Josh then addresses practicalities: "Absolutely no smoking, no drugs and alcohol, and above all NO NEGATIVITY. Always listen to your instructors and especially to the buddy who has been assigned to you." These words make me acutely aware of Jim standing there next to me.

Joshua continues, "These rules may seem a little intrusive, but they just make things run smoothly around here. Okay, got it?!"

"YYYYYYEEEEEAAAAAAAHHHHHHH!"

"Great! . . . Now we're going to have breakfast in small groups. Before we break up, let me teach you the 'choo-choo,' our special little chant. Now grab the hands of your neighbors next to you and move your hands up and down like this. Ready? All together now:

"Chew-chew-chew, chew-chew-chew, yeah, yeah, POW!"

"Ohhh, that's *pathetic!*" Josh teases the crowd. "Let's do it again. This time put your whole heart and soul into it. Show me that you're awake. Okay. Ready, set, go!

"CHEW-CHEW-CHEW, CHEW-CHEW-CHEW, YEAH, YEAH, POOWWW!"

We practice the choo-choo at least one more time before dividing up. Each small group is made up of about seven members, guys and gals. We sit on large blankets sprawled out on the grass. On cue, wait staff arrive to distribute our breakfast trays. Today's course is granola, orange juice, coffee (or tea), and a half of a banana. To my surprise, my server, a person I'd never met before, addresses me by my first name.

I'm in Annie's cell group, which consists of Annie the group leader, a vivacious redhead with green eyes and freckles; Jim and me of course; and four others: two guys and two gals. The latter two pairs are presumably mentor/mentees like Jim and me. The other newcomer male besides me is 18-year-old Charlie. He stands out with his long black hair flowing down to his shoulders like an Apache warrior. He's happy-go-lucky and oftentimes funny. When Annie asks "Charlie, what's your impression of Boonville so far?" he turns into Dorothy. "Toto, I've a feeling we're not in Kansas anymore. We must be ooooooovvver the rainbow!" His quick wit hits everyone's funny bone. But Charlie's talent for blurting out famous movie lines will get him into trouble later. During lunch one time, he holds up a baby carrot and imitates Otter from *Animal House*:

"Vegetables can be really sensuous, don't you think?"

The other newbie in Annie's Group is Piper. She's the chatty type and can be jarringly blunt.

"What do you think of Boonville, Piper?" asks Annie.

"Wellllll, I don't know, " replies the 21-year-old brunette from Sweden. "The folks around here are nice and everything, but they're kind of . . . er, well . . . obnoxious and pushy."

"Look, Piper, I know exactly where you're coming from. I felt the same way when I first came here. But you gotta give us a chance. Trust me, the more you take part, the more you'll see how great things are here."

All eyes turn to me. "Ted, what do *you* think?"

"I see it like this," I reply confidently. "It's kinda like a *game* and I mean that in a good way. You pretend it's the perfect place and it becomes so. In other words, you make it real by believing it."

"Well . . . yeah . . . That's insightful, Ted."

"Can I say something else?"

"Sure."

"You get what you put into it. It's like what the Beatles said on *Abbey Road*. "And in the end, the love you take is equal to the love you make."

"Bravo, Ted! Everyone, let's give Ted a hand."

"Yyyaayyy!" the rest of Annie's group cheers, though Piper and Charlie seem to do so half-heartedly. From that day forward, I'd be recognized for my knack for backing up Boonville with the appropriate song lyrics. Another time, when Charlie was called out for being negative. I interject the words of an Elvis Costello song: "C'mon, Charlie, what's so funny about peace, love, and understanding?"

☾ ☾ ☾

AFTER BREAKFAST, EVERYONE HEADS OVER to the Chicken Palace. Besides being the men's sleeping quarters, the former hen house serves as a lecture hall. When Jim and I arrived, people were already singing their hearts out.

"*To be alive and feelin' free and to have everyone in our family / To be alive in every way / Oh, how great it is / TO . . . BE . . . ALLLIIIIIIIIIVVVE!*"

WHOOOSH! I'm transported back to the late '60s! I'm a third-grader at St. Suzanne School in Cody Rouge. The Family is singing one of the songs we used to sing at the guitar Masses. Thumbing through the rest of the songbook, I discover other classics from that era like "Pass It On" and the all-time favorite "Kumbaya."

After the songfest, a thirtyish Jewish woman with big round glasses stands up next to the chalkboard. Her zany mannerisms remind me of *SNL*'s Gilda Radner. "Now we're going to talk about the Principles of Creation." With passion and polish like Dr. Durst the night before, "Bethie" introduces a different topic: Religion.

Like Dr. Durst, Bethie is a perfect speaker, funny, interactive, and direct. She efficiently maps out rhetorical points with geometric shapes, bullets, and arrows.

"God is invisible," she says. "We can't see God but there are many things in this world which we can't see, yet we know they exist. Radio waves, x-rays, and the air we breathe can't be seen, BUT we know they exist by studying their effect. In the same way, we know God exists from observing a perfectly designed universe." Here, she restates the classic "argument from design" or "teleological argument," proposed by Aquinas, but takes it much further.

"God reveals and expresses himself in the universe. By the way, referring to God as 'Him' is just a manner of speaking. The dualistic nature of the universe—'masculine' elements and 'feminine' elements seen in things like the stigma (male) and pistil (female) in flowers, positive (male) and negative (female) ions in molecules, and so on—reveals that God is both male and female."

According to the Divine Principle, science proves religion.

Next comes the giant leap from natural revelation (via science) to divine revelation (via the Bible). Bethie now appeals to Genesis 1:28: "Then God blessed them and said, 'Be fruitful and multiply; fill the earth and subdue it; and have dominion over the earth.'" This one verse is the basis of a teaching called the Three Blessings which is the foundation of the entire Divine Principle.

CHAPTER 40

SIN REVISITED

Boonville, the afternoon of July 21, 1979 (same day).

THE "PRINCIPLES OF CREATION" LECTURE lasted about an hour. A sanguine, arm-flailing, chalk-wielding Bethie ended it by driving home the Three Blessings, how they apply to everything. Annie's group reconvened outside under the big oak tree. Charlie's member-buddy is Hector; Piper's is Ursula.

Annie begins. "So, what did you get out of the lecture? Hector?"

"I'm amazed at how the Divine Principle is so logical and scientific. I used to be skeptical about everything but I'm not anymore."

"Ursula?"

"I thought it was great! I've heard this talk many times before, but I always get something new out of it."

"Charlie?"

"To tell ya the truth, I think you people are kinda sneaky. Why do you guys hide the fact you are religious?"

"I hear what you're saying, Charlie. That's because we figured you'd get turned off right away. You must admit, you probably wouldn't hear us out otherwise."

"Well, I suppose."

"Piper?"

"I like the idea of everybody working together for world peace. But what I *don't* like is the idea that us females are compared to *negative* ion charges. Sounds sexist to me. Oh, one other thing: If God is all powerful, couldn't he make a rock that even he himself can't lift?"

"Wow, great question! Save that thought. We'll discuss it later. Ted?"

"During most of the lecture, I was blown away. I mean, the stuff Bethie was saying fit right in with Karma™."

"You mean Hinduism?

"No, Karma™ is the name of the religion my buddy Randal and I made up. Our core tenet is God is Love, and Love is the basis to everything. Bethie made some points that I'd maybe like to borrow, like the idea of Yin and Yang."

My brief presentation of Karma™ received a warm reception for the most part. They did grimace a little when I told them that Asbury Park is the Holy City and Commack is the unholy city.

ᴄ ᴄ ᴄ

AFTER LUNCH CAME THE NEXT LECTURE. The speaker is a blonde named Jennifer whom I'd seen around a lot and found attractive. She has a nice figure and big glassy blue eyes. I love the passionate way she strums her guitar. I wanted to ask her out but realized at one point she's out of my league. Come to find out, her full name is Jennifer *Morrison*. She's the younger sister of Kristina and Matthew!

Anyway, Jennifer gives a talk called the Fall of Man. It centers around Genesis 3:15, the familiar tale of how sin entered the world via Eve and the serpent. Like the Catholic Church, the Family holds that Adam and Eve are real people, but most aspects of the story aren't literal. For example, the snake, the tree, and the fruit are all symbols.

Now Jennifer introduces an interesting new twist. The Fall of Man resulted from the illicit relations between the angel Lucifer and the first woman. From the Catholic perspective, this is a novel interpretation. The traditional view is that mankind fell because of pride, not lust.

Rajneesh had flat-out rejected the idea of the Fall. He teaches that unbridled lust is a good thing. Have sex whenever, wherever, and with whomever you want. The old doctrines concerning sin, repentance, and disciplining yourself not to sin induce guilt and shame which are psychologically damaging. We must celebrate pleasure, not denounce it!

☾ ☾ ☾

AFTERWARDS, WE GO AROUND THE CIRCLE of Annie's group to share reactions. Piper breaks down into tears as she talks about her broken romantic relationships. Charlie rants about the sad state of the world.

When it's my turn, I recount how Professor Dutton's lecture on Nietzsche inspired me to be the antichrist for a month. Using Jesus as my reference point, I would do the exact opposite of what he would do—like be unforgiving and rude, harbor resentment and hatred toward everyone I meet (especially Jocks and those I perceived as shallow), practicing all seven deadly sins, etc. (except the ones that can get you arrested). I'd single out certain individuals to despise for no reason. I'd go around school hunched over, gritting my teeth, clenching my fists, scowling, sneering, giving people the evil eye.

"What was the point of that?" asks a shocked Annie.

"The experience. Just to see what it's like," I reply.

CHAPTER 41

DURST RETURNS

Boonville, the evening of July 21, 1979 (same day)

H ERE'S A RUNDOWN OF SATURDAY'S agenda. Everything begins and ends exactly on time.

8:00 a.m.	—	Family and guests awake
8:45	—	Exercises/Singing
9:30	—	Breakfast in groups
10:15	—	Introduction Lecture
11:45	—	Hike, lunch in groups
1:00 p.m.	—	Dodge ball
2:00	—	Creation Lecture/Ideal World
3:15	—	Group Meeting
3:45	—	Creation Lecture/Man's Responsibility
5:00	—	Group Meeting
5:30	—	Fall of Man lecture/Testimonials
7:00	—	Dinner, create songs in groups
8:30	—	Song Festival, Campfire
9:45	—	Staff Testimonials
10:45	—	Group Meeting
11:00	—	Family to bed

☾ ☾ ☾

THE DAY'S BIGGEST EVENT IS PRECEDED with chatter. "He's coming! He's coming!" (Again, these are grown people talking like eight-year-olds.) No, they're not expecting Santa Claus or a surprise visit from their M&Ms-dispensing Uncle Ernie. No, they're not anticipating Christ's Second Coming (not this time). They're talking about the return of Dr. Mose Durst. Everything is scripted for best dramatic effect. The build-up is enormous. To prepare for Durst's imminent arrival, the assembly in the Chicken Palace goes through another round of jubilant songs, chants and cheers. At present, a guy named Nathaniel leads:

"Good evening, everybody!"
"GOOD EVENING!"
"What does everyone want?"
"TRUTH!"
"And what?"
"RIGHTEOUSNESS!"
"When do you want it?"
"NOW!"

The vehement replies make the whole room shake. Ecstatic people grab each other's hands and hold them up high. Then Nathaniel suddenly declares the presence of Our Conquering Hero who'd just inconspicuously slipped into the back of the room.

On cue, Dr. Durst ambles up to the podium and chalkboard with his signature Cheshire-cat grin. The cheers almost break your eardrums. He's modestly soaking up the adulation like a sponge. Then with a flick of his wrist, the crowd becomes stone silent.

"What is our *nature*?" his voice bellows out. "Are we just blinking lights in the dark, just coming and going, or are we part of something bigger?"

As he continues his talk, my heart is bouncing in my chest like a tennis ball. The professor's message is one of great hope. He speaks of the incredible opportunity to be a pioneer and help construct the ideal world. And just to think, I, Ted Granger, could play a major role. Kristina Morrison, the radical clinical psychologist from Michigan, had confirmed I have what it takes to be a special contributor to the cause!

CHAPTER 42

SUNDAY NIGHT TESTIMONIES

Boonville, the evening of July 22, 1979 (the next day).

ALL OF SUNDAY, THE MOMENTUM LED up to Boonville's big campfire event starting at sundown when the appeal is made to us weekend attendees to stay for the week-long training session. All the lectures, group discussions, and songs throughout the day converge on the theme of "taking responsibility" and "making the right choices."

Jim Corner, my constant companion for forty-eight hours, had asked me the big question privately. But it is really a team effort on the part of the whole Family.

The eloquent Dr. Durst, who did all the day's talks, had created a sense of urgency: "The time is *now* to actualize the truth.". . . "Follow conscientious common sense.". . . "Participate in this glorious historical moment." . . . "Get in on the ground floor of the emerging Heavenly Kingdom." . . . "Fulfill your destiny!"

The Family is careful to avoid saying anything that can be construed as coercion. In this regard, they walk a fine line. They say things like, "Whether or not you stay in Ideal City Ranch is entirely up to you." At the same time, they lay a heavy guilt trip on you if you decide to leave.

☾ ☾ ☾

FACES GLOW BRIGHTLY IN THE WARM, flickering light of the bonfire in the open field. Hearts smolder. Spirits lunge to the stars. The adage "It feels like I died and went to heaven" sounds especially stale to one who thinks they're in a *literal* heaven on Earth. The term "falling in love"—which is thrown around a lot here—comes closer to describing the feeling, though at this point in my life, I had never experienced falling in love, only imagined it. But I had never been through a weekend quite like this one. In terms of being an hour-long high, it was beyond sensational. The sensations aroused by all the intense singing and rhetoric comes close to the elation felt at the two Springsteen concerts I attended. Words fail me when I try to describe the sensation of being constantly bombarded with the love of a swarm of perpetually happy people for two days in a row.

While the metaphors "heaven" and "falling in love" denote extreme joy, they also suggest peace-of-mind. I can't say I feel peace. Instead, I feel discombobulated and uneasy. The people here say they've never been happier in their lives and their words seem credible. Folks indeed appear content. At the same time, the bombast, the ginned-up emotions come across as real as plastic flowers. I'm mentally exhausted. There's a gnawing sense that the carefully managed flame in the fire pit—a metaphor for what's going on at Boonville—could turn into a raging wildfire in a matter of seconds. Things said here sound way too superlative, too over-the-top, and fanatical.

The highlight of the evening is testimony time. The advanced members had shared theirs all weekend in the context of the small and whole group sessions. Like Pentecostals at a revival meeting, they disclosed how their lives dramatically changed since they joined the Family. Their stories—often cringe-worthy given their personal nature—follow the "Amazing Grace" template: "I once was lost but now I'm found." *Now* the void is filled by the Family and the Divine Principle. Their sincerity shines through these accounts. It significantly offsets the phoniness.

Now before the whole group, sitting around the campfire, it's the newbies' turn to "testify." Their words had been carefully prepared ahead of time lest something embarrassing slips out and spoils the mood of the evening. Those who are about to speak have made the commitment to stay a week. Those who had decided to leave are instructed to keep their mouths shut.

Since it's her turn to speak, all eyes are on Piper.

"Tonight, several people said they had found 'what they're looking for' at Boonville. Not me. I've been hurt so many times, I was starting to think real love doesn't exist, so I wasn't looking for it. Sure, I love my mom, my best friend, and my dog, but that's about it. My so-called love life has been a disaster. When I first heard about Ideal City Ranch, it sounded too good to be true. I thought, 'Everyone loving everyone else? That's crazy! How is that even possible?' Well, Family, you won me over! You showed me that brotherly and sisterly love is real. I'm yours. I love you. I love you all very much. So, I decided to stay the week."

Visibly moved, everyone bursts out into song:

"WE LOVE YOU, PIPER, OH YES, WE DO! WE DON'T LOVE ANYONE AS MUCH AS YOU. WHEN YOU'RE NOT WITH US, WE'RE BLUE. OH, PIPER, WE LOVE YOU!"

Uproarious claps and cheers follow. After three others give their testimony, Charlie is next in line. He says the following:

"No offense, guys, but when I first came to Boonville, I thought you folks were certifiably nuts."

"HA-HA-HA-HA-HA-HA-HA-HA-HA-HA!"

"I honestly didn't want to come here but my sister Karen dragged me kicking and screaming, 'Why should I waste a weekend at some farm out in the sticks when I could be getting *wasted*?"

"HA-HA-HA-HA-HA-HA-HA-HA-HA-HA!"

"If you want to know the truth, that's all I lived for: partying. Well you guys forced me to confront myself and what's going on in the world. Dr. Durst and the other speakers made me realize this world needs saving. They gave me hope that I, one person, can make a huge difference. They made me realize life is more than getting drunk and high with my buddies."

"YYYYYYYYAAAAAAAAYYYYYYYY!"

Now it's my turn. I swallow hard as I stand up.

"Ted, what do you have to say?"

"Yeah, I too thought you people were weird at first. But I changed my mind when I met Kristina at the dinner back in San

Francisco, particularly when she said you're a '60's radical group. To make a long story short, the thing that makes me want to stay the week is the thing Bethie said about Boonville being a greenhouse. You might say it was the *Greenhouse Effect*..."

CHAPTER 43

THE LAST MAN

Boonville, late that evening.

EVERYONE WENT TO BED. ALL IS quiet except for the sound of the crickets and owls. Before falling asleep, I asked myself, *did I make the right decision?* The answer was yes. *I must do it for the experience!* For that very reason, Randal would approve. Or would he? Over the past eight months, he has changed.

Sticking to his New Year's Resolution, he quit smoking marijuana. He not only improved his grades, he made the Dean's List. He regained his academic mojo by studying harder, hanging out with the right people, and doing everything in moderation. He definitely turned the corner. I should've been happy for him, but I was not. His occasional drinking and snorting cocaine didn't bother me. It was the fact that he had become *boring*. True, he was into Punk Rock, but he didn't espouse anarchy or nihilism. He wasn't into the *movement*. In the late 1970s, British punk rockers took to the streets to fight racism.

The old Randal was an aspiring philosopher-king. He came up with his own version of Plato's Republic and Huxley's Brave New World. He had Nietzsche's will to power. He wanted to win friends and influence people so he could carry out his ambitious agenda. He thought of himself as the Übermensch like Raskolnikov did. For the sake of his grand designs, he took big risks. That's why he thought it was imperative that we hitchhike to New York instead of taking the bus.

After the New York trip, our expectations were higher than the clouds concerning our next trip—to California. We talked about it a lot, agreeing that it had to be achieved come hell or high water. We swore on it as if our lives depended on it. We would never be able to forgive ourselves if either one of us, or both of us, became faint-hearted, caved to social pressure, and backed out.

But in late '78 and early '79, Randal showed signs of having second thoughts. At one point, he came right out and said that he must do the responsible thing: stay home and work during the summer to help pay for college. This of course left me deeply sorrowful. What's more, I thought Randal was being a certified wuss, taking the advice of his meddling parents. Why should *he* help pay for the expensive tuition? That's *their* job.

The new Randal is not the intrepid tight-rope walker in *Thus Spoke Zarathustra*. He is the exact opposite: Nietzsche's Last Man, a bland, mediocre person who does everything in moderation, is responsible, obedient, safe, well-nourished, and cooperative. He *conforms.*

CHAPTER 44

"I'M A PRISONER..."

Boonville; July 23, 1979.

I STARTED TO GRASP THE CONCEPT of responsibility at Boonville. Up to that point, the R-word was the most hated word in the English language. Now I knew I had to save mankind. In his final lecture Sunday evening, Dr. Durst had made a good case against individualism and personal freedom. "When individuals do their own thing," he said, "we *all* suffer. Worse yet, given mankind's present condition—with nuclear weapons, pollution, and all—we face the real threat of going extinct. Saving humanity from itself will require collective action."

"Free will is a wonderful thing, but here's the rub: We must acknowledge the grave peril we're in and choose to sacrifice our freedom for the common good. When you're on a sinking ship and the captain cries, 'ALL HANDS ON DECK!' is it time for a coffee break?"

"NOOOOOOOO!"

"Is it time to space out and do your own thing?"

"NOOOOOOOO!"

"Is it time for mutual cooperation and teamwork?"

"YYYEEEEESSSSS!"

"The responsibility lies in each and every one of us," Durst concluded. "We can't afford to be self-centered anymore. God is willing to take 99 percent of the responsibility for the Kingdom of Heaven on Earth. But God can't do it alone. Man must assume one percent of the responsibility. To fulfill his one-percent share, he must give one-hundred percent."

Now that Piper, Charlie, and I committed ourselves to the Family (at least for the time being), we knew what was expected of us: Follow the rules, adapt to every social norm, always reciprocate respect and affection toward others. Of course, you're obligated to always follow the lead of your member-buddy. You're expected to volunteer to do things, even if you're not asked to do so. Willingness to carry out even the humblest tasks—such as taking out the trash, washing dishes, and cleaning toilets—was a sure sign of your steadfast devotion to the cause. You were compelled to express yourself exuberantly; sing, cheer, and chant as loud as possible; take part in every activity with great intensity.

The "great intensity" part goes along with what Dr. Durst said about "giving one-hundred percent." In one's relationship with fellow humans, "you pour yourself out," another popular phrase at Ideal City Ranch. As a young man, I learned this from Bruce Springsteen.

There's a reason why the New Jersey rock star has such devoted fans. Bruce performs each concert with his E Street Band like his life depends on it. Every ounce of energy is drained out of his wiry frame, as he runs back and forth across the stage, leaps into the air occasionally and does this thing where he slides on his knees making his electric guitar wail. After doing several encores following his famously long shows (sometimes extending to four hours), Springsteen melts to the stage floor like he's a mass of burning lava (requiring a band mate to dump water on him.) The last words muttered to his adoring audience are "I'M A PRISONER. . . A PRISONER OF ROCK AND ROLL!"

After you spend one-hundred percent of yourself, after you fully absorb every word in every lecture delivered, one would think that the recreational activities are designed to help you relax so you can "recharge your batteries." Not so at Boonville! Even a dodgeball game is seen as an opportunity for players to physically max themselves out like Bruce Springsteen in concert.

"OKAY, ONE-TWO-THREE, EVERYBODY, HUDDLE!" our team captain Joshua orders. "Remember, always, always be positive and chant every second so that we'll love bomb them right out of the game!"

A half dozen cheerleaders are selected to chant "DODGE WITH LOVE, DODGE WITH LOVE." Of course, the opposing team does the same thing, except their chant is "FIGHT, FURY, FIGHT." Both teams and their huddle with an earsplitting "CHOO-CHOO," and continue to fire at their opponents on all cylinders. The game is frighteningly aggressive and brutal. The ball slams torsos, limbs, and heads at full veracity. After one such skirmish, I found myself nursing a two-diameter-inch bruise on my right thigh. As the old Nazareth song goes, "Love hurts."

ᴄ ᴄ ᴄ

THE GREENHOUSE IDEA WAS INSPIRED by something Bethie said in one of her lectures. On Saturday morning, she gave the analogy of a seed breaking through the soil as a sprout.

"When he was a little seed," she said, "he knew everything about being a seed. He was secure. Breaking out is scary. The seed was afraid to break out of his secure, familiar surroundings but was glad he did when he found out how beautiful the world was above ground. Our Family is that way. Like that little seed, you have maximum creative potential. This weekend is a great chance to open yourself up, to be all those things. All that wonderful potential. . ."

These words coincided with a certain fantasy, one influenced by the "pop psychology" craze in the '70s. Self-help books like *I'm OK, You're OK*, *Your Erroneous Zones*, and *Looking Out for Number One* topped all the best-seller lists. According to Maslow's Hierarchy of Needs, you first meet your survival needs and then climb to the summit of your personal development, a state-of-mind called self-actualization. It was all part of the Human Potential Movement which combined New Age ideas with psychology. Self-improvement oriented, it saw people as having unlimited "potential."

At last, I found an environment where I could completely "wipe the slate clean," meaning I'd rid my mind of all the negativity wired into my brain since birth. Once I do that, I could reprogram myself to be supremely strong, positive, and *able*. I would *grow* into a healthy plant. I'd be powerful. I'd be able to out-able the ableists. I could rise up the ranks to become an Übermensch!

CHAPTER 45

"I'M YOUR SPIRITUAL FATHER"

Boonville; July 24, 1979.

LIKE EVERY OTHER BUILDING AT BOONVILLE, the restroom, a modest wooden cabin labeled "Brothers" was built for utility not for looks, but at least it had plumbing and electricity. And it was meticulously clean. Shelves have a copious supply of toilet paper, shaving cream, and toothbrushes. And whoever maintained it kept the lines of communication open to users. One time, I entered one of the stalls and a hand-written sign on the wall greets me.
"DEAR BROTHERS, PLEASE LOVE THIS TOILET. . . IT DOESN'T LIKE WASTEPAPER."
My chuckle breaks the tension that's been mounting between Jim Corner and me for quite some time. But, despite that, my rant picks up where it left off.
"Jim, are you coming into the stall with me to watch me s***?!" The issue here is Jim following me around everywhere I go—*even to the john*. He never let me out of his sight for two seconds the whole time I was at Boonville! I tolerated it for a while, but at one point I just blew up. The constant surveillance by not just him but the others is starting to wear on me.

"Okay, Ted, I see where you're coming from. It's just the way we do things around here." I can tell he is embarrassed.

Overall, I like Jim personally. He's one of the reasons I ended up staying here a while. My favorable impression of him at Fisherman's Wharf had lasted even to now. He is wiry and relatively short. Judging by how he grips my hand, he's surprisingly strong. With his chiseled facial features and ruddy complexion, I picture him as the rugged outdoors-type like Daniel Boone. Beside that, he's a talented guitar player. My favorite song from his repertoire is "Joy to the World" (the Christmas hymn, not the Three Dog Night tune.) He plays it with precision and flourish like a friggin Andrés Segovia.

Jim had been working odd jobs and taking classes off and on, but he wasn't sure what he wanted to do for a career (that is, before he met the Family). He doesn't have the kind of problems others around here have. Like my natural parents, his folks have stayed together through thick and thin. He's the middle child of three siblings. I believe his dad is an electrician or something. The worst thing that ever happened to him was he recently broke up with his girlfriend.

After we leave the lavatory, we make our way back to the Chicken Palace to rejoin the group session in progress. Though I've calmed down considerably, I'm still irritated.

"What would you do, Jim, if I just decided to walk out of here?"

"I guess I'd feel very hurt. After all, I'm your spiritual father."

SOMETIME DURING THE FIRST WEEK, I notice subtle changes in the nomenclature. My "member-buddy" is now my "spiritual father." Annie, my red-headed group leader, is now my "spiritual mother." Unlike her counterpart, I hardly ever see her. Every now and then, she'd check in on me or slip me an encouraging note.

In my estimation, Jim is doing a fine job playing concerned papa. In some ways, he's better at raising me than my real dad. For one thing, he spends much more time with me: that is, every single waking hour, seven days a week.

Good parents always want the best for you. Their sincerity is clear. They wait on you hand and foot but expect you to eventually stand on your own two feet. Behind every rule there's a principle:

For instance, "Wash your hands" and "Eat your peas" are all about the principle of good health. "Come in when the streetlights are on" and "Wear your helmet" are all about the principle of safety. At Boonville, the overarching principle is *order*.

"FOLLOW DIRECTIONS AND YOU'LL HAVE A VERY ENJOYABLE WEEK!"

"Atta boy, Ted! Job well done!" Jim often says accompanied with a pat on the back. When I mess up something, he'll say "That's okay, you'll do better next time." Some of his fatherly instructions are explicit such as "Hey, let's really clap and sing loud" or "Ted, you got to participate one-hundred percent." Some are implicit like "Wasn't Dr. Durst's lecture great?" My spiritual dad often gives me nonverbal cues like raised eyebrows or a gentle poke in the ribs when my attention span or enthusiasm start to wane. "Come on, Ted, *Listen*. You're spacing out again" is heard regularly.

The wise parent teaches by word and example. The docile child learns and follows until he is mature enough to parent children himself. The process repeats itself for generations. It's been that way since time began. The same interaction goes on between one's *secondary* parents, namely teachers, bosses, law enforcement officials, religious figures, tribal leaders, scientists, and college professors.

Family members end their prayers with the phrase "in the name of True Parents." As a Catholic, it was always "in the name of the Father and the Son and the Holy Spirit." Protestants say, "in Jesus' name." At one point, I got the notion that the "True Parents" meant Jim and Annie! This obviously felt strange since Jim and Annie are mere mortals. And the more I thought about it, the more I got the sinking suspicion that the pair is supposed to *replace* my natural parents! This reminds me of John Hancock practically divorcing his blood relatives and making the Greeley gang his new family.

ᴄ ᴄ ᴄ

WORK DETAIL TIME GAVE ME THE opportunity to try different things like construction, farming, and food prep. In addition, I got to see Jim in a different context.

Annie's group was once assigned kitchen duty. Charlie and I prepped salads. Piper and Hector made peanut-butter-and-jelly sandwiches. I overhear Jim talking to Ursula in the back room. The subject of the conversation is the designated overseer of our operation, a certain Richard Q. Davies from Kensington, England. Now, Richard—who, for some odd reason, pronounces his name RRRRRRRRRRRICHARD (heavily rolling the R)—is the thespian type and, as such, has the annoying habit of "hamming it up" on stage and off. Putting on my psychoanalyst hat, I surmised he lacked attention growing up. Anyway, RRRRRRRRRRICHARD leads us with a CHOO-CHOO and starts singing "Blue Skies"— the old Irving Berlin show tune—maniacally waving his arms like an orchestra conductor. His eyes are wide, glazed, and practically popping out of his head. His perma-smile is broad and toothy.

"OKAY, EVERYBODY SING ALONG WITH ME. BLUE SKIES SMILING AT ME / NOTHING BUT BLUE SKIES DO I SEE!"

Personally, I would have thought nothing of it. Singing at Boonville is almost as common as breathing. Doing so with gusto and exaggerated emotion is not only acceptable but encouraged. As far as the song choice, numbers from hit musicals like *Oklahoma*, *Man from La Mancha*, and *West Side Story* are often crooned. But, for some odd reason, RRRRRRRRRRICHARD rubs Jim the wrong way.

"Somebody ought to talk to him," Jim goes off. "Why does he act like that? He's gonna turn people off."

CHAPTER 46

HEAVENLY DECEPTION

Boonville; July 25, 1979.

"WE HAVE A FEW RULES HERE. THEY ARE REALLY GOOD RULES. FIRST, NEW PEOPLE ARE NOT TO TALK TO EACH OTHER."

The activities at Boonville were highly regimented like those of an anthill. Rules and procedures had to be strictly obeyed. Any deviation from the schedule was a cause of great concern among the rank-and-file. Individuals going rogue—refusing to take part in the activities, speaking out-of-turn, and doing things independently without permission—were pulled aside and reprimanded. At least initially, they were chided in a nice way. The nonconformist would be told something like "You won't gain the full experience of the week if you don't follow along." If you continue to rebel, however, serious measures had to be taken.

Those who had decided to stay a week or more at Boonville were allowed time to be alone for forty-five minutes or so in the afternoon. This was *your* time. If your assigned spiritual parent was confident that you're "mature" enough to stay put, you could be autonomous for this special time. Your spiritual mom or dad could have a much-needed break. Within limits of course, you were free to do whatever you wanted. You could do stuff like pray, write letters, or attend to your personal hygiene.

While returning from the washroom, I chance upon Charlie pacing back and forth next to the Chicken Palace. He looks glad to see me.

"Hey, Ted, wanna go sit in my car and chill for a while?"

"Sure."

At the time, I didn't think twice about it. The Family had not yet gotten through my thick skull that it's absolutely forbidden to speak to a fellow newcomer on my own. Charlie and I broke this rule when we were still relatively self-governing and not yet robots.

We mosey over to Charlie's '74 Ford Pinto parked in a lot next to the apple orchard. The fact he had his vehicle available on location intrigued me. It would be very easy for him to hightail out of Boonville at any time.

We enter the hot compact car and roll down the windows. Charlie in the driver's seat reaches for a Pall Mall and lights up. He takes a long puff and triumphantly exhales.

"Man, I've been dying for a smoke!" he exclaims as he grabs an 8-track and slips it into his car's aftermarket audio player. The tape is *Who Are You?* by the Who. Charlie carefully adjusts the volume to prevent us from being discovered. The conversation naturally veers to one of the big topics of the year: the untimely death of the Who's drummer:

"Keith Moon, *Reverend Moon*. No relation," I quip.

Then Charlie makes his voice sound ominous like the Wizard of Oz: "PAY NO ATTENTION TO THE MAN BEHIND THE CURTAIN!"

Both of us burst out laughing. Private joke. It all started when I commented that the Family has all the markings of a cult, but Charlie and I agreed that it's not. In fact, the very notion struck us as funny. We started joking that we are in the Moonies and Reverend Moon is the Wizard.

☾ ☾ ☾

JIM CORNER MUST HAVE HAD A HECK of a time parenting me. I'd often make random, off-the-wall comments like "This place seems cultish" and "When I leave here, I'm going to . . ." and "Come on, who are you people, really?" Looking back, Jim was very skilled at stonewalling using snappy answers like "That's a question for another time" or "Wait and see" or "Be patient. You'll find out." One time, he gave a more elaborate answer: "When you learn more about the Divine Principle, the deeper meaning will be revealed. That's why it's so important that you listen to the lectures from start to finish and hear them over and over."

"Jim, who's the head of this organization?"

"Oh, ah, Dr. Durst of course." Jim finally answers a question I had asked numerous times! My guess is he realized that repeatedly dodging it might arouse suspicion. His reply isn't necessarily a lie. Durst—along with his wife—headed up the western division of the Unification Church.

"Jim, is this the *Moonies*?"

"No, no, absolutely not!"

The actual name of the group is "The Holy Spirit Association for the Unification of World Christianity," aka the "Unification Church." Members of this group don't call themselves Moonies.

On the Friday after my arrival at Boonville, everyone expects a fresh supply of potential recruits late at night on the Elephant Bus from the Bay area.

"Ted, always be mindful of what you say around them," Jim admonishes, "don't tell them any of the new stuff you learned this past week. For one thing, don't say we are a religion."

"But we *are* a religion. Isn't that being dishonest?"

"Well, yeah, it would be in most cases. But sometimes it's okay to fudge the truth a little for the sake of the Kingdom. Around here, we call it *Heavenly Deception*."

SPIRITUAL BOOTCAMP

CHAPTER 47

MRS. DURST

Ten miles east of Healdsburg, California; July 28, 1979.

THE NIGHT RIDE FROM BOONVILLE TO CAMP K took about an hour-and-a-half.

Camp K, the nine-acre site located in the Pacific coastal highlands, was where new recruits went to hear the intermediate-level lectures. It had a different theme than Boonville. Instead of the "greenhouse," it was the "spiritual boot camp." This depiction recalled spartan army barracks with drill sergeants making you do push-ups all day. It wasn't a place for babies. I looked forward to it because, in such a brutal environment, I could stretch myself to the limit so I could achieve Übermensch-hood. Contrary to expectations, however, I found Camp K to be a step up from Boonville. The AAA Travel Guide would probably give it a high rating. Its previous owner, the Camp Fire Girls organization, had put a lot of money into it to make it nice.

Located in a valley that cuts through the densely wooded coastal highlands, the training center is quite inconspicuous.

There were two prominent figures at the camp: Noah Ross and Onni Durst. Noah was the ever-present camp director and chief lecturer. He had a slight build, horn-rimmed glasses, and large ears. As public speaker, he was Dr. Durst minus the goofiness. His nerdy appearance was offset by his poise, deadpan humor, and remarkable athletic ability (judging by his killer dodge-ball performance).

Then there was Onni Durst. She only visited one time at Camp K when I was there, but she left quite an impression.

☾ ☾ ☾

"ALL HANDS ON DECK, EVERYBODY!" shrieked a sister. "Something supercalifragilistic is happening tonight. *Onni is coming!*" Thereafter, the camp underwent a meticulous cleaning from top to bottom (though it was spotless already). Family members ran around frantically, decorating the assembly hall with flower garlands, fruit baskets, and party favors. Who's the expected guest? Yeon-soo Lim aka Onni Durst, the wife of Dr. Mose Durst. All day long, it was Onni this and Onni that. The funny thing was, before the big announcement, I never knew this Onni person even existed, let alone understood her role in the organization. I had assumed that her husband had founded the organization singlehandedly and ran it all himself, but now I began to think this woman might actually be the commander-in-chief. People even joked that "poor" Mose was a henpecked husband!

Older brethren spoke of her reverently as if she were Mother Teresa, a living saint. I had pictured her as a frumpy plainclothes nun. Being a stalwart spiritual warrior, she'd have little time to deal with trivial things like her physical appearance. Her zeal for the Divine Principle and compassion for others was so all-consuming that she only sleeps four hours a day. One of her secrets to attracting crowds was her juggling act. Yet despite her eccentric personality and silliness, she managed to recruit top-shelf talent into her righteous "army," including Mose Durst, Kristina Morrison, and Noah. Moreover, she had amazing powers such as discerning spirits. In a split second, she could tell if you're closer to God or Satan.

The arrival of Onni and her entourage at Camp K was a bit of a culture shock. On one end of the spectrum, you had college-age kids like me roughing it in grungy clothes. On the other, you had formally dressed foreign dignitaries, mostly Asians, who had arrived in a black limousine. The male Asian chauffeur opens the car door and out comes a classy-looking Asian woman with shoulder-length black hair. About forty-years old, she is dressed in a light-blue pants suit which offsets a fancy gold necklace which features a purple-amethyst gemstone. Her gold bracelets and rings glitter in the sun.

Standing by Onni's side are Kristina and Dr. Durst. The faces of the trio beam in response to the warm reception they receive in the parking lot. Next to them are four stone-faced Asian men, presumably bodyguards.

The Family affectionately calls the Dursts "Omma and Oppa," which means "Mama and Papa" in Korean. Upon learning this, it suddenly dawns on me that THEY are the "True Parents," the perfect humans I'm supposed to emulate, not Jim Corner and Annie, as previously thought. It is them —Mose and Onni Durst— who I've been evoking at the end of my prayers instead of the Holy Trinity!

In the festive-looking meeting hall, songs are sung, prayers are said, and Dr. Durst steps up to the podium.

"I remember that evening like it was yesterday," he says wistfully. "Someone at school told me about this very unusual woman living in a tiny apartment on Dana Street. I knew I had to meet her. . ." Durst goes on to reminisce about his first impression of his future wife, her happy demeanor, warmth, and "directness in contrast to her warmth." At one point, he recalls asking her, "Why did you come to America?"

"'To end God's suffering,' she answered in broken English, "and to end the suffering of human history."

After his over-the-top gushy introduction, Dr. Durst hands the mic over to his wife. The applause makes the room rumble like an earthquake. He relegates himself to the sidelines as she now takes command.

In contrast to all the lectures I'd heard up to that point, Onni Durst's talk is completely unscripted. She spouts out a series of platitudes like "We must be value-makers and happy-makers," "Doubts no good," and "Get rid of ego." The most distinctive thing is her emphasis on "spiritual warfare," that one must constantly fend off evil spirits with prayer every moment of the day. In the middle of her speech, she yells "GET BEHIND ME, SATAN!" and starts kicking and karate-chopping spirits in the room! She also talks about the spirits of our dead ancestors cheering us on. I must admit, she gives me the willies. Unless I wasn't paying attention, the other presenters had glossed over this spiritual-warfare stuff.

There's a wide chasm between Onni the Image and Onni the actual person. Of course, I—like a drone bee amongst the other drone bees buzzing around the queen bee—cheered her like everyone else. But deep down, I'm not impressed. The "True Mother" is too strange for me to relate to.

CHAPTER 48

KRISTINA'S BIG ANNOUNCEMENT

Camp K; July 28, 1979 (same day).

K RISTINA MORRISON, THE NEXT SPEAKER, was as relatable as Onni is unrelatable. She's from metro Detroit! Kristina stands before the assembly with her arms crossed as she patiently waits for the rigorous clapping for Onni to die down.

"Brothers and sisters, I have some great news to share!"

"YYYYYYYYAAAAAAAAYYYYYYYY!"

"There are incredible things happening in our movement. Onni and I just returned from New York, and we are making major strides in building the Kingdom. Of course, we give full credit to our Heavenly Father. We couldn't have done it without his help."

"YYYYYYYYAAAAAAAAYYYYYYYY!"

"It was truly remarkable. Onni and I had arranged a meeting with hundreds of prominent leaders, professional people, and ambassadors of the United Nations. At the hotel, we hosted a banquet where we did a presentation about Project Volunteer. At first, they were skeptical about our ideas, which of course is understandable. What we do sounds so crazy."

"HA-HA-HA-HA-HA-HA-HA-HA!"

"It's amazing to see how many people of the highest level are now behind our work. It's just a question of networking."

"YYYYYYYYAAAAAAAAYYYYYYYY!"

"Great things are being written about us."

"YYYYYYYYAAAAAAAAYYYYYYYY!"

"All this has been part of the process to show the true ideal of *unification*. We've been able to turn the media around, turn college professors around, turn parents around and show them what we're really all about."

"YYYYYYYYAAAAAAAAYYYYYYYY!"

What is our key to success? We love-bombed them. We simply treated those cynics like human beings. We supplied them with free dinner and hotel reservations. We showed them a good time. It goes to show that showering people with love softens them up and makes them receptive. I'm telling you, friends, great things are happening!"

WHOOOSH! That's the sensation of my heart leaping.

Kristina continues, "Regarding what's happening, a word that Tolkien coined comes to mind: *eucatastrophe*. It means a catastrophe in reverse. The times they are a-changin,' brothers and sisters. A new era of world peace and love is unfolding before our very eyes!"

My thoughts then turn to Randal, the side of him who first proposed setting up our own Republic. Granted, our past discussions on this were pure tongue-in-cheek, but Kristina made me think that Utopia is not just a pipedream. It's not only possible, but it's *imminent*. Mankind is rapidly moving in that direction!

Man, oh man, I can't wait to tell Randal!

CHAPTER 49

LETTER TO RANDAL

Dear Randal,

I know you are probably wondering where I am so I'll tell you. I am staying at a place called Camp K in Northern California. Sorry, I haven't got in touch with you for quite a while, but I haven't had much time to myself lately.

You won't believe what I am about to say. I know a lot of crazy thoughts are going to run through your head and I hope they will be joyous ones. Well, imagine a place where everyone loves one another, a community where you can be completely yourself and feel so fulfilled in a constant process of growth.

No, I did not turn into a Jesus freak or a Krishna follower or anything like that. Let me explain what is going on here. This place is totally committed to love and truth, but in the intellectual sense, no fairytales or religious dogma. The week I have been here seems like a year because I have done so much growing in my mind and heart. All everyone talks about here is God and self: deep things. Everyone is so happy because there is so much giving and receiving going on. I got a chance to de-brainwash myself from so much bad karma.

I must tell you, there is something very important happening here: this organization wants to change the world, not by violence but by the very concept of love. And I didn't believe it myself. This community had been founded many years ago by a man named Dr. Durst, an extremely strong, determined, friendly sociologist who has really found the answers to the human struggle and so many here have been enlightened by this knowledge.

I know this has really blown your mind. This thing is really growing fast. The people at this camp are really turning people's heads fast. It's a miracle, really a miracle!

Randal, you and I, through the years, have been working on developing our philosophy of life. I have found this place has the same kind of idea that we had, even far better. I learned that if I want to achieve a goal, I have to act. It's achieved by doing not thinking about it all the time like I have been doing.

I'm planning on staying here for who knows how long because I owe it to myself, and you and my family and everybody. I must say though PLEASE DON'T TELL ANYONE else because they will all think I'm crazy. Best to wait. You can write me now at this address: Camp K /PO Box 1949 / Santa Rosa CA 95402.

Peace and love,
Ted

CHAPTER 50

POLITICS, POLITICS

Camp K, sometime in August.

NOAH ROSS'S PUBLIC SPEAKING SKILLS matched those of Dr. Durst which is saying something. This cool nerd inspires confidence! He's up there pointing to the blackboard and pounding his fist on the podium.

"The mission of the Last Days is to become united with God!" he cries. "NOW is the moment—the most important moment in human history. If we can realize God's plan, America will become great again. WE are the last hope for America. WE must win the love of the rest of the world! WE have to LOVE-BOMB the world. Don't you think?"

"YYYYYEEEEESSSSS!" screams the audience full-throated. Then Noah leads the chant "USA! USA! USA!"

Nice to hear! The United States of America is part of God's plan. But, come to find out, the "second Christ" will come from *Korea*. The first Christ failed in his mission to get married, have a family, and turn the world into a utopia. He got himself crucified before he could make any headway. So the new Korean Messiah will pick up where Jesus left off and finish the job.

"Proof? It's right there plain as day in the Book of Revelation!" Noah continues "Chapter 7, verses 2-4 says the seal of the living God will be placed on the foreheads of the 144,000 in the *East*, where the sun rises. Which among the nations of the East is chosen to receive the Lord? Since ancient times, the nations in the East have traditionally been the three nations of Korea, Japan, and China.

Uh-huh.

"Among them, Japan throughout its history has worshiped the Sun Goddess. It entered the period of the Second Advent as a fascist nation and severely persecuted Korean Christianity. Therefore, we can around Japan won't work in China, at the time of the Second Advent, would become a communist nation. That means Christ couldn't possibly return in China."

Sooo, the last man standing is KOREA! What's more, the final battle will be between South Korea (representing God) and North Korea (representing Satan).

"The future is in our hands. If we harness human resources for the common good, we can do anything! If we align ourselves with that ideal, we shape history! By acting in accordance with a universal value structure, we direct that destiny!"

"YYYYEEEEAAAAHHHH!"

"We can inspire America to return to its idealism. We can free ourselves from the things that threaten to destroy us—drugs, sexual sin, divorce, violence, and all the rest. The whole vision of America has been corrupted, but it can be revitalized so that the world will follow its righteous example."

"YYYYEEEEAAAAHHHH!"

"I know it's hard to relate to God," Noah continues, "but, if there is *one perfect man* who can relate to God, we can unite with him."

"YYYYEEEEAAAAHHHH!"

"Yes indeed, he can unite this country and eventually the world. God is counting on us. NOW is the time to respond. God can't do it without us."

"YYYYEEEEAAAAHHHH!"

On the blackboard, Noah maps out the major events in world history in chronological order using the typology of Cain and Abel. On the "Cain" side is atheism and communism trying to take over the world; on the "Abel" side is Christianity and democracy. Proof that we are "living in the Last Days" is presented. According to Noah, the world will soon experience a mega-war between the forces of God and Satan. Then a new messiah, along with his followers, will restore the Kingdom of Heaven on Earth.

"I tell you, that one perfect man—the Lord of the Second Advent—is alive and well and walking the earth!" With that, Noah starts to sing a familiar tune and everybody joins in: *"MY EYES HAVE SEEN THE GLORY OF THE COMING OF THE LORD. . .!"*

CHAPTER 51

CHARLIE

Camp K, sometime in August, 1979.

CHARLIE AND I HAD ONE MORE CHANCE to sneak off together during a break. The Eagles' "Hotel California" comes on the car radio. After the song is over, Charlie says to me with a smirk, "Y'know, this place kinda reminds me of the Hotel California: *'You can check out any time you like / But you can never leave!'*"

Laughter.

"*This could be heaven or this could be hell.*"

More laughs.

"Seriously, Ted, I just know you're going to be a great leader for the Family."

"Thanks, Charlie. What makes you say that?"

"A lot of people at Boonville and Camp K come across bogus, but you make the Divine Principle seem so natural and relatable."

"Wow! That's a high compliment."

"Really, man, thanks for not giving up on me. The past three weeks have been pretty rough. I was reprimanded three times for being a smartass. The higher-ups came close to kicking me out. But I was determined to stick with it. And it's all because of you, Ted."

"Me?!"

"Yeah and there's one thing that you said that stuck with me: that you can't know if something is good or bad unless you try it. Well, I tried the Family and now I'm feeling pretty good about it!"

Sadly, this was the last time the two of us got together one-on-one. Jim found out about our secret meeting and made triple sure Charlie and I never came in contact again.

A week or so later, I stumble upon Charlie outside in front of the assembly hall. He and others are sitting in a row getting haircuts like at a barber shop.

I'm stupefied. His long black hair once looked like that of an Apache warrior. After the "Family barber" got done with him, Charlie doesn't look like himself anymore. He now resembles a member of the Baptist church in my Detroit neighborhood and that's not a compliment. His face is radiant yet vacant. He has this sickening Howdy Doody smile not to mention crystalline eyes. I must admit, I liked the old Charlie better.

CHAPTER 52

THE TWO ME'S

My notes of one of Noah's lectures . . .

"VISIONARY SELF: There is such unity here, understanding, and giving and receiving, I can't refuse it. It is there to surrender to and enjoy. I can really grow in a place like this. I can really get to know myself and others.
INDIVIDUAL SELF: Be independent. TO HELL WITH THEM! I don't think I have to do what the crowd does all the time. Time to go. Read Jack Kerouac.
VISIONARY SELF: Dive into it. Surrender to it. Stay. Stay.
INDIVIDUAL SELF: Be different. Be unique. Leave!"
(As I'm dictating this, Jim leans over and notices what I just jotted down! He is witnessing in real time the Great Debate going on inside my cranium. He points to the "TO HELL WITH THEM!" and the "Leave!" passages and glares at me as he shakes his head disapprovingly. I immediately sense the danger that I'm losing a grip on my selfhood.)

CHAPTER 53

LETTER FROM RANDAL

Camp K, sometime in August, 1979.

IT'S AFTERNOON QUIET TIME. I'm sitting at the riverside taking in the beauty, staring at the dancing sparkles in the water. My mind badly needed a break after the intense lectures. My reverie is interrupted when the Family mail carrier walks up to me and hands me a letter. It has Randal's handwriting and return address! I anxiously open it and begin reading.

Dear Ted,
    I hope this letter finds you well. The one I got from you was a lot to take in.
    If I get this straight, you think you've found the perfect society. I've come to the conclusion that any utopia must become dystopian. For a utopia to work, everyone has to agree on everything... all the time... forever, and that's just not in our human nature. Eventually there's dissent, and that leads to either dissolution or coercion. Camp K does sound interesting, but sorry, I can't share your enthusiasm. It seems too good to be true, and to be honest, I think it's a cult. This Dr. Durst guy sounds like the Reverend Moon himself, or at the very least a slick con man. If I were you, I'd get the hell out of there.

Another thing: How can you expect me to keep this a secret from your family? Your parents call me practically every week to find out if I've heard from you. They're worried sick. You're putting me in a very tough position...

"HHHOOOLLLLLYYYYY CRAP!"

CHAPTER 54

THE RESCUE TEAM

Detroit, August 17, 1979.

RANDAL HAD ALREADY SPILLED THE beans and there was nothing I could've done to stop him. Shortly after his urgent call to my parents, an emergency meeting commenced at the Granger house. Those present wasted no time with small talk. The tone is sober and phlegmatic despite the fact my mom and dad are in a state of panic. Their many sleepless nights are etched on their faces. The revelation I'm at Camp K at least gives them the satisfaction of knowing where I am. But any consolation was squashed by the realization that the place may be another Jonestown.

The master of ceremonies is my brother Bart. A recent U of M grad, he is between jobs, so his time is flexible. Randal, on the other hand, has to work ten-to-six, but he came over to my parents' house as soon as he could. Waiting for him were some Top Hat sliders, French fries, and the latest news about me. "The Archdiocese is on the case," Bart related. "We also called the Sonoma County sheriff, but he said he couldn't do much since Ted's a legal adult."

The job of rescuing me fell to Bart and Randal. They seemed to have what it takes to plan and execute such a sophisticated operation. Everyone agreed that some research needed to be done beforehand. The two-man rescue team needed to learn more about whom they'd be dealing with. What tools would they need? (Shovels? Wire Cutters? Talking points?) The next day would be devoted to addressing these issues.

Bart and Randal know a little more about cults than my parents. Groups like the Hare Krishna, Scientology, and the Children of God tended to congregate in college towns like Ann Arbor where both guys had lived. Moonies were known to sell flowers and candy on street corners until two in the morning. Bart and Randal had read about Reverend Moon officiating over mass weddings at Yankee Stadium. Moon had personally picked mates for the hundreds of brides and grooms he married at the same time.

☾ ☾ ☾

THE HENRY FORD CENTENNIAL LIBRARY was where Randal had conceived his Republic. He arrives late in the afternoon still in his work clothes; Bart has been there all day. He looks wilted from hours of intense study. There's a stack of stuffed folders on the table in front of him as well as copies of several books and periodicals. In the proper hushed tones, the pair get right down to business.

"Man, I still can't believe Ted joined the Moonies," Randal whispers over to Bart as he shakes his head. "How could he be so friggin' gullible?"

"Yeah, not to mention stupid," says Bart.

"It's like something out of *Invasion of the Body Snatchers*."

"Try spy flicks."

"*Spy flicks?*"

Bart hands Randal an 8½ x 11 wire-bound booklet. The whole thing is typewritten, double-spaced. It's got a long, wonky title, but the word "KOREAN" jumps out. The publisher is none other than the "U.S. HOUSE OF REPRESENTATIVES." It's dated October 31, 1978. My brother asks Randal, "Are you ready for this?"

With Bart's help, Randal soon gets the overall gist. Reverend Moon, who started his church in 1954, is now a major power broker in South Korea. He rose to this lofty position being in the right place at the right time. His buddies in the Korean CIA and military helped him secure lucrative defense contracts (His company manufactures M-16 rifles and grenade launchers.) The South Korean government allows him to peddle influence in the U.S. and other countries. He had set up a vast, international network of organizations which are engaged in all kinds of economic, political, and religious activities. A lot of these ventures involve income tax fraud, money-laundering, and conspiracy.

"He's trying to take over the world!" Randal concludes with nervous laughter.

"Yeah and get this," Bart replies. "Moon actually said he's greater than Moses, Buddha, and Muhammad put together and he's 'ten times greater than Jesus.'"

"He reminds me of what'shisname . . . you know, the criminal mastermind in James Bond movies."

"Goldfinger?"

"No, the dude who sits in a leather chair and pets a white cat."

"Oh, *Blofeld*, Ernst Stavro Blofeld."

"Yeah! Oh, by the way, Randal, did you write Ted back?"

"Uh-huh, I did a few days ago. I hope he got my letter by now."

CHAPTER 55

THE ROARING SILENCE

Camp K; August 18, 1979.

RANDAL'S LETTER DISTRACTED ME all day. I was so obsessed with it that I couldn't concentrate on the lectures. My frequent "spacing out" prompted Jim to nudge me more often than usual. Whenever he wasn't looking (like when I was in the restroom stall), I pulled out the wrinkled, folded-up piece of paper and read it over again. I must've done this five times. The words that really stung me were "Ted, how can you expect me to keep this a secret from your family?" There had to be a way to prevent him from telling my parents (if he hadn't already done so). I decided to write Randal a second letter and mail it along with the green spiral notebook that I called the Truth Project.

In the letter, I tried to convince him that "Project Volunteer" is a completely respectable organization, not a cult. I suggested that my stay at Camp K was only temporary and that I could leave at any time. The Truth Project would help Randal put my weeks-long sojourn at Boonville and Camp K into perspective. It had reflections on the different religions and philosophies that I had dabbled in all summer, most notably that of Bhagwan Rajneesh. In my mind, the notebook would show Randal how open-minded, insightful, and discerning I was. My spell with the Family was just a brief interlude.

At the same time, I needed to get across to Randal that the people at Camp K are special: (1) The core tenets of their philosophy line up with Karma™. (2) They are implementing a utopia like his Republic. (3) They're using Behaviorism to create a new social reality like in B. F. Skinner's *Waldon Two*. This organization had Randal Stark written all over it! Now, if I could only convince Randal Stark.

There was something I wanted to include but decided to save it for another time: an invitation to Randal to come out and visit Camp K. As he once said, "You can't really know if something is good or bad unless you try it." I figured if he saw the place for himself, he'd be thoroughly impressed, and this would prompt him to join the organization. I imagined that the inner circle would immediately recognize Randal's cleverness, superior intellect, and will to power just as Kristina immediately spotted my unique gifts and talents that first night in San Francisco. Randal, like me, would be a perfect fit! He and I respectively would rise through the ranks quickly and join the elite Übermensch class calling the shots. I thought we'd have a blast working together with the other top leaders.

Ironically, while I was hatching these thoughts, I was considering *leaving* Camp K. The cognitive dissonance was almost unbearable. I yearned to be my own boss again, resume the hobo fantasy, and "read Jack Kerouac." I had the strong urge to keep exploring the United States and eventually the world via the Overland Trail. To prevent myself from going crazy, I came up with a solution of sorts. I would view my imminent departure and time away from the Family as a kind of sabbatical. I could have my cake and eat it too! I'd see America and the world—get the wanderlust out of my system—and come back to the Family when I'm ready.

There was another inner conflict that needed to be addressed. I liked the material taught in the early lectures but not so much the new stuff. I couldn't stomach the latest gobbledygook concerning Korea, the Lord of the Second Advent, etc. It just sounded preposterous. I came up with a solution to that dilemma too. In Plato's Republic, Socrates realizes that certain policies may upset some citizens (like dividing people into classes). So, to avoid civil unrest, he concocts a "noble lie," namely the "myth of metals," a religious concept. Maybe the Dursts, the Morrisons, Noah Ross, and the rest of the Family leaders are secretly atheists using a fake religion to keep everyone on the same page. If Utopia is the aim, then who cares if the faith that keeps it together is untrue? It still serves a good purpose. The Noble Lie is morally justified!

☾ ☾ ☾

AT THE SUMMIT OF A NEARBY HILL, Noah is teaching and leading the group in song with his guitar. He says, "Remember Moses who climbed the mountain to show God his faith." Everyone is holding hands in a big circle except for Noah in the middle. As we're watching the sun go down on the gorgeous valley below, he stops and admonishes us to bask in the beauty. Before this moment, it was hard to imagine him as the bearded, shoulder-length-haired hippie he once was. Now I can see it. The hippies I had met on the road like Rosie Smith, John Hancock, and those at the two Gulches showed me how to not only appreciate nature but to relish it.

"God is speaking to you through nature!" Noah continues. "He is telling you he loves you!"

Next, Noah directs our attention to the work of human hands, Camp K with all its buildings, utility poles, and powerlines. There's beauty in that too.

"Someday people from all over the world will come together in the New Jerusalem that we have built. Everyone will live in peace and harmony. When the world is restored to God, there will be bells ringing in the streets. There will be much celebration. Some may not understand what has happened, but they'll know that it is something good."

"YYYYYYYYAAAAAAAAYYYYYYYY!" everyone in the audience explodes in unison.

After everyone comes down from the hill, preparations are made for tonight's big event. It will be extra special because it's Saturday night when there's a lot of people from the big city staying overnight. All enjoy the fellowship and a vegetarian feast that can't be beat. After that, we congregate before the bonfire. There, we break up into small groups where we plan skits.

Each group is instructed to choose a popular song and rewrite the lyrics to fit tonight's theme, "finding truth and happiness." After that, each member of the respective team is assigned blocking to go along with the words. Our group did the tune of Johnny Cash's "Folsom Prison Blues" with these lyrics:

> *The heav'nly kingdom's comin,' it's rollin' 'round the bend.*
> *We ain't seen our Father since we don't know when,*
> *But we're gonna see him shortly, just you wait and see.*
> *Gonna bring His kingdom. He'll be so proud of me.*
>
> *We've been livin' in the darkness for six thousand years,*
> *Brought our Father sadness, sufferin' and tears.*
> *But we're gonna make him happy, take away his pain*
> *We're all bound for glory, oh won't you board this train?*

RRRRRRRRRRRICHARD is in our group. *Oh crap!* As usual he hams it up. What is particularly odd is him trying to imitate Johnny Cash with his thick English accent.

After we sing the final line about the train, we do a hearty "CHEW-CHEW."

"YYYYYYYYAAAAAAAAYYYYYYYY! BRAVO! BRAVO! BRAVO!" We get not only thunderous applause but a standing ovation!

After each of the other groups perform their skit, the whole group once again launches into song. Notable selections are "Gonna Build a Kingdom," "There's a New World Coming," and "I'll Never Find Another You." During the last song, "The Impossible Dream," my ecstatic brethren and I raise each other's hands skyward.

Next comes testimony time.

Ramona shares, "I admit I had intellectual doubts at first but decided to follow my heart. Now I'm so happy!"

"YYYYYYYYAAAAAAAAYYYYYYYY!"

Next comes Harold: "I never thought one could fall in love so quickly, but I love you all!"

"YYYYYYYYAAAAAAAAYYYYYYYY!"

Lucy is next: "At first, I had a hard time following the rules, but now there's no conflict. Everything is so peaceful here."

"YYYYYYYYAAAAAAAAYYYYYYYY!"

As I'm listening, I'm starting to think that what's being said is sounding a little repetitive, so I raise my hand.

"Okay, you over there in the U of M t-shirt," says the leader in front pointing at me.

"Ahem! Uh, er, hi everybody. My name is..."

"A LITTLE LOUDER, PLEASE!" shouts someone from the peanut gallery.

"OKAY. UH, MY NAME IS TED GRANGER. I'M FROM DETROIT, MICHIGAN. CAN YOU HEAR ME NOW?"

"That's good. Perfect."

"Uh, I want to do something a little different here. I want to share with everybody a letter I got in the mail this morning. It's from my buddy Randal Sturk."

"YYYYYYYYAAAAAAAAYYYYYYYY!"

"I must admit, um, it kind of shook me up at first. He was reacting to the letter I had sent to him a week ago describing this place. He sounds a little... worried."

"Yyyaayyy."

"After reading it over a few times and mulling it over for a while, I began to laugh my head off, realizing how totally off-base Randal is. Get this: he actually thinks I'm in a *cult*! Isn't that ridiculous?"

Silence.

"I got the letter right here."

I pull the letter out of my pocket before a stone-faced crowd.

"Okay, here we go... *'Dear Ted, I hope this letter finds you well... Camp K does sound interesting, but sorry, I can't share your enthusiasm. It seems too good to be true, and to be honest, I think it's a cult. This Dr. Durst guy sounds like the Reverend Moon himself, or at the very least a slick con man. If I were you, I'd get the hell out of there.'* Isn't that funny! Randal actually thinks I'm in the Moonies!"

Audience members look at each other utterly stupefied, mortified, and confused.

Silence.

"Yyyaayyy."

I saunter back to my seat with my head lowered. *Well, that went over like a lead balloon.* Jim, totally flabbergasted, says, "That was very nice, Ted... Only, do me a favor. Next time, please let me know beforehand what you're going to say."

The group leader gallantly jumps into the void. "Ooooo-kay, brothers and sisters, who wants to be next?"

CHAPTER 56

THE INFANT OF PRAGUE

Detroit, August 18, 1979.

O N THE RUGGED TRAIL HEADING BACK to my sleeping quarters in the main lodge, my heart sank into the pit of my stomach. My head felt like it was hit with a two-by-four. What could trigger such a reaction?

One of the higher-ups approaches us. Her flashlight blaring in my face makes me squint and shield my face with my hand. "Ted?" she inquires. "We've been looking all over for you."

"Huh? What?"

"Your *mother* has been trying to get a hold of you all night. She's been very persistent."

"OH MY GOD! SHE KNOWS!" Stunned, I look over to Jim who is barely distinguishable in the dim light. He studies my face with his beady eyes.

"Do you want to call her back right now or wait 'til tomorrow?"

"Ummm. I'll wait. Too late in the evening."

Mom probably was up way past 1 a.m. storming heaven on my behalf. Beside saying rosaries all night, she does novenas, special prayers that are repeated for nine consecutive days. There's a novena to Our Lady of Guadalupe, another to Our Lady of Częstochowa. Mom's novena of choice that summer was to the 400-year-old Infant of Prague, a wax-coated wooden statue of the Child Jesus. Originally from Spain, the 19-inch-tall figure was purportedly owned by St. Thérèse of Lisieux. Today, it resides at a magnificent basilica in the Czech Republic. Replicas of the original statue, outfitted in royal robes and a crown, are found in churches everywhere. The faithful in local parishes always make sure it's properly cared for, cleaned, and dressed.

One time I joked that it reminded me of a Kewpie doll from a carnival. My childe remark did not amuse my mother. Great miracles had been attributed to the Holy Child including narrow escapes. She told a story one time. During the War, a bomb had reduced a house in Italy to a pile of rubble. One of the survivors realized, to her shock and horror, that her month-old baby was trapped under the debris. A woman of faith, she turned to the Child Jesus. Then, with superhuman strength, she started lifting and slinging heavy chucks of wood, metal, and concrete like they were Styrofoam until she finds her daughter alive and well six feet under. The mom is Wonder Woman! But of course the Infant gets all the credit.

Whether it was divine intervention or not, something inside of me snapped. I suddenly "saw the light." I at once felt a strong urgency to leave Camp K and get home asap. The funny thing is I started to worry about my parents being worried.

☾ ☾ ☾

SATURDAY NIGHT'S FESTIVITIES wind down, and everyone gets washed up for bed as usual. Jim and I had been sleeping on the assembly hall floor along with most of the other men. The next morning, I wake up to find my spiritual father gone! There's a handwritten note next to my pillow. It reads:

"Ted, I'm really sorry that I can't be with you today. I must go back to the city to take care of some business. While I'm away, Zeke will be your point man instead of me. I hope you have a wonderful day! See you soon. Affectionately Yours, Jim."

This was the last time I heard from Jim Corner.

CHAPTER 57

MY FINAL DAY AT CAMP K

Camp K; August 19, 1979.

ON THE SABBATH, THINGS WERE DONE a little differently. The morning gathering was more like a church service; Noah's lecture was the "sermon." The rest of the day was more relaxed. Though I had convinced myself that the Family's religion is Plato's Noble Lie, Jim's sudden departure seemed like a gift from heaven. I felt liberated. As I went about my day, I felt less uptight not having a pesky spiritual parent constantly breathing down my neck. I engaged in all the activities with the usual zest and vigor, but I could think more clearly. I doubt if anyone suspected what I had up my sleeve. Instead of being hyper-geeked up about the Heavenly Kingdom, I acted that way because I looked forward to leaving.

Planning my escape was probably ten times easier than it would have been if Jim was around. He would pull out all the stops to get me to remain with the Family.

As Jim said in his note, a fellow named Zeke would be my point man while he was gone. I'm sure the leaders thought the arrangement was less-than-perfect given the fact Zeke and I barely knew each other. But the show must go on. Blond-haired and blue-eyed Zeke was originally from Christchurch, New Zealand. He was the cream of the crop, as they say. His build and mannerisms reminded me of a gym teacher. In Randal's Republic, he'd definitely be placed in the Jock category. I found him to be easy to get along with. His higher status in the group afforded him the privilege to live in one of the cozy cabins next to the creek as opposed to the assembly hall where Jim and I stayed. His cabin accommodated eight or so men. True, they were all packed in there like sardines, but it beat sleeping in an ocean of bodies like I had to do night after night.

About my imminent escape, the crucial thing I managed to do was hide my backpack in a strategic spot. At the assembly hall, everything except my sleeping bag and toiletries bag were packed and ready-to-go for the 2,400-mile trip back to Michigan. In moving it to Zeke's cabin, the backpack never arrived at Zeke's cabin. Making sure no one else was around on the trail, I slid it in the crawl space under one of the other cabins. Its location was important because, later, I would have to be able to retrieve it quickly without making any noise in the middle of the night. Moreover, it had to be along the escape route that I had mapped out in my mind.

I arrived at Zeke's cabin with just my sleeping bag and toiletries bag. No one noticed that I didn't bring along my backpack. I'm sure nobody there even knew I had one.

If I remember right, we did this thing in the afternoon called Heavenly Father's Birthday Party where we got together to eat cake and ice cream.

❦ ❦ ❦

I'M MINDING MY OWN BUSINESS, prepping for tonight's flight to freedom when an attractive brunette comes out of nowhere and grabs me by the arm. She's conservatively dressed of course, yet she is still within bounds of the current '70s fashion. She dons wide-legged jeans and a white embroidered blouse.

"Hhheeelllooo, there!" She greets me with an infectious smile. "Would you like to donate something to the ice cream fund?" The Maxwell House coffee can is shoved in my face.

"Huh? What?"

"It's for this day's big event: Heavenly Father's Birthday Party."

"Wwweeellll. I dunno."

"Would you? Oh, *could* you? Please. Please. Please..." She says this with a cutesy, baby voice as she bats her eyelashes, pouts her lips, and sways her head.

My complexion is as red as a firetruck.

"No, I just..."

"PPPllleeeaaasseee!"

Her eyes lock with mine. After that, she lowers them and slightly parts her lips. Then she leans toward me.

"Oh, my Lord," I mutter under my breath. Then the thought occurs to me, *Just give her the money. It might throw off any suspicion of me leaving.*

So, I proceed to pull out my wallet, open the billfold and hand her a wrinkled twenty-dollar bill.

"Oh, thank you! Thank you!"

Once the money is in her hand, Ice Cream Girl vanishes, no doubt in hot pursuit of another sucker.

Oh crap. What just happened. I've been seduced!

CHAPTER 58

PIPER

Same afternoon.

I STOP BY PIPER'S CABIN. THE SIGHT of her packing her suitcase floors me.
"What's going on, Piper?"
"Ted, I'm going back to San Francisco."
"Whoa, what brought this on? I thought you were one of the Family's rising stars."
Silence.
"Oh, (chuckle) I'm not leaving the Family! I'm just going to the city to hear the final series of lectures. I'm surprised *you're* not going, Ted"
"Maybe they forgot about me. Things have been quite out-of-whack since Jim left."
"Why did he leave?"
"I don't know. Weird huh? Well, have a nice trip, Piper." I reach over and give her a brotherly hug.
"Thanks, Ted, but I'm not leaving until after the movie."
"Great, I'll see you then."

CHAPTER 59

PETE MEETS JIM

Downtown San Francisco, the evening of August 19, 1979 (same day).

AROUND 7 P.M. ON BUSH STREET, a lone backpacker walks by Jim Corner standing outside a Victorian-style house.
"Hey, friend, where are you from?" asks Jim.
"Michigan," replies the blond-haired stranger.
There's a pause.
"Hey, I know someone else from Michigan!"
"Is his name Ted?" asks the backpacker.
"That's him!" Jim cries. "What's *your* name?"
"Pete."
"Hey, you're Pete LeBlanc! Wow. I heard so much about you!" exclaims Jim shaking his head in wonder.
Stupefied by their chance encounter and what it may mean, both young men vigorously shake hands.
"Yeah, Ted and I are the best of friends," says Pete. I can hear him adding "like Frankie Lee and Judas Priest," a reference to a Bob Dylan song. LeBlanc has this funny quirk. He's a Dylan quote machine.
Jim asks Pete, "Ted's at Camp K right now! Do you want to

come join him? I'm going back there tomorrow morning. You can ride with us."

"Yeah, I'm definitely interested."

"Great! First we have to talk to Kristina."

So, Jim and Pete enter the house, go up the fancy staircase and there's Kristina in the kitchen washing and drying dishes. Jim explains the situation and Kristina gives Pete the third degree. After pacing back and forth, contemplating what to do, she finally arrives at her decision. She walks up to my buddy and holds out her hand.

"Okay, that will be $20, please."

"I don't have $20."

Without pause, Kristina says, "Then you can't go to Camp K."

Her quick response showed that she probably knew the answer ahead of time. Pete got the impression that she didn't want him there all along.

CHAPTER 60

THE LAST TEMPTATION

Camp K, the evening of the same day.

IT'S A SLUMBER PARTY! THE ASSEMBLY HALL can hardly contain the gaiety. We're little kids all crouched down on blankets on the floor before a tripod projector screen. Popcorn is being passed around in large bowls.

The projector sputters, clicks several times, and stops. Even in the ideal world, s*** happens. Some film got bunched up in the upper loop causing the whole mechanism to go haywire. No worries. The person running the machine rotates the small knob that controls the lower loop, and the problem is fixed! Everyone cheers as the lights go out and images appear on the screen. The movie trailer...

"Come to a new world of music, a new world of adventure, and a new world of love!
Come to Shangri La!
At Last—A Picture for Everyone!
The ROMANCE of Lost Horizon *is touched with a magic all its own!*
The EXCITEMENT of Lost Horizon *grips you from beginning to end!*
The ADVENTURE of Lost Horizon *is as spellbinding as it is unique!*

The STARS of Lost Horizon *give the spectacular performances of their careers!*
The BEAUTY of Lost Horizon *is the wonder of faraway Shangri-la!*
The MUSIC of Lost Horizon *will make your heart sing!"*

I've seen this movie before on TV. I remember it quite vividly in fact. It's a cut above the rest but not in a good way. The first half hour is actually quite engaging. The world is on the brink of World War III; a group of refugees board a small plane to flee the escalating chaos; they crash land in one of the most far-flung places on Earth: the Himalayan Mountains. The weather is unbearable but strangers from out-of-nowhere bring the plane-crash survivors to safety at nearby Shangri-la, the "Valley of the Blue Moon." It's an earthly paradise. The weather there is just right, sunny and mild all the time (due to an unusual climate phenomenon caused by the mountains); the people there are always happy, healthy, and friendly. They age very slowly and live hundreds of years. (The typical hundred-year-old person looks to be about thirty.) When they start to sing and dance to Burt Bacharach songs, I begin to cringe, yawn, and daydream. Thoughts of my imminent escape from Camp K distract me as well as Piper next to me, her thigh and my knee touching.

I have mixed emotions about leaving tonight. The most potent argument for staying is the Family has the corner on truth. They have the fullest understanding of the meaning of life. What is life's meaning according to the Family? It's *family*. You must cherish it. You must be responsible for it. You must sacrifice yourself to serve, preserve, and protect it. Family first! Doing your own thing is at the very bottom of the priority list.

But *which* family do I choose? My imperfect blood family in Detroit—or the perfect family in Camp K?

❧ ❧ ❧

THOUGH IT'S WIDELY CONSIDERED ONE OF THE WORST movies ever made, *Lost Horizon* (the 1973 version) serves the Family's purposes well. It has a powerful message. Shangri-La (the perfect place where everyone is happy) is Camp K (another perfect place where everyone is happy). Who do you want to be: Richard

Conway, the main character in the movie who wants to stay in Shangri-La—or George, his foolhardy brother, who wants to leave? Richard is a man of the world, a diplomat, and a brilliant guy. He finds Shangri-La incredibly alluring and feels he's meant to be there. Tired of the rat race, he's glad he's found this utopian oasis, however strange it seems. Besides, there's a golden opportunity staring him in the face: The 300-year-old Lama (the supreme leader) who is about to die needs a successor. Richard is qualified to fill the position! He would not only rule Shangri-La; he would set up the new world order after "evil destroys itself" in the outside world.

As the Lama recognized Richard's extraordinary gifts and talents, Kristina Morrison saw something in me that first night in San Francisco. The Last Temptation was to remain with the group so I can eventually become the big cheese who orders people around.

George, on the other hand, sees Shangri-La as a prison. He never felt at home there. He senses evil within its alpine walls. Having been brought there against his will (along with the others), he feels violated. He tells their polite host Chang, "We wish to get back to civilization as soon as possible" to which Chang replies, "Are you so sure you are away from it?"

George and a reluctant Richard eventually leave Shangri-La through the same cave they had entered through weeks before. They once again face subzero temperatures and blizzard conditions. Not long after their departure, George's "twenty-year-old" girlfriend Maria reverts to her actual age, *eighty-something* and dies. Grief-stricken George runs off half-cocked and accidentally kills himself by falling off a cliff.

Was George a fool for leaving? The Family would say so. The risk was too great. He was bound to fail. Am I, Ted Granger, about to make the same disastrous mistake? Once I leave the safe haven of Camp K, will terrible things befall me?!

ᴄ ᴄ ᴄ

MOVIE NIGHT IS OVER. THE CROWD DISBURSES. Earlier, I had volunteered to stay up late for kitchen duty. The assigned task is washing dishes. When I'm done, practically everyone's in bed. Most of them are asleep. I go to the restroom to wash up and return to my cabin where I lie awake in my sleeping bag until 2 a.m.

CHAPTER 61

HARRY AND MARGE

Along State Highway 128.

A T ABOUT 2:30 A.M, AN ORANGE '74 AMC Gremlin pulls over to the side of the road and stops. *The moment of truth has arrived!* As I approach the vehicle, my stomach begins to turn. Will Camp K interventionists suddenly jump out and try to talk some nonsense into me? Or will I encounter some mutant lifeform(s) from the outside world?

Who's in there? I momentarily get my answer: The driver's door opens, activating the dome light switch. I let out a protracted sigh: *Wwwwwwwwwwhew!* I wipe the sweat from my brow with the cusp of my elbow as I observe a middle-aged, Caucasian male. He comes out of the Gremlin and steps into the red glow of his tail-lights. He winces and shakes his head at my grody appearance and kindly picks up my backpack and hurls it into his trunk and slams it shut. I walk over to the car where I behold a middle-aged, white female sitting in the front passenger seat. I say hello and climb into the back seat.

The driver mumbles something like "What in the hell are you doing out here at this time of night?" The woman expresses the same sentiment. When he starts driving again, I learn Harry and Marge are returning home from a watering hole in Healdsburg. They weren't exactly drunk but I can smell booze on their breath. As I proceed to tell them about my swashbuckling, ninja-like escape from the Moonies, the couple seem to forget I'm even there. I apparently caught them in the middle of something:

"Harry, I can't believe you think it's no big deal!"

"Look, honey, I only found out about the business trip a week ago. It came up at the last minute."

"WORK, WORK, WORK! It is always about WORK. Did you ever think about discussing it with ME first? Did you ever consider that there are MORE IMPORTANT things in life like OUR FAMILY—OR OUR MARRIAGE!"

"Did it ever occur to you, Marge, that I'm doing this for the US?! Look, I—er, we—need that promotion! Do you know what galls me? You never show any appreciation for the sacrifices I make!"

"Oh, come on, Harry, quit the martyr stuff, you know perfectly well that the *real* reason you canceled our family trip is you *hate* my mother!"

"Who said *anything* about that bitch?! You're not listening to me! You never do!"

While Harry and Marge are at each other's throats, the weirdest sensation comes over me. I can't fathom it. I'm sitting in the back seat of an AMC Gremlin, loving every minute of watching World War III commence. It's music to my ears!

Ahhhhhh, civilization!

CHAPTER 62

HOME AT LAST

Detroit, the afternoon of August 22, 1979 (2 days later).

WHILE IT TOOK TWO WHOLE MONTHS to get from Detroit to the West Coast, the ride back took only forty-eight hours. My worrying about my parents' worrying fueled my desire to get home at warp speed. Unlike the meandering path I took going West, my eastward course was practically a straight shot. Starting a half-a-mile down the road from Camp K, I hitchhiked through California until I got to Reno, Nevada. From Reno, I took the Greyhound bus the rest of the way back to the Motor City.

Leaving Camp K so abruptly was a shock to my system. It would be acutely felt for weeks, even months. I was like a strung-out heroin addict, needing a shot of love. I was a lot more self-disciplined than I was before which is not a bad thing of course. And I finally grasped the concept of responsibility. On the downside, I was an OCD basket case. The Family pounded into my brain that everything had to be perfect, I mean *absolutely* perfect (as in flawless) in every detail. This is in keeping with their emphasis on a literal interpretation of Matthew 5:48: "Be ye perfect as (God) is perfect."

This is obviously problematic in an imperfect world such as ours where nobody's perfect. The Family instilled in me the idea that I must participate in an effort (a "movement," as they say) to *perfect everyone on the planet*, in addition to perfecting myself! For a careless, lazy, foolhardy teenager—who only a month ago despised the word "responsibility"—that's a tall order.

Before the cult, I had reasoned that sin doesn't exist. After the cult: I'm hyper-conscious of my sins, i.e., falling short of the Family's extremely high standards. Guilt and shame weighed on me like I am wearing deep-sea diving gear. There were times I felt like jumping off a cliff. Before the cult, I'm determined to "explore my sexuality" in San Francisco. After the cult: I'm Sayyid Qutb at the church dance. This transformation is nowhere more plain than in grungy Reno where I have to wait around for the bus. The very sight of strip-club billboards and porn racks in the corner of my eye make me want to jump out of my skin.

From Reno, the bus line took me east down Interstate 80 until we got past Gary, Indiana, where we turn onto I-94 into Michigan. I finally make it to my destination, Downtown Detroit, sometime in the afternoon. There, I slip into a deep funk over how rundown our city has become with its ugly, neglected buildings scarred with graffiti. Then there are the poverty-stricken inhabitants. I'm gripped by the overwhelming burden of saving Detroit. Now, without the Family in my life, the task seems to be too much to bear.

From the Greyhound station, I take a local charter bus to the corner of Plymouth Road and Grandville Street. I made it to my neighborhood Cody Rouge! I'm glad to see Sicily's Pizzeria and our local gas station. I go into Sicily's and order a large pizza. From Grandville, I walk down Plymouth to Piedmont, one street over, *my* street. There's an underlying depression on seeing the urban blight starting to creep in even there. I turn right and stride south one block to Elmira Street, where my house is, at the corner of Piedmont and Elmira.

Wearing my tattered army-surplus jacket, I'm hunched over under the heavy load of my stuffed aluminum-framed backpack. I'm looking disheveled, weary from the 2,400-mile trip, malnourished, pining for the pizza I am carrying. With a shambling gait, I knock on the side door. I behold my mother peering through the two panes of glass. Her face goes from looking haggard to astonished to ecstatic in a split second. She explodes like a supernova and opens the door. "TTTTTTTTTTTTTTTEEEEEEEEEEEEEEEEDDDDDDD DDDDDDDDD! OH MY GOD. OH MY GOD. OH MY GOD. IT'S A MIRACLE. IT'S A MIRACLE. PRAISE THE LORD. PRAISE THE LORD. THANK YOU, JESUS. THANK YOU, JESUS." I'm bombarded with hugs and kisses. I proceed to enter the kitchen where I find my dad, Bart, and Randal standing with their jaws on the floor. Utterly confounded by my presence, they bask in the joy of the moment. The prodigal son has returned! Shout it from the mountaintops! Prepare the fatted calf! (Well, we'll settle for a pepperoni pizza.) I'm informed that I was in the Moonies (which I can't even comprehend. It would take *days* before I come around to accepting it.) My eyes look weird. I had arrived not a moment too soon: Bart and Randal were *minutes* away from leaving for the airport to fly to California to rescue me from the cult! Randal and I shake hands, embrace, and study each other's faces for a few seconds.

"I guess we have a lot to talk about, man," Randal says.

No truer words have ever been spoken! In the weeks and months ahead, there would be many talks. In one of them, we decide to go on another hitchhiking trip.

After an intense homecoming celebration, I finally go to my room and collapse into bed. Totally sapped, I must've slept twelve hours. With *Lost Horizon* still heavily on my brain, I dream I'm Richard Conway regaining consciousness in a hospital bed. I'm somewhere in mainland China, a town at the foot of the Himalayas. Nuns are checking my vital signs as I keep repeating nonsensical things regarding "home." An ELO song starts playing in my dream. Its lyrics go, "My Shangri-la has gone away / Faded like the Beatles on Hey Jude."

The song ends with a lengthy fade like "Hey Jude" with vocalist Jeff Lynne and a female opera singer taking turns echoing the recurrent line: "I wwwiiiillllllll return to Shangri-laaa!"

EPILOGUE

"I've seen the future, brother / It is murder "

— Leonard Cohen (1992)

IT'S SEPTEMBER OF '79. I'M RUBBING my eyes like Rip Van Winkle waking from a long dream. The outside world feels different from how it was before I joined the Moonies. It's as if a decade had gone by. There's no Disco on the radio. A peculiar new song called "My Sharona" has topped the Billboard charts. Another one, "Rappers Delight," by the Sugarhill Gang is unlike any music I have heard before. Is it even music?

The seismic shift is nothing compared to what I noticed in Dearborn upon my return. I'm sitting at my usual spot in the UM-D cafeteria and here comes Zainab. The sight of her makes me choke on my Hardee's cheeseburger. My classmate who typically wears tight blue jeans and a flashy, pointy-collared, polyester blouse—is now sporting a black chador!

"Hi Ted, what d'ya think?" she asks and then does the three-sixty twirl.

There's a long pause. I couldn't believe my eyes. Finally. . .

"Zainab, what the heck?

Obviously tickled by my reaction, she says, "I decided to get more serious about my faith." She then tells her story of her recent reconversion to Islam. Her joy is mixed with sorrow as she expresses disappointment over her parents not understanding her decision. Her mom shrugged it off, saying to her dad, "Oh Zainab is just going through a phase." Her dad said, "She's taken a giant leap backward in time!"

"On the contrary, Ted, I feel totally liberated now. The trouble with Western culture is women are treated as sex objects. Now that I'm wearing my chador, men see me as a person, not just a body."

Zainab was not alone. There was now a good number of other "born-again Muslims" around. This was the beginning of a new trend, one that has lasted even to this day. The Iranian Revolution inspired many Muslims in our area to don traditional clothes. According to Zainab, Sheikh Mohammad Jawad Chirri (pronounced SHUR-ee), the leading spokesman of the local Muslim community, traded his customary suit-and-tie for a clerical robe and turban and grew a beard. Today, opinions about Iran may have changed, but the Muslim faith remains strong in Dearborn.

Less than a month after my Moonie experience, I ran across an article in *The Detroit News*: The crazy rumors about Bob Dylan "getting saved" turned out to be true! They were confirmed with the release of his new album *Slow Train Coming* which I'd pick up at School Kids Records in Ann Arbor. As I played it for the first time in Randal's dorm room, I was impressed by its slick production and cool guitar work by Mark Knopfler of Dire Straits. Of course, the record would be played non-stop once I returned home. The impression it made was phenomenal. The album's single, "Gotta Serve Somebody," still gives me chills. It's a direct affront to *Demian*'s admonition to serve both God and the devil at the same time. "Gotta Serve Somebody" says you must pick one or the other.

Dylan had made several references to Jesus throughout his career. The one that stands out to me is the line in the song "Idiot Wind" about the "lone soldier on the cross" who mysteriously wins "the war—after losin' every battle." Though not a Catholic, Bob now embraced a brand of Christianity which emphasizes regular Bible study, the end times, and spiritual rebirth. It had a vibrant and hip vibe like that of the Jesus freaks (hippies who became born-again Christians). It appealed to me because it promised to lift me out of my despondency. Following the lead of Dylan whom I'd considered the coolest man on the planet, I decided to experience this religion for myself. So, on a Wednesday evening, I went to a small church called the Lord's House in Livonia and responded to the altar call. It would have a lasting effect. A year later (after that hitchhiking trip to California with Randal), I announced to the world I was born-again.

What ever happened to Reverend Moon and Bhagwan Rajneesh? What are Pete and Randal now? Most important of all, where is Ted Granger?

Reverend Moon

THE MOONIES ARE STILL AROUND today, but their numbers have drastically dwindled. Even before Sun Myung Moon died in 2012 at age 92, his surviving wife and children have been fighting over who gets what of his vast business/political/religious empire.

Besides failing to rule the world, the True Father turned out to be a crummy dad. He was a workaholic, always too busy to spend time with his kids. His wife Hak Ja Han, the True Mother, was just as bad or worse: She was a *shop*aholic, an absentee mom. Raised by yes-men at a luxurious estate in Tarrytown, New York and given everything money could buy, the thirteen Moon children ended up spoiled brats and perhaps even cursed. The first-born son Steve was a womanizer and drug addict who died relatively young. One son died in a car crash, another committed suicide.

Then there's Sean Moon, the True Parents' youngest son. The True Mother controls the original core church, but Sean—who considers himself his father's rightful successor—thinks he's entitled to everything. She allegedly told him she is literally "God" and had Sean excommunicated. He in turn called her the "Whore of Babylon" and used his pastoral authority to unmarry his parents and remarry his father in the spirit world with another woman who is still alive.

Before his congregation in Newfoundland, Pennsylvania, Sean parades around in kingly attire. Besides a royal robe, he wears a

EPILOGUE 229

crown made out of *bullets*. He had discovered in the Book of Revelation that Christ will rule his earthly kingdom "with a rod of iron" which means the AR-15 semiautomatic. He and his followers are well-armed to fend off the forces of globalism. Members of his Church frequently have their rifles blessed in church, scaring local residents. Congregants also wear crowns like their leader, except theirs look like they're made out of tinfoil.

Back to the Reverend Sun Myung Moon himself. He was found guilty of tax evasion in 1981 and served thirteen months in prison. It was later found out that Moon, the "perfect man," had committed adultery, the worst possible sin according to his Divine Principle.

Bhagwan Rajneesh

BEFORE I JOINED THE MOONIES, I seemed destined to join the Rajneeshees. What would my life be like if I had chosen to become one of them? In 1979, the Nietzsche-inspired cult leader was still living in India and his utopia in central Oregon, Rajneeshpuram, didn't exist until 1981. He would become world famous for being the sex guru who owned 93 Rolls Royces. He was a media sensation. Dogged by scandal, the shameless "holy man" was kicked out of the United States in 1985. After that, no other country would have him. His plane couldn't land anywhere until his native India reluctantly took him back. In poor health, he stayed there until his death five years later. Unlike Moon, Rajneesh (who renamed himself "Osho" in his dying days) remains popular today.

Bhagwan and his group leaders used psychotherapy combined with ancient Eastern meditation to create the "new man." Minds were expanded with continuous chanting, yoga-style breathing exercises, Rolfing, primal screaming, Sufi dancing, psychedelic drug trips, staring into lights for extended periods of time, and so on.

Add group sex to the mix. No, raise it up another notch: *violent* group sex. Participants scream at each other, tear each other's hair out and literally beat each other to a bloody pulp! Like in *Brave New World*, everything ends up in an orgy. Violence and sex go hand and hand. Sex is performed for mere physical pleasure and no other reason, certainly not for love. What about for procreation? Well, words like "procreation" are meaningless, along with "mother," and "home." They're obsolete terms banned from the English language just like in Huxley's dystopia. Regarding family (Oh sorry, "family"), abolish it! Get an abortion. Practice contraception. Better yet, get sterilized.

Netflix's six-part documentary *Wild Wild Country* (2018) focuses on Rajneesh's utopian city in the Oregon desert. Lots of juicy stuff here: voting and immigration fraud, wiretapping, arson, kidnapping homeless people and drugging them, attempted murder of three individuals including the U.S. District Attorney, 750 people being poisoned with salmonella chopped into salads at local restaurants and grocers, the largest bioterrorist attack on American soil up to that time.

New Republic columnist Win McCormack claims the Netflix miniseries *still* "doesn't capture... the evil of the Rajneesh cult." He cites what was left out: strong evidence of battery and sexual assault committed amongst members; deadly substances being stockpiled. (For what purpose? Maybe to fulfill Rajneesh's prophecy about the coming global holocaust?) And then there's the mistreatment of children. Oh, yeah, the *children*. I forgot about them.

Pete LeBlanc

PETE HITCHHIKED ABOUT 4,000 MILES after we split up in Boulder. In 1980, he traveled 8,000 miles across the U.S. and Canada. Then there was the 7,000-mile motorcycle trip in 1981 across the U.S. and Canada. After getting the wanderlust out of his system, he ended up settling down in Colorado and eventually Hawaii. "I am still a nonconformist," he said in 2022. "I'm the sort that refuses to try to adopt the thinking of others who consider themselves to be nonconformists but are no different than anyone else. My Bible education through the organization known as Jehovah's Witnesses has taught me to think with my own mind, but to educate myself regarding the mind of Christ."

When asked, "How does it feel to be rejected by the Moonies?" he responded, "Well, being broke can have its perks."

Randal Stark

"HOW ARE YOU DOING these days, Randal?"

"I'm drifting aimlessly, Ted"

"Very funny."

"I'm only partially kidding. I wish my younger self had had passion and direction and wasn't so falsely self-assured. But I'm also self-aware and understand that that was never in my psychological makeup."

"What happened to you?"

"Well, reality. At some point during my first semester at U of M, I realized *I'm not that smart.*"

"Oh, come on, Randal. You're effing brilliant. Give me a break."

"No really, Ted. Back in '78 when I arrived in Ann Arbor I had really high expectations for myself. I assumed I was smarter than everyone else. It didn't take me long to realize that's not true. For all our scheming and philosophizing, we never came up with an original thought. We unwittingly repackaged other peoples' ideas and sold them as our own."

"So what would be your final testament to the world?"

"I've got to give that some thought. But I'm curious, where do you think I am now?"

"All things considered, you are content, blessed with a wonderful family, and living what used to be called the American Dream. You've had a zig-zag career but have always managed to land on your feet. You are dumbstruck by how fortunate you are."

"All true, but I also must live out the rest of my life. I find it hard to stay true to the faith, meet new people, and try new things. It's stultifying."

"You far surpassed me in terms of ambition. You hitchhiked around Europe and lived in France for a while."

"Vanity of vanities; all is vanity!"

"Are you Ecclesiastes?"

"I guess I could be Ecclesiastes, but I really don't think I'm that cerebral."

"What about God's grace?"

"Grace sustains, but it has to be replenished or it dries up. The marathon run is exhausting. I'm somewhat haunted by Rev. 3:15-16."

"But check out verse 17. You realize you're 'wretched, pitiful, poor, blind, and naked.' That's your redeeming trait."

"That's why I'm only *somewhat* haunted by it. You asked for a final testament. I don't know how final it can be. It changes. Currently, I think I would have to go with this quote from Marion G. Harmon: 'Everything happens for a reason. Sometimes the reason is you're stupid and make bad decisions.'"

Ted Granger

COVID ALMOST KILLED ME but I'm okay now. When I thought I reached the end, I was actually glad to leave this messed-up world behind. But the fact people still needed me down here saddened me. I'm talking about my family, my *blood* family, my wife and kids.

Since my Moonie experience, I realized I can't solve all the world's problems. The perfect world doesn't exist on this side of the Jordan. My modus operandi is to stand firm and hold fast to the traditions passed on to me and to impart the faith to the next generation. I'm a link in a human chain. Like my parents before me, I storm heaven with prayers for my kids. They need all the help they can get. This world is effing dangerous!

Now that mankind has the technology, is Utopia just around the corner?

Never say never but judging by the present situation, it will take a million years. Our present dystopia is a combination of Huxley and Orwell. We're also living out the story of the Tower of Babel. With all our advanced technology, we're trying to build our way to heaven, but we humans have ended up more scattered and confused. What's more, our so-called smart people are dim-witted, conniving nimrods. Even if our rulers were all-knowing philosopher-kings, only a handful of people would listen to them. Why? Human nature. People don't like being told what to do.

After all is said and done, I stand by the words of an old friend: "I have God and I have family—what else do I need?"

THE END

AFTERWORD A

THE VANISHED IMAM

THE TRAVELER NEVER REALLY LEAVES HOME! I tote the Motor City around with me everywhere I go like my pocketknife. In the same way, my grandparents brought Poland to Detroit and the Arabs brought the Middle East. With the help of Zainab, I gradually got to understand the different groups.

Of course not all Arabs are Muslims. A good number are Christians and none-of-the-above. Aside from the Shia and Sunni split, UM-D professor Sally Howell identifies a huge chasm between Muslims who arrived in America in the 1970s (which I'll call the '70s-wavers) and those who had been living in Detroit since about 1900. She makes her case in her book *Old Islam in Detroit*, a recommended read.

The Lebanese '70s-wavers had been hugely affected by the Lebanese Civil War and the Palestinian-Israeli conflict. Most of them are Shia. Their harrowing accounts of war-related violence are too horrifying to contemplate. Their ability to leave their tragic past behind and start a new life here in the States is a testament to human resilience.

Many of the Shia '70s-wavers originated from southern Lebanon, the hilly region north of Galilee which features cities like Bint Jbeil, Tyre, and Nabatiyeh. It's literally a nation within a nation. Jabal Amil, as it's been called, has its own national identity and cultural heritage which goes back centuries. The widespread practice of the Shia religion distinguishes it from the rest of Lebanon. That being the case, they have a strong connection with Iran and Iraq where most of their holy sites are.

Jabal Amil was once considered the backwater of Lebanon. Desperately poor and illiterate, the people living there ranked on the very bottom of the social ladder. Sadly, the ineffective and even negligent Lebanese government had deprived them of funds needed for hospitals, schools, and even clean drinking water. The main reason they were discriminated against was probably their religion. While the Lebanese constitution supposedly recognizes Christians and Muslims as equal partners, the Shia Muslims were treated like second-class citizens.

The Shia homeland—located north of Lebanon's southern border—isn't very safe. Starting in 1968, it became a war zone for two bitter adversaries: the Palestinian militia and the Israeli army. The people of Jabal Amil initially stayed out of the conflict, wanting to be left alone. They didn't appreciate the rag-tag Palestinian guerrillas trespassing on their land and setting up military bases which all but guaranteed Israeli counterattacks. But they especially didn't like the Israelis' heavy-handed approach to weeding out the guerrillas. So, the Shias of Jabal Amil—tired of being sitting ducks—reluctantly joined the Palestinian resistance.

ENTER MUSA AL-SADR (BORN 1928), the Shia leader who served in Lebanon from 1960 to 1978. True, al-Sadr had formed a movement in '75 to fight the Israelis. True, he used fiery rhetoric to galvanize young men to take up arms. However, the more I learned about him, the more I saw the opposite of a man of war. In fact, he reminds me of a Catholic saint like, say, St. Vincent de Paul who founded orphanages and other charitable organizations. Or St. Martin de Porres, the patron saint of social justice (how the Catholic Church defines the term.) Or St. John Paul II the philosopher-pope who championed (1) the dignity of the human person, (2) individual rights and freedom, and (3) the importance of interfaith dialogue.

His full name is *Sayyid* Musa al-Sadr. "Sayyid" literally means "lord" or "master," but it also denotes being blood-related to the Prophet Muhammad. Another thing about names: Sometime in the 1970s, his admirers started to call him *Imam* Musa al-Sadr. Nowadays, the term "imam" has lost its import due to inflation if you will. Now it's applied to any religious leader. In the old days, calling a man "Imam" raised eyebrows. Critics feared it elevates the designee to the level of the venerable Twelve Imams or even the anticipated Mahdi, which is considered heresy. Interestingly, the only other public figure given the title in the '70's was Ayatollah Khomeini. And people naturally drew the connection between al-Sadr's mysterious disappearance and that of the Twelfth Imam.

ᒼ ᒼ ᒼ

WHO WAS THIS RARE SPIRITUAL LEADER? A man of many gifts and talents. A brilliant scholar from one of the most celebrated clerical families in Iran, he earned degrees in Law and other disciplines at major religious and secular universities. He had extraordinary people skills. Those of all walks of life, from floor sweepers to heads of State, found Sayyid Musa to be warm, gracious, and amiable. He was strikingly handsome, and people looked up to him in more ways than one: He was six feet and six inches tall. With these and other traits, he could have enjoyed a safe and prosperous life among the very privileged. Instead, he chose to live modestly amongst the so-called "wretched of the earth," tirelessly pleading their case before Lebanon's parliament and wealthy elite. Al-Sadr, a human dynamo in many ways, chose to identify himself with the powerless, to live dangerously speaking truth to power.

His fellow countrymen, many of them Christians, often said Sayyid Musa reminded them of Jesus Christ. Why? Obviously, his commitment to the poor, but there are other reasons. First off, unlike the other religious leaders, he wasn't boring. Folks reacted to the uncommon things he said and did with utter amazement. For example, he shocked people's smug sensibilities when he violated their deeply ingrained taboos. Fellow clerics weren't thrilled. In the same way the Jews shunned the "unclean" Samaritans in Jesus' time, the Shias scrupulously avoided Christians in fear of *najas*, moral contamination. On top of that, strict dietary laws prevented them from eating anything touched by a Christian. In the port city of Tyre where he served, Sayyid Musa learned of a Christian ice cream vendor who couldn't get by because no one in the Shia-dominated town would buy anything from him. After Friday services at the mosque, Sayyid Musa casually tells his flock that he wants to take a walk. His listeners look at each other puzzled, but they accept his invitation to join him. At one point during the outing, jaws drop and heads shake: The revered sayyid orders a cold treat from you-know-who!

Secondly, like Jesus, Musa al-Sadr has an "aura of mystery" about him that fascinates and befuddles. He defies categorization. He is firmly rooted in the traditions of the fathers and yet he proposes a totally new way of thinking (in line with the Islamic concept of *Ijtihad*). So, is he conservative or progressive? Sayyid Musa's tendency to "break the rules" upsets the religious establishment, yet he accepts and works within the framework of the Lebanese political establishment, rejecting the zealotry of the communists and the Palestinian guerrillas. So, is he a radical or a moderate?

Thirdly, like Jesus, al-Sadr is considered dangerous. He draws crowds with his magnetic personality, knack for public speaking, and dramatic flair. He's extremely popular, so much so that he infuriates the elites because he threatens their agenda and their influence over the people. Perhaps his most audacious moves involve getting too friendly with the Christian leaders (who are disliked for political as well as religious reasons). He delivers sermons in *churches*. At least one sermon points out the parallels between Imam Hussein's martyrdom and Christ's crucifixion. He even dares to set foot in the Vatican to attend the induction of Pope Paul VI!

☾ ☾ ☾

WHAT HAPPENED TO MUSA AL-SADR? He goes to Tripoli to meet with Libyan president Muammar Gaddafi. No one knows precisely what they had planned to discuss, most likely it concerned the Palestine/Israel situation. Possibly but least likely, it had something to do with Iran, the powder keg about to explode. Gaddafi, a colorful personality to say the least, wasn't exactly al-Sadr's kind of guy, but both men were key players in the Middle East.

The Imam with his two companions were last seen in public leaving a Tripoli hotel on Friday, August 31, 1978, never to be heard from again.

AFTERWORD B

THE POLISH POPE

IT WAS SATURDAY, JUNE 2, 1979, only two and a half weeks before leaving on my hitchhiking trip to California with Pete LeBlanc. My mother and I sit glued to the TV watching live coverage of Pope John Paul II's pilgrimage in Poland. Mesmerized, even I knew it's a game-changer.

For my entire life, I had heard stories of how my relatives were oppressed by the Germans and the Russians in their native land. If the Nazis were the worst, the communists came in close second. After Stalin died, Russia's iron grip loosened a little but not by much. If you uttered the slightest criticism of the government, you risked being harassed by the secret police. If you didn't take heed, *you* could end up disappearing.

Karol Wojtyła, once he became pope, tricked the communists into having him return to Poland for a nine-day public tour. (The regime had worried that the "rock star" might stir up an insurrection.) To make matters worse, the date chosen to start the visit—the eve of Pentecost—had powerful symbolic significance.

As every informed Christian knows, Pentecost is "the birthday of the Church," the celebration of the moment in history when the Holy Spirit came down. Ten days after Jesus ascended into heaven, his disciples stayed in a house in Jerusalem where they heard a violent wind and saw "tongues of fire" appear over each other's heads. Everyone there experienced a strange welling up inside—something like a driving force or energy. It transformed each of them from being timid and afraid—to be bold and confident. It prompted the disciples to go out into the streets to preach the gospel at risk of life and limb. In doing so, they miraculously spoke in languages they hadn't learned before.

Two thousand years later, John Paul II does Mass in Warsaw's Victory Square. A crowd of a million-plus have shown up, not to mention half the world watching the event via satellite. During his homily, the cameras zero in on the faces of the people. Many are teary-eyed and, to my surprise, I turn to see my usually stoic mother bawling. Here are the pope's words:

"And I cry—I who am a Son of the land of Poland and who am also Pope John Paul II—I cry from all the depths of this Millennium; I cry on the vigil of Pentecost:

Let your Spirit descend!
Let your Spirit descend!
and renew the face of the earth,
the face of this land!"

WHOOOSH! Practically everyone grasped the double message when he said "Pentecost." It was the tipping point, activist Lech Wałęsa would later testify. Everyone from able-bodied young laborers to little old ladies with babushkas took the pontiff's words as marching orders. From that moment forward, the Polish people took charge of their own destiny. They would become a formidable spiritual army. After getting their souls right with God, millions bravely resisted the corrupt communist regime—and, eventually, the Soviet Union, one of the world's two superpowers (the other of course being the U.S.). The imminent uprising, largely non-violent, was a real-life eucatastrophe.

"How many divisions (of soldiers) does the Pope have?" Soviet dictator Josef Stalin once wisecracked. However, a decade after John Paul made that speech, Stalin's successor Mikhail Gorbachev would receive the answer. Gorbachev, the last Soviet leader, admitted that the pope's visit to Poland in '79 had marked the beginning of the end of his career.

Musa al-Sadr and Pope John II have strikingly similar philosophies. Both emphasize (1) the dignity of the human person, (2) individual rights and freedom, and (3) the importance of interfaith dialogue.

Both men reminded their people—the Polish and Lebanese Shia respectively—of their intrinsic worth and gave them hope they would rise above their oppressors. And the people took their words to heart and made things happen.

When al-Sadr said, "Our name is not *Matawlah* (a derogatory term comparable to the N-word); our name is 'men of refusal,'" he reminded the Shia of Lebanon of their proud cultural heritage. At the same time, he imparted a new identity by renaming them. In a similar way, John Paul gave his fellow Poles a sense of pride being who they are. It was like he was saying our name is not *Polack*.

ENDNOTES

Prologue / Escape from Paradise

6, **...the first religion to be called a "doomsday cult:"** John Lofland. *Doomsday Cult: A Study of Conversion, Proselytization, and Maintenance of Faith.* (Hoboken, NJ: Prentice-Hall, 1966).

6, **Moonies...most sophisticated (of) the cults:** Flo Conway and Jim Siegelman. *Snapping: America's Epidemic of Sudden Personality Change.* (New York: Dell Publishing, 1979), 36.

Chapter 1 / Lucky Break

12, **(Ford) Pinto... on sale on September 11:** "It Happened on September 11th: Ford Pinto Hits the Market." Article. *This Day in Automotive History.* https://automotivehistory.org/first-ford-pinto/. Accessed 13 Sept. 2022.

13, **"Danger is how you find God:"** Bhagwan Shree Rajneesh. *Ecstasy: The Forgotten Language.* Pdf file. 1976. https://oshofragrance.org/db/books/files/Ecstasy%20-%20The%20Forgotten%20Language.pdf. 17. Accessed 4 Apr. 2023.

13, **"Disastermania:"** "Behavior: The Deluge of Disastermania." Article. *Time.* https://content.time.com/time/subscriber/article/0,33009,916649,00.html. March 7, 1979. Accessed 4 Apr. 2023.

13-14, **The story of Guadalupe:** Editors of *Encyclopaedia Britannica.* "Our Lady of Guadalupe, Patron Saint of Mexico." September 12, 2022. https://www.britannica.com/topic/Our-Lady-of-Guadalupe-patron-saint-of-Mexico. Accessed 14 Sept. 2022.

Chapter 3 / Greeley, CO

19, **The Promise of the Prairie (statue in Greeley, CO):** *Waymarking.com.* December 6. 2009. https://www.waymarking.com/waymarks/wm7V9T_Promise_of_the_Prairie_Greeley_CO. Accessed 14 Sept 2022.

20, **Greeley...striving to be a utopia:** David Boyd, *A History: Greeley and The Union Colony OF Colorado.* (Greeley, CO: The Greeley Tribune Press, 1890). A remarkably detailed (and readable) first-hand account of the ambitious endeavor.

"The Origins of Union Colony and Utopian Socialism." Article. *Greeley Tribune.* May 13, 2020. https://www.greeleytribune.com/2014/09/18/historical-hindsights-the-origins-of-union-colony-and-utopian-socialism/. Accessed 15 Sept. 2022.

20-21, **Sayyid Qutb (1906-1966):** founder of Islamism. a religio-political ideology. A leading member of the Muslim Brotherhood, Qutb wrote *Milestones* (Ma'alim fi al-Tariq), the manifesto of the radical Islamist movement.

21, **Americans... primitives "living in jungles and caves:"** Sayyid Qutb. "The America I Have Seen." Pdf file. https://www.cia.gov/library/abbottabad-compound/3F/3F56ACA473044436B4C1740F65D5C3B6_Sayyid_Qutb_-_The_America_I_Have_Seen.pdf. (Kash ul Shububat Pub, 1951). 7. Accessed 5 Apr. 2023.

21, **Desperate situation in 1979:** Philip K. Verleger, Jr. "The U.S. Petroleum Crisis of 1979." The Brookings Institution. Pdf file. https://www.brookings.edu/

wp-content/uploads/1979/06/1979b_bpea_verleger_okun_lawrence_sims_hall_nordhaus.pdf. Accessed 15 Sept. 2022.

24, **Poverty Gulch:** Dan Grajek. *The Last Hobo.* (Dearborn, MI: Round Barn Media, 2016), 19.

Chapter 4 / How Randal and I Got the Idea to Hop a Train

25-26, **The hobo...very symbol of freedom:** Colin Beesley. "The American Hobo." *northbankfred.com.* https://www.northbankfred.com/colin1.html. Accessed 15 Sept. 2022.

Chapter 5 / The Miracle

30, **Holden Caulfield:** Emily Temple. "Holden Caulfield, Egotistical Whiner or Melancholy Boy Genius?" *Literary Hub.* July 2, 2018. https://lithub.com/holden-caulfield-egotistical-whiner-or-melancholy-boy-genius/. Accessed 15 Sept. 2022.

30-31, **Demian:** Hermann Hesse. *Demian.* (New York: Bantam, 1970).

31, **Übermensch:** Jack Maden. "Übermensch Explained: The Meaning of Nietzsche's 'Superman.'" *Philosophy Break.* June 2022. https://philosophybreak.com/articles/ubermensch-explained-the-meaning-of-nietzsches-superman/. Accessed 15 Sept. 2022.

32, **St. Paul, Minnesota ...Crow ...Black Hills:** Grajek, 98, 123, 171.

32-34, **The miracle:** Id., 217-267.

Chapter 7 / Conversation with Rosie

40, **"A controlled man is a dead man:"** Bhagwan Shree Rajneesh. *Ecstasy: The Forgotten Language.* Pdf file, 1976. https://oshofragrance.org/db/books/files/Ecstasy%20-%20The%20Forgotten%20Language.pdf, 16-17.

Chapter 8 / The Apron Strings Speech:

The real "Randal Stark" contributed to this chapter.

Chapter 10 / The New York Trip

54, **1977 Blackout:** James Barron. "45 Years Ago Tonight, a Blackout Struck New York City." Article. *The New York Times.* July 13, 2022. https://www.nytimes.com/2022/07/13/nyregion/new-york-city-blackout.html. Accessed 5 Oct. 2022.

Chapter 11 / John Hancock

56, *Thus Spoke Zarathustra*: Friedrich Nietzsche. *Thus Spoke Zarathustra.* (Mineola, NY: Dover Publications, 1999).

Editors of *Encyclopaedia Britannica.* "Thus Spoke Zarathustra: Treatise by Nietzsche." *Encyclopaedia Britannica.* https://www.britannica.com/topic/Thus-Spake-Zarathustra. Accessed 5 Oct. 2022.

56, **"The Bible of the future:"** Osho (Bhagwan Shree Rajneesh), *In Love with Life: Reflections on Friedrich Nietzsche's Thus Spake Zarathustra.* (Maharashtra, India: Osho Media International, 2015), 6.

57, **The Grand Experiment:** Grajek, 19.

58, **Hippie trail:** Rory Maclean. "Legacy of the Hippie Trail." Article. *The Guardian.* August 13, 2007. https://www.theguardian.com/commentisfree/2007/aug/13/legacyofthehippietrail. Accessed 11 Apr. 2023.

Chapter 12 / Commack, NY

59, **The notorious Commack Motor Inn:** "Commack, New York." *Wikipedia.* https://en.wikipedia.org/wiki/Commack,_New_York#cite_note-13. Accessed 5 Oct. 2022. Also "Commack Motor Inn" is synonym for "dirty place." https://urbanthesaurus.org/synonyms/dirty%20place. Accessed 5 Oct. 2022.

Chapter 13 / Moon Gulch

61, **Charles Fourier:** The Man Who Made Happiness. http://mumm.ninthenrichelen.ie-clopedia.org/entry/Charles_Fourier. Accessed 5 Oct. 2022.

62, **Expo 67:** https://www.parcjeandrapeau.com/en/expo-67-universal-exposition-montreal/#information. Accessed 5 Oct. 2022.

64, **Lost Horizon (book):** Hilton, James. *Lost Horizon.* Kindle Edition. (New York: Open Road Integrated Media, 2011).

Chapter 14 / Asbury Park

67, **Blue Mind:** Wallace J. Nichols. *Blue Mind: The Surprising Science That Shows How Being Near, In, On, or Under Water Can Make You Happier, Healthier, More Connected, and Better at What You Do.* (Boston: Back Bay Books, 2015).

Chapter 17 / Breakfast at Sambo's

72, **Skylab:** Andy Harris. "When Skylab Made Us All a Little Chicken Little" Article. *A Paperboy's Archive.* http://www.paperboyarchive.com/2019/07/when-skylab-made-us-all-little-chicken.html. Accessed 5 Apr. 2023.

74, **It's this Iran thing:** James Buchan. *Days of God: The Revolution in Iran and Its Consequences.* (New York: Simon & Schuster, 2013).

Christian Caryl. *Strange Rebels: 1979 and the Birth of the 21st Century.* (New York: Basic Books, 2014), 83-94, 107-116, 137-154, 289-302.

Chapter 21 / Dearborn, MI

89, **Dearborn has the highest concentration of Arab Americans in the United States:** (source information forthcoming).

89, **"The Muslim capital of the West:"** Imam Hassan Qazwani. *American Crescent: A Muslim Cleric on the Power of His Faith, the Struggle Against Prejudice, and the Future of Islam and America.* Kindle version. (Dearborn, MI: Islamic Center of America (ICA), 2013), 113. BTW, Imam Qazwani's memoir is an invaluable source because: (1) He led the ICA after Sheikh (Imam) Mohammad Jawad Chirri. (2) He offers an Iraq Shia perspective.

89-90, **The Sunni and Shia split:** Qazwani, 199-245

90, **"Cultural Muslim:"** "A religiously non-practicing or secular or irreligious individuals who still identify with Islam due to family backgrounds, personal experiences, or the social and cultural environment in which they grew up." *Wikipedia.* https://en.wikipedia.org/wiki/Cultural_Muslims#:~:text=Cultural%20Muslims%20or%20Nominal%20Muslim,in%20which%20they%20grew%20up. Accessed 10 Apr. 2023.

Chapter 22 / Vanity Fair

93, **Some would attest the (Grateful) Dead is a religion:** A fascinating first-hand account of Grateful Dead fans' fervent religiosity can be found in Fr. Donald Calloway's book *No Turning Back.* (London: Marian Press, 2010), 117-122.

94, **Hippie lore:** Ann Charters, editor. *The Portable Beat Reader.* (New York: Penguin Classics, 1992). An anthology of the Beat/hippie founders, Jack Kerouac, Allen Ginsberg, and others.

Os Guinness. *The Dust of Death.* (Westmont, IL: InterVarsity Press, 1973). A thorough philosophical examination of hippie thought and Leftist ideology in the 60's and 70's.

Tom Wolfe. *The Electric Kool-Aid Acid Test.* (London: Picador, 2008). In my opinion, this book best captures the mind of the hippies.

Chapter 23 / Go Blue!

95-97, **Philosophy 101:** Regarding Philosophy, there are far too many sources to list here. The best and most user-friendly I found are:

Will Durant. *The Story of Philosophy: The Lives and Opinions of the World's Greatest Philosophers.* (New York: Pocket Books, 1991).

Peter Kreeft. *Socrates Children: The 100 Greatest Philosophers.* Volumes I-IV. (South Bend, IN, St. Augustine's Press, 2019).

Richard Tarnas. *The Passion of the Western Mind: Understanding the Ideas that Have Shaped Our World.* (New York: Ballantine Books, 1993).

96-97, **Professor Paul Thagard:** Paul Thagard. *The Brain and the Meaning of Life.* (Princeton, NJ: Princeton University Press, 2010), 1-12.

97, **"Why don't you kill yourself?:"** Thagard, 1.

98, **Pope John Paul I:** George Weigel. *Witness to Hope: The Biography of Pope John Paul II.* (New York: HarperCollins, 1999). 246-247.

98, **Cardinals in the Vatican have reconvened to select a new pope:** Weigel, 247-256.

101, ***Brave New World*** **by Aldous Huxley:** Editors of *Encyclopaedia Britannica.* "Brave New World, Novel by Huxley." *Encyclopaedia Britannica.* https://www.britannica.com/topic/Brave-New-World. Accessed 5 Apr. 2023.

Chapter 24 / The People's Republic of Boulder

102, **Anti-nuke demonstration in the Black Hills of South Dakota:** *The Last Hobo,* 171-215.

Chapter 27 / Sister Mary Fisher

113, **The Greening of America**: Christopher A. Reich. *The Greening of America*. (New York: Bantam, 1971).

114, **Marxism 2.0**: (aka cultural Marxism, neo-Marxism, critical theory, etc.) Hicks, Stephen. *Explaining Postmodernism: Skepticism and Socialism from Rousseau to Foucault*. (Ockham's Razor, 2013).

James Lindsay. *Race Marxism: The Truth About Critical Race Theory and Praxis*. Kindle Edition. (New Discourses, 2022). Besides addressing Critical Race Theory or "Race Marxism," the book touches on the other forms of Marxism regarding gender, same-sex attraction, etc.

Dennis McCallum, general editor. *The Death of Truth*. (Bloomington, MN, Bethany House Publishers, 1996).

Chapter 28 / The Shadow of Death

116, **The Pope... a stone-throw away from (Grandma's) front porch:** Charles Sercombe. "Between the Lines ...When the Pope Came to Hamtramck." Article. *The Hamtramck Review*. September 21, 2018. http://www.thehamtramckreview.com/between-the-lines-when-the-pope-came-to-hamtramck/. Accessed 5 Apr. 2023.

117, **Our Lady of Częstochowa: "The Miraculous Icon of Our Lady of Czestochowa:"** Marian Valley (Shrine) website. http://marianvalley.org.au/miraculous-icon-our-lady-czestochowa/. Accessed 11 Apr. 2023.

117-118, **Jonestown disaster:** Daniel J. Flynn. *Cult City: Jim Jones, Harvey Milk, and 10 Days That Shook San Francisco*. (Wilmington, DE: Intercollegiate Studies Institute, 2018), 185-201.

Chapter 29 / A Sign from Above

119, **"Yazid:"** Slang term for any tyrannical person referring to Yazid ibn Mu'awiya ibn Abi Sufyan (646-683) aka Yazid I, the caliphate leader who ordered the killing of Muhammad's grandson Husayn ibn Ali, the Third Imam according to Shia Muslims. A pivotal event in their history.

120, **They're looking at the Moon to see Ayatollah Khomeini's face:** This was going on among Shias worldwide in November of '78. Caryl, 224.

120, **Khomeini is the Chosen One:** Throughout 1978 and 1979, a few Shia Muslims thought the Ayatollah was the Twelfth Imam returning to Earth to usher in the Millennium. Caryl, 223.

Dearborn's leading Muslim cleric, Sheikh Mohammad Jawad Chirri (1905-1994), apparently believed in this notion. [See Sally Howell. *Old Islam in Detroit: Rediscovering the Muslim American Past*. (Oxford, England, Oxford University Press, 2014), 259- 260.]

Chapter 31 / Christmas

124, **Lufthansa Heist in New York City:** Editors of *Encyclopaedia Britannica*. "Lufthansa Heist Theft [1978]." *Encyclopaedia Britannica*. https://www.britannica.com/event/Lufthansa-heist. Accessed 5 Apr. 2023.

Chapter 32 / Ma Prem Nando

127, **Like Zarathustra...I descend from the mountain:** In Nietzsche's *Thus Spoke Zarathustra*, the Persian prophet comes down the mountain to recruit followers. But this Zarathustra is not the historical figure from the fifth century B.C. but the mouthpiece of Nietzsche who had made it his life mission to dethrone the Christian God (and, by extension, the gods of all other religions including Allah and Science).

130, **"To be an individual is the hardest thing in the world:** Osho (Bhagwan Shree Rajneesh), "Osho Quotes on the Individual." https://www.oshoquotes.net/2012/11/osho-quotes-on-individual/. Accessed 5 Apr. 2023.

130, **"The worst group of all is husband and wife:"** *Ecstasy: The Forgotten Language*, 28. "I have never come across a couple who is not bad. Persons are beautiful but couples are ugly."

Chapter 33 / New Years

131, **Disco died:** Derek John. "July 12, 1979: 'The Night Disco Died' — Or Didn't." Article. National Public Radio (NPR). https://www.npr.org/2016/07/16/485873750/july-12-1979-the-night-disco-died-or-didnt. Accessed 6 Apr. 2023.

132, **Wilayat al-faqih (the Guardianship of the Jurist):** Imam Ruhollah Khomeini, *Islamic Government*. English translation by Hamid Algar. Pdf file.
https://www.iranchamber.com/history/rkhomeini/books/velayat_faqeeh.pdf (Tehran, Iran: Institute for the Compilation of Khomeini's works, Publication date unknown).

Chapter 35 / Caliph-ornia

138, **Spanish explorers...named (California)...:** Ruth Putnam and Herbert Ingram. *California: The Name*. Berkeley: University of California Press, 1917).

139, **Jim Jones had close ties with high-ranking city politicians:** Flynn, 80-85, 108-111, 218-222.

140, **(Encounter with) two beaming young men:** My experience is corroborated with countless other testimonials, most notably:
David Frank Taylor, *The Social Organization of Recruitment In the Unification Church*. Graduate Student Thesis (1978). https://scholarworks.umt.edu/cgi/viewcontent.cgi?referer=&httpsredir=1&article=6585&context=etd. (ProQuest LLC, 2014.) 38-39, 69-71. Accessed 8 Apr. 2023, David used the participant observation method to gather information that corroborates with my experience.
Christopher Edwards. *Crazy for God*. (Hoboken, NJ, Prentice-Hall, 1979), 9-18.
Steven Hassan. *Combating Cult Mind Control: The Guide to Protection, Rescue and Recovery from Destructive Cults*. Kindle Edition. (Freedom of Mind Press; 4th edition, 2015), 50-51. Steven joined the New York branch of the Unification Church in 1973 where the recruitment techniques were slightly different than those used in California in 1979. BTW, he spent over two years in the cult and became a leader. Years after leaving the organization, he became a highly-respected cult expert and psychotherapist for cult victims and their families.

Chapter 36 / North Beach Crossroads

142, **Sayyid Qutb...revert(s) to the Islam (in) San Francisco:** Anonymous. *The Lives of Hasan Al Banna and Syed Qutb*. Pdf file. Publisher unknown (Muslim Brotherhood?). https://ia600204.us.archive.org/32/items/TheLivesOfTheTwoRevivers-HasanAlBannaSyedQutb/TheLivesOfTheTwoRevivers-HasanAlBannaSyedQutb.pdf. Internet Archive, 18. Accessed 8 Apr. 2023.

143, **"The Condor Where It All Began:"** Historical Marker Data Base. https://www.hmdb.org/m.asp?m=9238. February 7, 2023. Accessed 8 Apr. 2023.

143, **City Lights Bookstore:** Besides selling them, City Lights also published books. One offering—*Howl and other Poems* (1956) by Allen Ginsburg—caused quite a stir. It called for the full-scale liberation of inclinations originating from below the belt. After it was first read aloud at a nearby gallery, one observer noted that those in attendance knew "at the deepest level that a barrier had been broken, that the human voice and body had been hurled against the harsh wall of America." (Michael McClure)

143, **San Francisco...the porn capital:** Joe Kukura. "Remembering When San Francisco Was the Porn Capital of America." Blog article. *Broke-Ass Stuart*. https://brokeassstuart.com/2015/04/30/remembering-when-san-francisco-was-the-porn-capital-of-america/. September 16, 2021. Accessed 8 Apr. 2023.

143, **AIDS, the deadly sexually-transmitted disease, was spreading like wildfire in San Francisco (in 1979).:** L.D. Saunders, G.W. Rutherford, G.F. Lemp, J.L. Barnhart, "Impact of AIDS on Mortality in San Francisco, 1979-1986." *National Library of Medicine*. https://pubmed.ncbi.nlm.nih.gov/2384868/. Accessed 8 Apr. 2023.

Chapter 37 / The Dinner Meeting

145, **The Dinner Meeting** Edwards, 18-24.
Barbara and Betty Underwood. *Hostage to Heaven*. (New York, Clarkson N. Potter, Inc, 1979), 40-41. Barbara (along with her mother Betty) tells the story of her four-year involvement with the sect and journey out of it. Her behind-the-scenes look of the Moonies' San Francisco branch proved to be a valuable source.
Taylor, 39-43, 70-73.

Chapter 38 / The Ride to Boonville

Edwards, 24.
Taylor, 43-45.

Chapter 39 / (Dis)orientation

Edwards, 25-34.
Taylor, 45-53.
Underwood, 37-60.
159, **Small groups:** Taylor, 78-82.
161, **Bethie's lecture 1:** Sun Myung Moon. "Exposition of the Divine Principle, 1996 Translation" https://www.unification.net/dp96/. Part I, Chapter 1: The Principle of Creation.

The Three Blessings in a nutshell:
(1) FIRST BLESSING: "Be fruitful."
- The spiritual mind—also called the conscience—must have dominion over the body.
- Perfect dominion over our own lives leads to maturity. The mature person reaches his fullest potential and perfection.

(2) SECOND BLESSING: "Multiply."
- After reaching perfection, men and women must marry and have a family. Through obedience to the will of God, a husband and wife create a relationship of true love, based on the true love of God.
- God's plan is for ideal families to form ideal societies that will form ideal nations.

(3) THIRD BLESSING: "Have dominion over the earth."
- The family unit not only embodies the image of God completely; it also encapsulates the rest of creation.
- A WORLD UTOPIA: Eco-friendly, agape-driven, and theocentric mankind builds a beautiful paradise on Earth—the Ideal World. Everything is unified. Everyone is one, big, happy family.

Chapter 40 / Sin Revisited

163, **Jennifer's lecture:** Sun Myung Moon. "Exposition of the Divine Principle, 1996 Translation." https://www.unification.net/dp96/. Part I, Chapter 2: The Human Fall.

164, **Rajneesh... teaches...have sex whenever, wherever, and with whomever you want:** Not entirely true. Rajneesh didn't allow same-sex attraction in his organization. I guess it violated his strict moral code.

Chapter 41 / Durst Returns

166, **Mose Durst:** "Mose and Onni Durst: Their Legacy," *How Well Do You Know Your Moon,* a tumblr-blog dedicated to reporting on the Unification Church. https://howwelldoyouknowyourmoon.tumblr.com. Accessed 12 Apr. 2023.

Underwood, 64-66, 128, 247.

166, **"What does everyone want?..."** Taylor, 57.

166, **"What is our nature? Are we just blinking lights..."** Id,, 52.

Chapter 42 / Sunday Night Testimonies

167, **Appeal ... to us weekend attendees to stay for the week-long training session:** Ibid., 108.

168, **"Falling in love:"** Id., 59-60.

Chapter 43 / The Last Man

From Nietzsche's *Thus Spoke Zarathustra:* "Alas, the time of the most despicable man is coming, he that is no longer able to despise himself.

"Behold, I show you the last man. 'What is love? What is creation? What is longing? What is a star?' — thus asks the last man, and he blinks.

"The earth has become smaller, and on it hops the man who makes everything small...'We have invented happiness' — say the last men, and they blink."

Chapter 44 / "I'M A PRISONER..."

174, "**The responsibility lies in each and every one of us:**" Taylor, 97, 102, 106.

175, **Dodgeball game:** Id., 54.

175, **Love Bomb:** Id., 83.

175, "**When he was a little seed....**" Id., 40.

Chapter 45 / "I'm Your Spiritual Father"

178, **Member-buddy (concept):** Id., 82.

179, **(The concept) of True Parents:** Id., 130.

Chapter 46 / Heavenly Deception

181, "**We have a few rules here. They are really good rules:**" Taylor, 9.

183, **Heavenly deception (concept):** Underwood, 188-189.

Chapter 47 / Mrs. Durst

187-188, **Noah Ross:** Taylor, 140-141.

188-190, **Onni Durst (Yeon-soo Lim):** "Onni Durst: The Dragon Lady," "Mose and Onni Durst: Their Legacy," Articles. *How Well Do You Know Your Moon.* https://howwelldoyouknowyourmoon.tumblr.com. Accessed 12 Apr. 2023.

Gordon Neufeld. *Heartbreak and Rage: Ten Years Under Sun Myung Moon.* (Virtualbookworm.com Publishing, 2002). 42-43.

Underwood, 59, 62-69, 74, 102, 119, 125, 128, 147, 155, 222-223.

Chapter 48 / Kristina's Big Announcement

191-192, **Kristina Morrison (Seher):** Bruce Sutchar. "Kristina Seher's 60[th.]" Pdf file. TParents.org. May 20, 2006. https://www.tparents.org/Library/Unification/Talks2/Seher/Seher-060520.htm. Accessed 12 Apr. 2023.

"Kristina and Onni Believed We Could Reach Perfection in Three Days," "The Creative Community Project in Its Own Words." Articles. *How Well Do You Know Your Moon.* https://howwelldoyouknowyourmoon.tumblr.com. Accessed 12 Apr. 2023.

Kristina Morrison Seher. "Boonville, California, 1970." Pdf file. *Tparents.org.* 2011. https://www.tparents.org/Library/Unification/Books/Tribute-2011/Tribute-080.pdf. Accessed 12 Apr. 2023.

Chapter 49 / Letter to Randal:
  Actual letter from "Ted" (Dan Grajek) to "Randal."

Chapter 50 / Politics, Politics
  Taylor, 125-127.
  195-197, **Noah's lecture:** Sun Myung Moon. "Exposition of the Divine Principle, 1996 Translation" https://www.unification.net/dp96/. Part II, Chapter 6: The Second Advent.

Chapter 53 / Letter from Randal:
  Reconstructed by "Randal" from memory.

Chapter 54 / The Rescue Team
  204, **Bart hands Randal an 8½ x 11 wire-bound booklet:** U.S. House of Representatives. "Investigation of Korean-American Relations: Report of the Subcommittee on International Organizations of the Committee on International Relations." October 31, 1978. https://archive.org/stream/investigationofkoounit/investigationofkoounit_djvu.txt (Washington D.C: U.S. Government Printing Office, 1978). Accessed 12 Apr. 2023. The definitive source on the Moon organization and its political connections in the 70's.

Chapter 55/ The Roaring Silence
  208, **At the summit of a nearby hill, Noah...:** Taylor, 147-149.
  208, **"There will be bells ringing in the streets...:"** Id., 56.
  209, **Johnny Cash's "Folsom Prison Blues" with (rewritten) lyrics:** Id., 103.

Chapter 56 / The Infant of Prague
  212, **Great miracles...:** Bob and Penny Lord, "The History of The Infant of Prague." Article. *Journeys of Faith Catholic Media.* May 21, 2019. https://www.bobandpennylord.store/blogs/news/the-history-of-the-infant-of-prague. Accessed 12 Apr. 2023.

Chapter 59 / Pete Meets Jim:
  From interview with "Pete LeBlanc." November 18-19, 2021.

Chapter 60 / The Last Temptation
  220, *Lost Horizon* **(1973)... one of the worst movies ever made:** Harry Medved and Randy Dreyfuss. *The Fifty Worst Films of All Time (And How They Got That Way.* (New York: Popular Library, 1978).

Epilogue
  228, **Zainab's recent reconversion to Islam:** Those living outside of Dearborn are often surprised to hear Zainab's "feminist" interpretation of her religion, but living here I have observed that her thinking is not unusual. BTW, the most well-in-

formed, fair, and readable literature I found on Muslims is John L Esposito. John is a Professor of Religion and International Affairs, and of Islamic Studies at Georgetown University. He wrote many well-received (non-sensationalist) books on Islam and the beliefs, values and attitudes of individual Muslims such as *What Everyone Needs to Know about Islam, Islam: The Straight Path,* and *The Oxford History of Islam,*

228, **Sheikh Chirri**...traded his customary suit-and-tie for a clerical robe and turban and grew a beard. Howell, 267.

228, **Bob Dylan (born-again Christian):** Rudy Maxa. "Bob Dylan Knocks on Heaven's Door." Article. *The Washington Post.* May 27, 1979. https://www.washingtonpost.com/archive/lifestyle/magazine/1979/05/27/bob-dylan-knocks-on-heavens-door-accepts-christ-says-a-west-coast-pastor-as-the-music-biz-and-the-stars-fans-await-an-album-to-explain-it-all/78a25f0a-c879-4539-81db-d4866c3f0508/ Accessed 15 Apr. 2023.

229, **(Whatever happened to) Reverend Moon:** Mariah Blake. "The Fall of the House of Moon: Sex Rituals, Foreign Spies, Biden Offspring, and the Unification Church's War-torn First Family." Article. *The New Republic.* November 12, 2013. https://newrepublic.com/authors/mariah-blake. Accessed 15 Apr. 2023.

229, **The thirteen Moon children ended up spoiled brats and perhaps even cursed:** Nansook Hong, *In the Shadow of the Moons.* (Boston: Little, Brown, and Co., 1998). The memoir of Nansook, the "child bride" of Rev. Moon's firstborn son Steve, is probably the best inside look of the Moon family.

229, **Reverend Moon's (son) Sean Moon:** Tom Dunkel. "Locked and Loaded for the Lord." Article. *The Washington Post.* May 21, 2018. https://www.washingtonpost.com/news/style/wp/2018/05/21/feature/two-sons-of-rev-moon-have-split-from-his-church-and-their-followers-are-armed/ Accessed 15 Apr. 2023.

231, **(*Wild, Wild Country*)... "doesn't capture. . . the evil of the Rajneesh cult:"** Win McCormack, "Outside the Limits of the Human Imagination." Article. *The New Republic.* March 17, 2018. https://newrepublic.com/article/147657/outside-limits-human-imagination. Accessed 15 Apr. 2023.

231, **(Whatever happened to) Pete LeBlanc:** "Pete" himself contributed to this section.

232-233, **(Whatever happened to) Randal Stark:** "Randal" himself contributed to this section.

232, **Revelation 3:15-16 (NIV):** "I know your deeds, that you are neither cold nor hot. I wish you were either one or the other! So, because you are lukewarm—neither hot nor cold—I am about to spit you out of my mouth."

Afterword A / The Vanished Imam

234, **A huge chasm between ("old" and "new") Muslims (in Detroit):** ... Howell, 219, 220-221. 258-267.

234-235, **The (Lebanese Shia) '70s-wavers:**

Howell, 258-267.

Gregory Orfalea. *The Arab Americans: A History.* (Northampton, MA: Olive Branch Press, 2006). 207-212.

Linda S. Walbridge. *Without Forgetting the Imam: Lebanese Shi'ism in American Community*. (Detroit: Wayne State University Press, 1997).

235-238, **Imam Musa al Sadr:** Fouad Ajami, *The Vanished Imam: Musa al Sadr and the Shia of Lebanon*. (Ithaca, NY: Cornell University Press, 1987). In spite of fact that this biography was disavowed by the Imam's family, they approved the material presented in this book *Moon People*.

Mary Catherine Bateson. "A Martyr to Moderation." Article. *The New York Times*. May 25, 1986. https://www.nytimes.com/1986/05/25/books/a-martyr-to-moderation.html. Accessed 12 Apr. 2023.

Daniel Buttry. *Interfaith Heroes*. (Canton, MI, Read the Spirit Books, 2008), 102-104. In this book, al-Sadr is counted among history's greatest interfaith heroes such as Mahatma Gandhi, Martin Luther King, Jr., and Ju, Francis of Assisi.

Raed Charafeddine. "The Universalism of Imam Moussa Sadr: A Relevant Approach to Contemporary Uncertainty." Article. RaedCharafeddine.net. March 5, 2013. https://raedcharafeddine.net/download/the-universalism-of-imam-moussa-sadr-a-relevant-approach-to-contemporary-uncertainty/. Accessed 12 Apr. 2023.

Maryam Gomshad and Rasoul Safarahang. "Study of the Place of Peace in Imam Musa Sadr's Thoughts." Pdf file. *Science Arena Publications Specialty Journal of Politics and Law*. https://sciarena.com/storage/models/article/gBjtq9oKqXUq8QQKSILZQd-MwdgU8dJ3OEBDmzwp9vllL22URBkUoMylZixQ5/study-of-the-place-of-peace-in-imam-musa-sadrs-thoughts.pdf (Qom, Iran, University of Mumbai Qom, 2018). Vol. 3 (1): 47-56. Accessed 12 Apr. 2023. An example of how al-Sadr's philosophy still resonates in our time.

Imam Musa al-Sadr. *We Have Come Together For the Sake of Mankind*. Text of a sermon delivered on February 19, 1975 at St. Louis Cathedral of the Capuchin Fathers in Beirut, Lebanon. (Dearborn, MI. Sadr Foundation, 2022.)

Walbridge, 38, 67, 79, 119, 132. This book documents al-Sadr's influence on Dearborn residents.

Afterword B / The Polish Pope

239, **(Pope John Paul II) tricked the communists into having him return to Poland for a nine-day public tour:** Weigel, 291- 325.

Richard A. Spinello. "The Enduring Relevance of Karol Wojtyła's Philosophy." *Logos: A Journal of Catholic Thought and Culture*. Volume 17, Number 3, Summer 2014. 17-48.

"**Our name is not *Matawlah* (Imam Musa al-Sadr quote):**" Ajami, 126.

ACKNOWLEDGMENTS

I would like to thank the following people for making this project possible.

— Joe Cheff, one of my closest friends and all-time greatest sparring partner. He truly earned the title of Chief Editor. When I asked him "to be brutal" with the earlier manuscript, he did not disappoint!

— My other dedicated editors. Joe Polgar, Joan Kettel, Tim Jr. Grajek (my son), and Judy Mulholland.

— Tim Grajek, my brother, who challenged me to do the illustrations myself. His beautiful work on my first book served as the template for this book.

— My other brother Alan Grajek for his ongoing support.

— Visual artist Dale Trujillo, long-time friend, equal partner in producing the gorgeous front cover.

— Andy Grajek (my other son) who helped proof-read.

— Friend Dave Armstrong for a great first review.

— Hamid El Sadr—President of Sadr Foundation USA—and his family. Bright stars in a dark world, they are beyond inspiring! Their thumbs-up on this project is humbling to say the least.

— Diane Chiola who is always willing help out somehow.

— Paul Crepeau. I'm so grateful that we have had a chance to rekindle our friendship during the process of writing this book. Paul was very helpful in jogging my memory and filling in gaps of the story. He also helped in proof-reading.

— Joe Polgar, my oldest and all-time closest buddy. During the production of this project, he showed much fortitude facing his and my smug younger selves.

— Lori, my wife, and her parents Rolf Wunderlich and the late Janet Wunderlich, who had encouraged me every step of the way.

ABOUT THE AUTHOR

DAN GRAJEK GREW UP ON DETROIT'S northwest side. By age twenty, he had hitchhiked to New York once and California twice. Once he settled down, he earned a Bachelor's degree in Psychology at the University of Michigan, Dearborn (UM-D). For over 20 years, he worked in Graphics and Marketing for auto-related companies. Later in life, he returned to UM-D to earn his Master's degree in Education. Fascinated with the community he lives in, he decided to write his Masters Degree thesis on Ameen Rihani's *The Book of Khalid*, the first Arab-American novel. Dan taught high school English at a residential detention facility for young women in Dearborn Heights. In addition, he substitute taught in the Dearborn area for 15 years. His first book, *The Last Hobo* (also about his road-trip adventures) was released in 2016. His favorite accomplishment was marrying into a violin-making family. He is married to Lori and has three sons—Andy, Justin, and Ben.

BONUS SECTION

Excerpt from the prequel
THE LAST HOBO: *A clueless Detroit kid hitchhikes across America the summer the seventies ran out of gas*

★★★   NEWLY REVISED SECOND EDITION   ★★★

LEARN what happened Fourth-of-July week 1979 and how Ted became a real hobo. WITNESS the lunacy at Poverty Gulch, the anti-nuke rally in the Black Hills of South Dakota, hopping a train in Nebraska, and much more. Based on a true story!

INTRODUCTION

"THE WORST OF TIMES"

"It was the best of times, it was the worst of times, it was the age of wisdom, it was the age of foolishness."

— Charles Dickens, A Tale of Two Cities

Sunday, July 8, 1979

PETE AND I WERE IN THE NEBRASKA PANHANDLE when the newspapers broke the story. A top secret memo, wired to President Jimmy Carter, was leaked. It read:

> "I do not need to detail for you the political damage we are suffering from all of this... This would appear to be the worst of times."

Written by one of Carter's top advisors, this ominous message captured what average Americans were already thinking: Across the nation, fights were breaking out at gas stations that were out of gas. Truckers on strike were shooting at each other. Prices were skyrocketing. People felt threatened by a new Iran, nuclear power, the list goes on.

America wasn't very happy. The term "worst of times" must've evoked grim memories of the Great Depression and the days immediately after Pearl Harbor.

Mr. Carter's response? A speech. On July 15, the President would tell the American people on national television:

> "The erosion of our confidence in the future is threatening to destroy the social and the political fabric of America."

★ ★ ★

IN SPITE OF ALL THIS ANXIETY and doom-and-gloom, I, along with my buddy Pete LeBlanc, set out to have a good time on a road trip! At one point of our serendipitous journey, we got picked up hitchhiking by a *train*! The engineer graciously let us ride with him in the cab of his locomotive.

Later on though—after we got off at Sidney, Nebraska and raised our thumbs up again—things took a turn for the worse. An irate highway patrolman forced us to get off the Interstate where hitchhiking is illegal. He suggested we instead take Highway 30, the road less traveled.

The history buffs in Dearborn, Michigan where I live would be delighted to know that U.S. 30 is the legendary Lincoln Highway, the first coast-to-coast main road. There, you'll find lots of enchanting ruins like the ones you see on old Route 66, but there's virtually no traffic. Our situation was so dismal I was tempted to burn a giant S.O.S. in the nearby wheat field so at least planes could spot us.

The ghost road had a companion: About fifty yards or so—running along 30—were railroad tracks. I could smell the creosote a mile away. It took me back to my old Detroit neighborhood, Cody Rouge, where I first dreamt of being a hobo.

"Holy Mother of God!"

A rumble and then a thunderous toot pierced the stillness. "A train is coming!"

Pete and I gazed east and recognized the headlight in the distance getting bigger! Pete snapped out of his reverie. You could see a sudden spark of life animate him. Neither of us had to say anything. We sprinted through the knee-high grass toward the rails.

As I got closer, I could see all the distinguishable features of the locomotive. It was yellow with gray trim, the branding colors of Union Pacific. It rumbled along like some mighty mongrel beast with its procession of cars in tow.

"Should we? Should we do it?" Pete is the first to verbalize what we are both contemplating. My mind oscillates, trying to decide if hopping a train is a good idea.

Dangerous? Hmmmmmm
Slow enough? Hard to tell.
Not a moment to spare. Gotta act NOW.
"YYYEEEEAAAHHH, LET'S DO IT!" I scream.

We run up the ballast and alongside the passing boxcars and flat cars, ripping off our 30 lb. backpacks. Pete flings his pack on an empty car and I follow suit.

Okay now, grab and hoist. Grab and hoist. Grab grab grab grab grab grab grab grab grab grab...
Can't. Keep. Up.
ZZZZZZOOOOOOMMMMMMM!

We watch with apprehension as one car passed, then two, then three and before we knew it, the caboose rattles by, leaving us breathless, perplexed and finally stunned over the fact *all our belongings* had just disappeared into oblivion!

Eyes bug out. Jaws drop.
"Sh*t! Sh*t! Sh*t! What are we gonna do now?!" I bewail breathlessly with clenched fists. "All our stuff is gone. We're screwed!"

JUST TO THINK, I WAS IN "HEAVEN" only hours before! I mean the intense joy I felt riding with that friendly engineer in that locomotive across the prairie.

Besides denoting a state or place in the afterlife, heaven also means "the realm of perfect ideals." You try to home yourself in on it—but you can't most of the time.

On my trip from Michigan to California in 1979, I thought two places might possibly be "heaven on earth"—Poverty Gulch and Boonville.

Poverty Gulch was a place in the woods where a a big party was held. Boonville was a farm run by the Moonies, a religious cult!

Poverty Gulch and Boonville are a pair of opposite bookends in my mind. The "books" they hold up and support on the shelf are little stories within the context of a big story.

Now I present the first "bookend"... POVERTY GULCH.

Made in the USA
Middletown, DE
04 July 2023

34511335R00156